Advance Praise for One Day Stronger

"A compelling story of a struggle for economic survival that strives to get beyond ideological polarization and highlight ways that unions, businesses, and governments can help ordinary people. An inspiring saga of grassroots political cooperation."—*Kirkus Reviews (starred review)*

"A captivating and comprehensive account."—*BookLife Reviews*

"Tom Nelson is a compelling storyteller. He's a change-maker in an era when we need them. And someday soon he'll be a terrific U.S. senator."—Larry Tye, *New York Times* bestselling author of *Demagogue: The Life and Long Shadow of Senator Joe McCarthy*

"*One Day Stronger* is exactly the story American needs right now. It is not just an account of saving a plant, but of respecting the dignity of work, the value of tradition, and the possibility of change. May Appleton Coated be a model for the future of American manufacturing!"—Anne Marie Slaughter, CEO, New America

"*One Day Stronger* does a great job of explaining the collective worker power that comes through a union, including the power to save a company. Not enough attention is given to the *future* of the labor movement, and Tom Nelson does a powerful job of just that. The more we look at what made us the greatest nation on the planet, the more we ensure we'll continue to be."—Congressman Mark Pocan (D-Wisconsin), co-chair Congressional Progressive Caucus

"An important story, a portrait for a new kind of leadership, a blueprint for a return to we-are-all-in-this-together."—Jon Geenen, formerly international vice president, United Steelworkers

"*One Day Stronger* is one of the best books, if not the best, about the paper industry and perhaps about American Industry in general."—Gerry Ring, Professor Emeritus, University of Wisconsin–Stevens Point

"Thomas Nelson's *One Day Stronger* is a must read for Americans who are looking to political and community leaders to push back against unbridled capitalism and its pattern of ruining our nation's heritage of innovation and worker skill. In his gripping first-person story of Appleton Coated, we can see a brighter future for American manufacturing, led by committed unions and skilled political leadership."—Dr. Michael Hillard, University of Southern Maine, author of *Shredding Paper: The Rise and Fall of Maine's Mighty Paper Industry*

"Wisconsin is a historic union state. It has never been more vital to understand the role that organized labor has played in our past, that it plays in our present, and that it must play in our future as a laboratory of democracy. Too many powerful figures in politics and the media neglect or openly dismiss the contribution made by Wisconsin's labor organizations. Tom Nelson pushes back against that neglect and dismissal. He reminds us that Wisconsin doesn't work without working people and the unions that represent them."—John Nichols, National Affairs Correspondent, *The Nation*

"In *One Day Stronger*, Tom Nelson has masterfully captured the importance of American manufacturing to a community and its citizens, along with the devastating impact of a potential mill closure. As a key participant in the fight to save the former Appleton Coated Mill, Tom vividly portrays the raw emotion and relentless determination of the workers, their union, and elected officials, as they worked to save this vital piece of their community."—Dennis Delie, Secretary Treasurer, Wisconsin AFL-CIO, United Steelworkers Local 2-213

One Day Stronger

One Day Stronger

*How One Union Local Saved a Mill
and Changed an Industry—
and What It Means for
American Manufacturing*

Thomas M. Nelson

Rivertowns
B O O K S

Printed in the United States of America • March, 2021 • I

Cloth: ISBN-13: 978-1-953943-00-2
Paperback: ISBN-13: 978-1-7339141-8-5

LCCN Imprint Name: Rivertowns Books

Cover design by Ryan Biore. Front cover photo © Danny Damiani—USA TODAY NETWORK.

Rivertowns Books are available online from Amazon as well as from bookstores and other retailers. Requests for information and other correspondence may be addressed to:

Rivertowns Books
240 Locust Lane
Irvington NY 10533
Email: info@rivertownsbooks.com

Contents

To the men and women

of Appleton Coated,

past, present, and future

Introduction:

One Night in Kaukauna

I T WAS A WILD WINTER'S NIGHT in Kaukauna, Wisconsin. Just above the hill from the city hall on Kenneth Avenue, sleet and high winds pummeled my dad's minivan, where I was sitting and scribbling notes on 4 × 6 cards like a nervous high school debater. This was the first weekend of my first political campaign, a race for a seat in the state assembly, and I was anxiously prepping for my very first campaign stop. The audience would be the members of Thilmany Pulp and Paper Local 10 of the Paper, Allied-Industrial, Chemical, and Energy Workers Union (PACE), the paper workers' union before its merger with the United Steelworkers (USW). I desperately needed their endorsement if my campaign was to have any shot.

My speech was a debacle. I was overdressed, I paced the floor awkwardly, and I never took my eyes off the cards. Eventually I was interrupted by the presiding officer. "Okay, I think we've heard enough. If anyone has questions for—what is your name again?"

"Tom Nelson," I replied, my voice trailing off after the first syllable.

"Right. If you have any questions for Tom Nelson, you can talk to him after the meeting." I stuck around for sloppy joes and beer, but I'm sure I didn't win over a single voter.

That night in 2004 was an inauspicious start for my political career, made worse by the fact that the people I'd failed to connect with were *my* people. I'd grown up in a neighborhood across the river from the Appleton Coated mill, my dad started his Lutheran mission church in a nearby elementary school in 1980, and many of my friends' moms and dads worked at the Locks mill, as it was colloquially known. Now, I couldn't even get the paper workers to listen to my speech. It was heartbreaking.

Thankfully, I rebounded from that terrible start. It made me realize I had a long way to go to build up my street cred. I turned my obsessive-compulsive tendencies into a strength, knocking on every door in Wisconsin's fifth assembly district at least once—and in the case of Kaukauna and my hometown of Little Chute, three times. My 22,000 home visits paid off. Local 10 not only came around, it anchored my campaign—donating office space, deploying half their membership into the field, dropping literature, knocking on doors, and sticking up yard signs. My personal bonds with the paper workers and their families were rekindled and solidified. On election day, I squeezed past my incumbent Republican opponent with a margin just big enough to stave off a recount.

Organized labor and the paper workers in particular would become cornerstones of my public service. Wherever it has taken me—so far, to the state assembly and a county executive's office—I've always been there for them. I've fought hard for the paper industry and its workers as a state assemblyman and as county executive of Outagamie County, and I launched my campaign for Congress in 2016 right outside the plant gate.

So in 2017, when Appleton Coated faced certain death in the wake of a brutal receivership sale, I joined with the community to fight back. Led by the USW, we challenged the sale of the mill to an industrial scrap dealer. The ingenuity of our legal and political strategy reflected a new three-part model of labor, management, and government working together to revitalize a troubled industry and rekindle its potential, saving the kinds of jobs that helped build the American middle class in the first place.

You'll read the whole story in the chapters that follow. But first, I want to say why I think it matters.

It wasn't until the early years of the twenty-first century that Wisconsin's paper makers began to suffer some of the same economic woes that had already begun to hobble other American manufacturing industries. As the paper mills began to close, the communities that depended on them suffered—and not just monetarily. As authors Anne Case and Angus Deaton observe in their seminal work *Deaths of Despair and the Future of Capitalism*, "Jobs are not just the source of money; they are the basis for the rituals, customs and routines of working-class life. Destroy work and, in the end, working-class life cannot survive."

Longtime labor leaders like Kaukauna native Jon Geenen have witnessed the societal change first-hand. He explains it this way:

> It was a central part of our upbringing, the idea of social solidarity, that you've got a responsibility to have the backs of your co-workers, the backs or your neighbors, to have the backs of everybody in your community. Today, I think we have lost the central tenet of what we stood for—people coming together to make our lives a little bit better.

The idea of "social solidarity" that Geenen describes is a national trait that goes back to our founding. In the classic 1835 book *Democracy in America*, written after a tour of our young republic,

French aristocrat and political scientist Alexis de Tocqueville observed, "Municipal institutions constitute the strength of free nations." He vividly described the way Americans seemed to instinctively join forces in support of worthy causes: "As soon as several of the inhabitants of the United States have taken up an opinion or a feeling which they wish to promote in the world, they look out for mutual assistance; and as soon as they have found one another out, they combine. From that moment they are no longer isolated men, but a power seen from afar, whose actions serve for an example and whose language is listened to."

Tocqueville was so impressed by this behavior that he made it the basis of a guiding principle: "Among the laws that rule human societies there is one which seems to be more precise and clear than all others. If men are to remain civilized or to become so, the art of associating together must grow and improve in the same ratio in which the equality of conditions is increased." We saw that in America during the New Deal Era and World War II, when "the Greatest Generation" pulled together to conquer enormous challenges at home and abroad.

Unfortunately, in recent years, the American talent for "associating together"—that is, for social solidarity—has been badly eroded. Economic, political, and social trends all play a part. Paper companies like Appleton Coated, Kimberly-Clark, and many others have been rocked by unfair foreign competition, over-production, managerial failure to respond quickly to changing markets and technologies, and ever-increasing pressures from Wall Street and the financial sector. When companies die, so do the communities that have grown up around them.

The best way to resist these forces is by building strong, vibrant, and resilient communities where everyone is welcome and secure. Saving paper mills like Appleton Coated and Kimberly-NewPage is important—and a crucial role in the effort to save them is played by organized labor. In addition to the relative handful of longtime, dedicated executives still found in U.S. companies—people like the owner-managers of Appleton Coated—great industrial unions like the USW contribute essential resources to the battle for long-term industry and community survival, including organizational skill, political clout, institutional memory, technical expertise, and a network of human connections that runs deep and broad.

Thankfully, northeast Wisconsin is one region that has so far managed to withstand some of the destructive trends that have ravaged much of our nation. Labor union membership, shrinking across the country, has held its own among the region's industrial and trade craft unions, including the USW. Other worker groups in the state continue to support unions, like the teachers in school districts like Green Bay, where my sister proudly—and voluntarily—pays dues and attends meetings in the old spirit of social solidarity. The story of how the USW and its local allies saved the Appleton Coated mill is another reflection of the continuing power of unions to serve not just their members but the entire society.

The Wisconsin paper industry can point the way to a brighter future for American manufacturing as a whole—provided we acknowledge the crucial role that workers play and embrace a labor-management model that fairly rewards owners and employees alike.

Organized labor is the solution, the paper industry is the model, and Appleton Coated is the proof.

Part One

Into the Breach

1.

On the Brink

"**S**O, YOU DO KNOW that one of your paper mills is about to go under?" my friend Tim Nixon asked me, just above the din of clanging pots and pans at the back of Green Bay's Vintage Cantina restaurant. It was lunchtime on Thursday, September 14, 2017, a crisp early autumn day along the city's bustling Washington Street corridor. Sitting across a metal and Formica table, Tim reminded me of Fezzik, the character André the Giant plays in *The Princess Bride*. Tim could be Fezzik's burly little brother, except that instead of being an outlaw from Greenland like Fezzik, he is a senior partner at one of Wisconsin's largest law firms.

"Which mill?" I asked Tim.

Why did I ask that? Was it a coping mechanism? I knew the answer: Appleton Coated in the village of Combined Locks.

"What do you mean, which mill?" Tim shot back, as if cross-examining a witness.

The Appleton Coated mill, one of the mainstays of the surrounding Fox River Valley's historic paper industry, was in big trouble. On August 18, a top-of-the-fold headline in the *Appleton Post Crescent* had seemingly sounded the death knell of the 127-year-old paper mill: "Appleton Coated seeks buyer, files for receivership."

In a sickening twist of irony, the story directly underneath that one reported, "State Assembly gives OK for $3 billion offer to lure Foxconn," the $39-billion Taiwanese electronics firm best known for supplying parts to Apple, to a site in southeastern Wisconsin. Governor Scott Walker had negotiated the deal with Foxconn CEO Terry Gou, and Walker's fellow Republicans in the state legislature had rubber-stamped it. A Foxconn facility would create jobs, but not high-quality ones like those at Appleton Coated and Wisconsin's other paper mills.

From Harrisburg, Pennsylvania to São Paulo, Brazil, Foxconn had a history of seeking gullible governments willing to dole out tax breaks for jobs that rarely appeared as promised. Along with this came a troubling labor and environmental record. Working conditions were so bad at one Chinese Foxconn facility that fourteen employees committed suicide. In exchange for the $3 billion in local and state incentives, Foxconn said it would deliver Wisconsin 13,000 jobs and invest $10 billion in a facility as big as seventeen football fields. Of course, no one really knew whether this time Foxconn would deliver on its promises. But Scott Walker was willing to bet the state's future—and his re-election—on it.

Meanwhile, a company with a history of providing solid jobs for Wisconsin workers was on the brink of collapse—and was getting no help from Walker or anyone else in his administration.

Despite challenging periods including the present, paper manufacturing has long been Wisconsin's most reliable employer, the industry that has withstood the test of time. Along the lower Fox River between Lake Winnebago and the port of Green Bay, over a dozen mills dot the banks. With $13.2 billion in collective annual output, the mills power a regional economic ecosystem of converting operations, printers, pulpers, transport companies, wood yards, and scores of other paper-related businesses. What's more, each mill sustains a local network of enterprises patronized by its employees, from hardware and grocery stores to doctors' and dentists' offices. The Fox Valley is not just the paper capital of Wisconsin, the Midwest, or the country; it's home to the highest concentration of paper mills in the world. Next to the Green Bay Packers and cheese, paper is what defines Wisconsin best—culturally, historically, and economically.

And while other industries have come and gone, unable to take root, paper has prospered. It has been with us for nearly a century and a half, and with a reasonable amount of support—government assistance that would amount to a small fraction of the Foxconn deal—it should be with us for as long again. Existing and innovative paper applications ensure that national and global paper markets will keep increasing, and, as a renewable resource, paper can be a core element of a Green New Deal.

But now one of the proud exemplars of that great papermaking tradition was in danger of dying forever, taking with it jobs and a way of life that had long sustained an entire community—Combined Locks, one of the smaller towns of Outagamie County, which I began serving as county executive in 2011. In most factory and mill towns, there is no other major employer. The local economy rises or falls with the wage structure of the factory or mill. Losing the mill would be devastating.

Ever since the August announcement that Appleton Coated had filed for receivership, I'd been thinking back to the closing of the NewPage paper mill in 2008. The village of Kimberly had already been struggling when NewPage shut its doors. Today, a nearby shopping center and strip mall are almost vacant. Most business expansion happens on the edge of the village, a mile from its downtown. If Appleton Coated went the same way as NewPage, another town and its residents would be plunged into economic decline.

Of course, Tim Nixon and I were both well aware of this history. We both understood the seriousness of the dilemma faced by Appleton Coated, its workers, and the entire community of Combined Locks. But there didn't seem to be much we could do about it. I said as much to Nixon as we sat together that day in September.

Tim's interest in the case was more than that of a concerned citizen. As the state's top bankruptcy attorney, Tim had represented clients on every side of a long list of insolvency cases, and he was involved in the Appleton Coated cases as well—in this case representing a creditor, Kaukauna Utilities. But no matter which side or interest he represented in a case, Tim always did all he could to save the business. "That's not because I'm a nice guy," Tim will say with a self-deprecating wink. "It's because you are generally better off keeping the thing together. In disasters, even the banks rarely get paid in full. If I can make it *not* a disaster, the pie gets bigger and my client gets paid, and so do others, including workers."

That combination of common sense with idealism is typical of Tim Nixon. He's a classic blue-collar kid who rose to the top of his profession, including arguing cases before the U.S. Supreme Court, but always remembered where he came from—just as my mother always reminded me to do. Tim's dad was a union official in the Western Union office where he worked, and Tim's mom worked for one of the nation's largest United Steelworkers (USW) locals for twenty-fve years. And he is proud of his union roots, to say the least. He likes to claim, "I had AFL-CIO tattooed on my ass when I was born."

In many ways, Tim personifies the unique and rich tradition of Wisconsin's progressive politics. The same ethos that spurred the careers and contributions of Fighting Bob LaFollette, Gaylord Nelson, Russ Feingold, and Gwen Moore can also be found in Tim Nixon. As counsel to the fee examiner in the 2009 General Motors bailout, he kept a legion of corporate attorneys honest by ensuring federal tax dollars went toward making cars, not consultancy and legal fees.

So I was very interested in what Tim had to say about the Appleton Coated case. Over the years I've known Tim, I've learned a lot from him about how businesses go under and the complicated legal and financial entanglements that arise in their wake. In Tim's experience, most insolvency cases result directly from poor management decisions. Although managers will blame a hundred things, in nearly every case the underlying problem is that they have failed "to understand and respond to market forces," as Tim puts it. He and I had spent hours diagnosing the troubles of Appleton Coated, which Tim felt fit the pattern perfectly. The company had stuck with white grade paper for too long, even as the market for that product steadily shrank. Years before, they should have shifted into producing brown grades for cardboard packaging, a sector with better margins and increasing demand thanks to the huge growth in e-commerce that was delivering countless boxes of goods to consumers every year. When Appleton Coated fell into receivership, Tim wasn't surprised.

But he also wasn't ready to give up on the company.

"You're the county executive," he reminded me. "You have what, six hundred jobs at stake? An economic machine that keeps one of your communities alive. Look what happened with NewPage in Kimberly. That was a big deal. This will be bigger!" Tim slapped the table with his palm and almost knocked over the basket of nachos between us.

"I know all that," I replied. "But aside from lighting them up with a few press conferences, what can I do?"

Tim had an answer—one that only an expert steeped in bankruptcy law would have been able to suggest.

In filing for receivership, Appleton Coated had surrendered functional control to its chief creditor, Pittsburgh-based PNC Bank. A court-appointed receiver had legal control, but PNC called the shots. Such arrangements are applications of the "golden rule": he or she that has the gold makes the rules.

Wisconsin's 1937 receivership law, known as Chapter 128 for the number of the statute, was originally designed to give individuals and enterprises in financial straits an easier route than going through the more expensive and complicated bankruptcy process. Receivership's roots date back to the late nineteenth century, when so-called assignments for the benefit of creditors were first codified. Today, creditors, shareholders, and attorneys have increasingly been pushing businesses through receivership. Unlike Chapter 11 bankruptcy in federal courts, receivership in state courts has no restructuring costs, because there is nothing to restructure—it is like hospice for a business. It puts a court-appointed receiver in total control, subject to the wishes of the largest secured creditor, which in Appleton Coated's case was PNC. The receiver can shut down a business and sell it without any regard for the workers or the business itself. The results are often brutal.

Yet hidden inside this dismal process was a hopeful, little-known provision of Chapter 128. As Tim explained to me over lunch that day, unlike in most other states, Wisconsin's receivership law allowed people and groups with standing—that is, anyone affected by the potential business closure—to object to a sale. Those with standing to object could include employees, vendors, creditors, chambers of commerce, or elected officials—like me.

This was exciting news. It meant I might have more than the bully pulpit of public office to use as a weapon to fight for the paper plant and its workers. I might also have a legal tool at my disposal. Of course, there was no guarantee it would work. But even having a ghost of a chance felt a lot better than the sense of helplessness I'd been laboring under for the last month.

Tim and I talked through the practicalities. The court-appointed receiver for the Appleton Coated mill was Michael Polsky, the state's go-to receiver in large, complicated cases. Tim credited him with reviving Chapter 128 as a viable alternative to bankruptcy in Wisconsin in the 1990s. Polsky's responsibility as receiver was to monetize the mill's assets and sell them at auction to the highest bidder, whether that was someone who would keep the mill running as a going concern or an industrial scrap dealer who would scoop it up for a relative pittance and profit by collecting on accounts receivable, then selling the machinery and other physical assets.

The auction had already been scheduled and was less than a week away. Tim felt that the prospects for a sale to a company that would keep the mill running were scant. Many potential going-concern buyers had looked at the mill, but with only twenty-two business days between the receivership filing and the auction, they hadn't had time to complete a normal due diligence process. Tim believed the likeliest bidders would be industrial scrap dealers. After all, it was a lot easier to figure the immediate and near-term return on monetizing the accounts receivable and the physical assets than it was to figure the long-term return on running the mill.

The plan Tim suggested was simple. If the mill went to a scrap dealer, as Tim expected, I would file a formal objection with the court. The goal would be to win time for the mill to find an alternative buyer, someone who would keep it intact and run it as a mill. That was our one hope to save the plant and, with it, the village of Combined Locks.

"Let's do it," I said.

When my lunch with Tim was finished, I phoned Doug Osterberg, CEO of Appleton Coated, who got his general counsel, Ed Bush, on the line, too. I'd known them both for years. Quiet and unassuming, Osterberg was not your typical CEO who bounces around from job to job, industry to industry, caring less for the business than for the stock option packages he can claim. With a few brief detours, Doug had spent his entire career at Appleton Coated and its previous incarnations under a series of owners. He knew every nook and cranny of the facility. He also knew the names of every worker from the broke hustler to the machine tender, as well as their years of employment, their spouses, and their kids' ages. He was smart, and he cared.

Circling the closed loop of a condo subdivision southeast of Green Bay while looking for a campaign friend's house, I excitedly shared Nixon's suggestion that I use my standing as county executive to object to any sale of the mill to a scrap dealer. Osterberg and Bush were intrigued to learn that Chapter 128 allowed for such an objection, but they weren't ready to support my involvement.

Next, I needed to check in with the United Steelworkers (USW), the international union that represented the Appleton Coated workers in USW Local 2-144. I called Jon Geenen. Jon was a longtime friend who'd grown up in Kaukauna, just down Highway 96 from me. Now he was the USW's international vice-president. Our labor and political philosophies complemented each other well. It turned out he was already acquainted with the objection provision in Chapter 128. "We've looked at the angle. We don't think it'll help," he told me.

I was sorry about Geenen's pessimism, but not surprised. The 2010s were a tough decade for labor, especially in Wisconsin. In 2011, his first year as the state's forty-fifth governor, Republican Scott Walker had signed Act 10, which gutted collective bargaining rights for public sector employees. In 2015, the state legislature, dominated by the Republican Party thanks in large part to extreme gerrymandering, also passed a so-called right-to-work law hamstringing crucial labor organizing tools, and later that year eroded prevailing wage statutes that set wage floors for trade craft workers. The antilabor legislation winnowed union ranks, drained treasuries, and crushed spirits.

So none of the three allies I'd called to share Nixon's idea was overly excited about it—though none raised any serious objections. That was okay with me. This was a strategy I could implement on my own. And given my role in local politics, I knew I could use the tool of a formal objection not just to claim a day in court—and maybe throw a monkey wrench into the receivership process—but also to generate publicity, sympathy, and citizen engagement on behalf of the Appleton Coated workers.

I would have loved to have their enthusiastic support from day one. But I had already made up my mind that I was going to go ahead.

With that simple decision—a long-odds gamble driven by the lack of any better options—Tim Nixon and I would set in motion a complicated saga that would lead to an unlikely outcome, one with important lessons to offer for countless other American communities facing the same forces of devastation that were confronting Combined Locks.

2.

Like Day into Night

TIM NIXON WAS RIGHT in saying that a business like Appleton Coated almost never becomes insolvent unless management has made some serious mistakes. But I also knew enough about the company's history to realize that the slide toward insolvency had been years in the making and had involved a number of complex issues. One of the key turning points had occurred less than three years earlier, when the mill's most recent corporate owner, French company Sequana, one of the world's largest paper makers, had tried and failed to sell it.

Sequana had invested considerable resources in Appleton Coated in the past. However, by 2013, the parent company was not healthy enough financially to make the further investments the mill needed to remain competitive. In fact, Sequana needed to divest the mill as a preliminary to refinancing its corporate debt in France, where it had already closed several mills. It would close Appleton Coated, too, if it could not find a going-concern buyer. But that outcome would leave Sequana responsible for the mill's pension fund. Selling to another paper maker was the only way Sequana could hand off responsibility for the pension fund and be sure it would never be asked to make up any future shortfalls.

About eighty percent fully funded, Appleton Coated's pension fund was in good shape compared to many American pension funds. The mill's pension fund included two pension plans, one for unionized employees and one for nonunionized management and administrative employees (including CEO Doug Osterberg and his senior executive team), with both plans funded on an equal basis. To remain in good standing with the federal Pension Benefit Guarantee Corporation (PBGC), the fund usually required annual contributions of $1 to 3 million. When the fund's investments did exceptionally well, the required contribution was lower, even zero.

A going-concern buyer would have to assume responsibility for the annual pension fund contributions along with liability for potential environmental cleanup costs at the mill and its two landfills. Thanks to a deal signed by prior management, the mill was also locked into a so-called load stability agreement with the local municipal power utility, Kaukauna Utilities, and the state municipal power utility consortium, Wisconsin Public Power Incorporated (doing business as WPPI Energy). Under the terms of the contract, the mill was effectively "selling at wholesale and buying back at retail," in Doug Osterberg's words. The pension fund obligations, the potential environmental cleanup costs, and the power contract were all negatives for potential purchasers of the mill, but the pension obligations were the biggest problem by far.

In good times, the mill could comfortably pay its pension and energy costs while remaining profitable. The wild card was notoriously unpredictable pricing for pulp, the raw material for papermaking. Fully integrated mills, in industry parlance, controlled this cost by having their own pulping machinery. Appleton Coated had once had a pulp mill, but it was one designed to make base stock for telephone directory paper, now an obsolete product. Appleton Coated managed to keep the pulper running until 2000, after which it had to buy pulp fiber on the open market. Any going-concern buyer would want to add pulping machinery that was suitable for the mill's current and future product mix, but making such a multimillion-dollar investment would stress cash flow even further on top of the pension and energy costs.

There was one way for the mill to shed the pension obligations and the power contract: insolvency. An insolvency procedure would nullify the energy contract and allow the mill to shift full responsibility for the pension fund to the PBGC. However, this required a change of ownership. Sequana could not put its Appleton Coated division through bankruptcy or receivership, and then repurchase the mill without the pension obligations and the power contract. Only new owners purchasing after insolvency could secure those benefits.

By 2013, for all these reasons, Sequana was eager to sell the mill to a going-concern buyer and so escape its pension, energy, and environmental obligations.

To make Appleton Coated as attractive as possible to prospective buyers, Sequana had the mill hire the consulting firm of Alvarez & Marsal to find ways to improve the company's finances. Doug Osterberg and his management team worked with Alvarez & Marsal to carve out $15 million in annual cost savings, including job cuts, wage reductions, and operational improvements. Alvarez & Marsal then marketed the mill for sale.

The results were disappointing. A number of going-concern paper makers looked at Appleton Coated, but they all shied away from buying it, mainly because of the pension fund obligations. An alternative might have been to sell the mill to a private equity (PE) investment firm. But Sequana distrusted PE firms as potential buyers, because it feared pension obligations might boomerang back on their company. The French company did not think a PE firm would work as hard as a strategic buyer running the mill as a going concern for the long term. If a PE buyer burned through cash and the mill entered bankruptcy, clawback provisions would allow the PGBC to demand pension contributions from the previous owner for up to five years after the sale.

In April 2014, Sequana stopped financing Appleton Coated's operations. One of the mill's outside lawyers said, "You are done making paper." But the mill managers weren't willing to give up without a fight. Scrambling creatively, they told suppliers they were delaying payments one week. The single week's delay allowed the mill to gather the cash to meet payroll and begin paying suppliers the following week.

Worried that Sequana would soon shutter the mill, even if it meant remaining responsible for pension shortfalls, Doug Osterberg told his management team, "We've got to get the facility away from them." It was CFO Marianne Sterr who suggested that the senior executives form a partnership to purchase the mill in what's called a management buyout (MBO). Believing they could run the mill profitably enough to position it for sale to a going-concern buyer within the next few years, Doug, Marianne, general counsel Ed Bush, and six other colleagues, including COO Ann Whalen, pooled their resources to come up with a low-seven-figure purchase amount. "We didn't mortgage our houses, but it was enough to hurt if things went bad," Doug said. The group formed a business entity known as Virtus Holdings LLC, signaling their honest intentions by naming themselves after the Latin word for virtue.

Selling to the executives appealed to Sequana, Marianne recalled, "because they knew we would continue to fund the pension plan, because our pensions were at stake along with everyone else's." Sequana was so eager to get Appleton Coated off its books with no risk of being sued later for pension costs that it not only said yes to the low purchase price but also offered to forgive $43 million of debt associated with the mill.

To complete the MBO, the management team needed financing for operating capital. Some of this would have to come from private sources. The team solicited loans from banks with commercial lending offices in Milwaukee and Chicago. Six banks expressed interest, and discussions advanced furthest with Wells Fargo. After months of courtship, Doug said, "I had a phone message from Wells Fargo on a Friday in the fall of 2014 saying the loan was approved and I'd have a loan sheet Monday. Then Monday rolled around, and they said, 'Just kidding.'" The timing was terrible, because Sequana was committed to divesting the mill in 2014, and the end of the year was fast approaching.

One of the five other interested banks was PNC, or to be more precise, PNC's commercial lending office in Chicago. Marianne Sterr called the business development officer she'd been in touch with at PNC Chicago, and she learned that PNC was willing to do a revolving monthly line of credit for three years for up to $15 million at any one time. However, because it was "a higher-than-normal-risk situation," in Marianne's words, PNC set a high interest rate of prime plus five percent. It also demanded two other onerous provisions. First, the loan covenant stipulated that Appleton Coated would make a monthly interest payment on a minimum loan balance of $10 million, even if the actual loan balance was zero. Second, the covenant stipulated that Appleton Coated would owe PNC a $750,000 prepayment penalty if the mill refinanced with another lender before the line of credit's three-year term expired.

These were tough requirements for Appleton Coated to have to meet. But at least it seemed that the needed financing was in place. However, at the last moment, PNC demanded even more.

Under what is known as debtor financing, the mill's healthy accounts receivable cash flow and any unsold inventory would serve as collateral for the combined loan and interest amount. This arrangement would ensure that PNC would be paid in full even if the mill went under or was sold to a third party. But as Doug Osterberg explains, "PNC came back to us after all that paperwork was signed and said, 'We also have to have all of the land, buildings, and equipment as collateral.'" Anxious to get the deal done before Sequana pulled the plug, Doug signed the mortgage on the dotted line, with all the mill's assets as collateral.

Supplementing the private financing from PNC would be public help from the state. The Wisconsin Economic Development Corporation (WEDC) supported the MBO by providing a $4 million loan for operating capital and equipment. This loan required only monthly interest payments, with the principal due as a lump sum on December 31, 2019. Even sweeter, WEDC would forgive $1 million of the $4 million principal if Appleton Coated maintained 600 or more jobs, unionized and nonunionized, until that date.

With these loans in place, Virtus Holdings completed the purchase of Appleton Coated from Sequana on December 18, 2014. It was the best possible Christmas present for the mill, giving it a new lease on life.

The mill performed well under Doug and his fellow owner-managers in 2015 and most of 2016. They attracted two serious suitors, a Taiwanese printer and specialty paper and containerboard manufacturer and a U.S. containerboard maker, but both wound up leaving the mill at the altar. Business conditions became more difficult in fall 2016, but overall operating results remained sound.

Appleton Coated's traditional core product was high-end printing paper—technically known as white coated free sheet (CFS) paper. The overall CFS market was shrinking, but Appleton Coated was a leader in the segment, supplying most of the CFS paper used on Hewlett-Packard industrial inkjet presses, which print corrugated packaging, magazines, retail signage and displays, and other commercial products. As a result, Appleton Coated's share of the market was continuing to grow. Doug Osterberg was also testing brown paper grades with promising results. These grades included liner board and medium corrugated board—standard cardboard box components—as well as a unique white-brown packaging grade that could open new markets and generate much-needed revenue. Some of Doug's colleagues in management were skeptical about switching to these less-familiar markets, but Doug himself was convinced they could open a path to long-term growth for Appleton Coated.

As late as March 2017, the outlook was good, according to Ed Bush. Ed had thirty-seven years of experience in the paper industry and knew it as well as anyone in the Fox Valley. "At that time," Bush recalls, "PNC was prepared to extend the mill's line of credit. They were actively courting us to sign a renewal." And they were willing to do so under "much more favorable terms," says Marianne Sterr. Her main contact at PNC had told her the year before that Appleton Coated was a "prize account." Other banks were also interested in doing business with the mill, and at lower interest rates. Although these opportunities were outweighed by the $750,000 prepayment penalty if Appleton Coated refinanced with another lender before the line of credit expired in December, they provided leverage for negotiating with PNC. They also offered an attractive fallback option if Appleton Coated and PNC could not agree on terms for renewing the line of credit.

But the mill's fortunes hung in a precarious balance. Business conditions had begun to deteriorate in late 2016 with a slight increase in pulp prices, which squeezed margins. In early 2017, Verso, North America's largest white grade paper producer with over fifty percent of the market, ramped up a brutal market-share war with extremely low pricing aimed at Appleton Coated, its most troublesome rival. Driving Appleton Coated out of business would clear the way for Verso to increase prices and enhance its profitability following a recent bankruptcy that had rid it of a crippling debt load.

Appleton Coated began to feel the pressure. A textbook publisher that had formerly ordered all its paper from Appleton Coated moved to diversify its suppliers, taking advantage of price cuts as producers fought for market share. Another important customer increased its use of electronic rather than printed communications. The merger of two large paper distributors added to downward pressure on pricing.

"When the numbers turned, they just turned like day into night," Ed Bush later told me. The financial decline was swift and merciless, catching management off guard.

"April and May were particularly bad months financially," Marianne Sterr says. As a result, Appleton Coated found itself breaching a PNC loan covenant on the mill's fixed charge coverage (FCC) ratio, a figure that indicates whether a company has enough cash to make debt payments. The mill's FCC ratio was calculated by taking earnings before interest, taxes, depreciation, and amortization (EBITDA) on a trailing-twelve-months basis; subtracting taxes, capital expenditures, and pension fund contributions; and then dividing by the interest payments on its loans. "As EBITDA dropped over the twelve months ending March and April 2017, the FCC ratio dropped below the minimum amount required by the loan covenants," Sterr explains. "The numerator was dropping, but the denominator was unchanged."

Appleton Coated fought back. It kept cash flow positive by lowering capital and operational costs, taking only those orders that were profitable and not running the machines just to keep them running. In particular, it turned down low-grade and smaller paper orders that strained gears and wore out rollers. Beyond this, it was hard to see how the company's finances could be shored up further. Most of the obvious cost trimming had already been achieved in 2013. Cutting a large number of additional jobs wasn't an option for two reasons. First, the mill continued to produce mostly white grades for the CFS market, which required many more workers than brown grades. Second, the WEDC loan's provision for forgiving $1 million of the $4 million principal required maintaining current staffing levels.

In the spring of 2017, with revenue plunging because of the changed operating environment, PNC broke off talks about renewing Appleton Coated's line of credit and pressed the mill to hire an outside consultant to validate its financial plan.

Marianne Sterr and her colleagues interviewed several consultants on PNC's approved list. They chose Michael Compton of Chicago-based Silverman Consulting, a leading corporate re-structuring firm. He got the nod in part because of his reported good work with Ariens Company, a family-owned manufacturer of mowers, snow blowers, and power brushes in nearby Brillion, Wisconsin. That experience suggested he would be a good fit for Appleton Coated.

Compton began work at Appleton Coated early in the summer. Although he was paid by Appleton Coated, he reported exclusively to PNC Chicago. Marianne Sterr expected Compton to analyze the mill's financial health and suggest "potential ways we could improve our operations and financial status." Instead, Compton focused almost entirely on Appleton Coated's projected shipping volumes for the rest of 2017.

Unfortunately, Compton displayed little knowledge of the paper industry, and he thought the projections contained a lot of hot air. Marianne explains, "Lead times for paper orders are rarely out more than two weeks, and most customers do not have purchase commitment contracts." Compton refused to accept this explanation for what looked like a relatively thin order book, and he discounted management's projections for orders of the brown grades the mill had been testing, despite the success of the trials. He also discounted management's positive discussions with both white grade and brown grade customers. From their time working under Sequana's ownership, Doug and his colleagues had successfully cultivated a number of high-margin customers. Management and the mill's dedicated employees had kept these customers happy by producing paper of unsurpassed quality. But if there wasn't signed paperwork in the order book, Compton made it clear in his conversations with management that he assigned little or no value to these superb customer relationships.

In late July, Compton sent his report to PNC Chicago. Appleton Coated management never saw the report, but they had to assume, in Marianne Sterr's words, that "the shipment volumes he used in his report were significantly lower than what we projected." Compton had also made it clear, as Doug Osterberg recalls, that "in his view receivership was the only path for the mill. He wouldn't talk about the cyclicality of the paper business, the signs that pulp prices were ready to tumble, or a possible Chapter 11 bankruptcy, which would have let us shift the pension fund responsibility and cancel the power contract—and keep operating—while we restructured."

It is hard to escape the conclusion that Michael Compton came to Appleton Coated with his mind already made up, and that his job was to justify the outcome the bank had already decided it wanted. In fact, on his first day at Appleton Coated, Compton had told Ed Bush that the mill was going to have to shut down, and he never expressed a more positive view, no matter what evidence management offered.

At the end of July, the balance on Appleton Coated's revolving line of credit with PNC stood at about $22 million, nearly eighty percent of its $27.5 million maximum. A seven-figure contribution to the pension fund was due in September, which would increase the loan balance. Otherwise, the last few months of the year would probably not change the financial picture much.

Yet PNC faced no risk of losing money on its line of credit to Appleton Coated. The bank had been making money hand over fist since the arrangement began, thanks to the high interest rate and the minimum monthly payments that were required even when the loan balance stood at zero. And the mill's healthy accounts receivable ensured that PNC would get every additional penny it was owed.

Perhaps the bank was worried that Appleton Coated's management would give themselves a special dividend or exorbitant pay raises before the line of credit expired. Such things do happen in MBOs and leveraged buyouts (LBOs) by unscrupulous managers and private equity firms. But Appleton Coated's management had always behaved impeccably. Their choice of Virtus as the name of their LLC was not slick branding; it was a sincere aspiration. In the months before business conditions worsened, the mill's "relationship manager" at PNC Chicago had been stunned to discover that Doug Osterberg and his team were not looting the business by paying themselves hefty dividends on their ownership shares—standard operating procedure in the private equity world. His jaw dropped in disbelief when Marianne Sterr said she and her colleagues were leaving the money in the business to position it for the future.

The Virtus Holdings team never took a penny out of the business except for their own salaries, which were on the low end for executives running a mill with $300 million in annual sales. True to their stated goals, they were looking to profit only when they could sell the mill to someone with the resources to capitalize on their efforts. PNC was apparently unused to dealing with business people with such high ethical standards. No doubt that helps explain why bank-approved consultant Michael Compton refused to trust the management team's expert sales projections.

Doug Osterberg and his partners knew PNC was disappointed by the mill's poor recent results, but they trusted that the bank would continue to finance them until the line of credit expired in December. At that point, the $750,000 prepayment penalty would also expire, freeing the mill to come to terms with one of the other lenders that had recently offered to provide financing. So the Appleton Coated management team saw no reason to believe that the mill was in imminent danger of closing.

Early in the summer of 2017, the Virtus Holdings partners had briefly considered shutting the mill of their own volition. If they did that while still officially in good standing with PNC, the bank would have to get its money back from the mill's accounts receivable. Meanwhile the owner-managers could sell the mill's assets, if possible, to a going-concern buyer who could conduct business without the drag of the pension obligations and power contract. However, this would have meant that the partners would still have been responsible for pension obligations and the power contract, more than counterbalancing any profit they might make on their ownership stakes by selling the mill's assets. A favorable ruling by the PBGC might free them of the pension responsibility, but that was a very uncertain prospect. If Virtus Holdings unilaterally shuttered the mill, the partnership would also still be responsible for repaying the full principal and interest on WEDC's $4 million loan. And PNC might sue, claiming that Virtus had breached its loan covenant by shuttering the mill without the bank's approval.

The owner-managers were also concerned about the mill's workers, both unionized and nonunionized. Ultimately, Doug Osterberg recalls, "We were not in the business of tearing things apart and scrapping. We were in the business of keeping people working—people we had known for years. We weren't going to close the mill."

A BALANCE SHEET WOULDN'T INCLUDE IT, but an excellent labor-management relationship was one of Appleton Coated's biggest strengths. It was why they made such great paper and had a solid base of high-end customers. Doug Osterberg led monthly Q&A sessions with any and all of the mill's workforce who could attend, almost always including the board of the mill's United Steelworkers Local 2-144. At these sessions, Doug and other senior executives took all questions, no matter how sensitive. Doug also tried to keep workers informed about the ongoing effort to find a buyer with enough resources to position Appleton Coated for the future. In fact, the executive team felt Doug was sometimes too spontaneously transparent in the Q&As, fearing that this could lead to misunderstanding when things were still in flux.

During the July Q&A, Doug mentioned that a paper maker who had recently toured the mill as a potential acquisition had said it would probably only want to run one of the mill's big paper machines and idle the other. If that happened, it would mean a layoff of around a hundred unionized workers. At this meeting, Doug also warned the employees that the mill had a rough patch ahead because of cash flow and financing issues, though he didn't go into detail on the rocky relationship with PNC Bank. An eternal optimist, Doug said they would come through things fine if all of them had faith in each other and kept working together. Among other things, they should all look for further opportunities to cut costs.

Tony Swanningson, Local 2-144's president at the time, was a man of faith, tested throughout his life. At a young age, he'd nearly lost his father, who worked at Appleton Coated before him, to an accident at the mill. Later he escaped certain death himself when his hand and upper torso got crushed by a machine. He had struggled through layoffs at three mills including Appleton Coated, watched his wife pass from a terrible illness, and in the wake of that loss battled alcoholism. He was the second coming of the Old Testament's Job—and like Job he would overcome each test and never lose faith. Swanningson was ready for anything. Local 2-144 could not have had a better leader at the helm.

Tony Swanningson says of the July Q&A, "Basically, we were told it was short term, that they were working with viable entities to either refinance the facility or sell it to another paper maker."

Millwright Nick Weyenberg, one of the younger paper workers, agrees with Swanningson. "They kind of gave the impression that we were going to be okay: 'We are not making money right now, but we got some new products coming up. We are going to get out of this and get back into making money and being profitable.'"

Despite the upbeat words from management, Swanningson had a Job-like premonition that things were not really so good and that major job losses would occur soon: "After the meeting, I kind of looked at everybody and I said, 'This feels awful familiar.' This might be my fifth layoff—the second from here."

On Tuesday, August 8, everything came to a head. With "an army of its lawyers and advisors participating," PNC held a conference call with Doug and his management team and "insisted we file for receivership the next day." PNC also insisted that the mill complete the receivership process within thirty business days, an unusually brief time period. The low FCC ratios in the preceding months— more precisely, the failure, because of the low ratios, to maintain a positive trailing-twelve-months EBITDA—gave PNC the right to "call the note," or, in Ed Bush's words, to "back up their trucks and take everything." The bank could do so even though Appleton Coated had never missed making a loan payment on time. PNC would not consider Chapter 11 bankruptcy, which would allow the mill to keep operating but also diminish the bank's overall profit on its line of credit. The bank had an iron grip on the mill, because of the way the line of credit contract had been amended at the last minute in December 2014 to mortgage all the physical assets as well as the usual collateral of accounts receivable and unsold inventory.

Stunned by this turn of events, all Doug and his colleagues could do was protest that they could not file for receivership without a forbearance agreement. In insolvency procedures, a forbearance agreement is a standard element that details the respective responsibilities of the creditor and borrower, usually including suspended or reduced payments by the borrower until the process is resolved. PNC's failure to prepare such a document in advance showed they were hell-bent on forcing receivership as quickly as possible, while leaving Appleton Coated no other options.

On Thursday, August 17, PNC supplied the necessary forbearance agreement, and Appleton Coated had to file for receivership the same day. The forbearance amounted only to stipulating that the bank would rely on the receivership process to get its money and would not hold the Virtus Holdings partners personally financially responsible. There was no leeway for the mill in the rest of the agreement.

The bank was technically not going to foreclose, no doubt because that step would have limited the ability to extract more fee income on top of the profits it had already made on the mill's line of credit. In return for financing operations and providing advisory services through the receivership period, PNC was to receive total fees of $50,000 per business day. This "cash burn plan," in Doug Osterberg's words, together with the foreshortened thirty-day timetable, left the management team without the resources needed to hire Wall Street advisors and pursue alternative financing. Doug later learned that PNC's appraisals, especially of projected sales and shipping volumes, were "outrageously low to justify their actions." At a stroke, the bank was also wiping out the ownership stakes of Doug and his fellow executives. Under receivership, they would be paid their salaries, but they would serve at the pleasure of the receiver and whoever bought the mill.

PNC had doffed its disguise as a financing partner and shown its true colors. How could the bank that had thrown the mill a lifeline just three years earlier—and later described it as a "prize account"—decide to rip it to pieces and devour it like a shark?

Perhaps PNC's extensive loan portfolio of other companies in the pulp and paper sector played a role. According to Doug, PNC had "big money, hundreds of millions" invested in Verso, Appleton Coated's chief competitor in the white grade paper market. Many people I spoke with during the receivership and while researching this book—workers, local officials, and senior paper industry executives—believed that PNC's true motivation for forcing

Appleton Coated into receivership was to goose its investment in Verso. As Marianne Sterr pointed out, "If Verso was able to remove any of their competitors from the market, they stood a better chance of raising prices and thus achieving better profitability. If Verso's profitability improved, wouldn't it make PNC's investment in them more viable?"

A person close to parties with intimate knowledge of the internal affairs of PNC and Verso told me that "multiple sources" said Verso pressed PNC to call Appleton Coated's note. According to this same source, Verso's senior executives had long considered Appleton Coated "a thorn in their side."

In any event, the net result of the financial squeeze put on Appleton Coated was a massive increase in the value of Verso's stock. From the beginning of the Appleton Coated receivership until the end of the year, during which time a similar mill in West Linn, Oregon, closed, the value of Verso stock would shoot up $16 from $4 a share to $20 a share—a remarkable fourfold increase. One year later (October 5, 2018), the stock would peak at $33.57. In 2019, the stock would come back down to earth, but it still hovered around $14 a share. For an industry racked with closures, bankruptcies, erratic pricing, and other challenges, Verso's turnaround was extraordinary.

PNC and Verso executives alike must have been well pleased with the outcome to that point in time (Verso would later run into difficulties again). Unfortunately, the managers and workers of Appleton Coated had been hung out to dry.

3.

Auctioning Off a Legacy

FTER THE CONFERENCE CALL with PNC, Doug called an all-facility meeting to tell the employees the bad news. That afternoon, Tony Swanningson, the president of the USW union local, received a briefing at the mill from a PNC representative, who portrayed the situation as an inevitable result of the FCC ratio's having dropped too low. Swanningson couldn't help thinking back to his first job—and his first layoff. Back in the mid-1990s, he'd been working at the Kimberly-Clark Globe mill in Neenah, the paper giant's flagship mill. "One day I went into work and we were told to shut the machines down. They rolled in a TV and played a taped message from the CEO of Kimberly-Clark," Tony recalls, rolling his eyes in disgust. "They had merged with Scott Paper Company, and because of the merger there was too much tissue on the market, and they had to close some facilities including mine. And that was it."

Like Tim Nixon, many Appleton Coated workers felt management should have responded sooner to market changes. Mike "Mack" MacDonald, the union local's secretary-treasurer, says, "The management team missed an opportunity in late 2016 and early 2017 to convert the mill [to brown grades]. We had the patents, we ran the trials—which were extremely successful—we had customers. But they waited too long. By the time they went to get financing, they were already in so much trouble that the bank was not willing to give them the chance."

Mill veteran Jim Weyenberg (Nick's father) agrees. "I don't think the owners could afford to buy the new pulper we needed to keep operating costs in line. They couldn't afford it or were unwilling to take the risk, probably more of the latter." He does not fault them. "They're all my age, probably most of them were ready to retire. They didn't want to take their life savings and stick it into a mill that might not survive." Indeed, the owner-managers in Virtus Holdings did not have the resources to make such a major capital expenditure. During the receivership, as before, they remained focused on attracting a buyer who did.

When Appleton Coated announced its receivership filing, PNC "took control over the facility," in Tony Swanningson's words. "No money was to be spent. Once a conveyor belt shredded and broke down. PNC was so cheap they refused to replace it. One of the supervisors went out and bought a couple rolls of duct tape so we could tape the belt and keep the rolls going."

Apart from that, things felt normal for the next two weeks. In Tony's words, "People still weren't seeing change. The facility was running; paychecks were coming." It also seemed as if the mill was making progress. Prospective buyers were walking through the mill, kicking the tires. Liberty Packaging, a growing paper manufacturer based in Becker, Minnesota, kept popping up in conversations as a prospective bidder.

"What was talked about most often was that a group of private investors would buy us and keep us running," Swanningson says. The promise of new products like corrugated medium, liner board, and an inventive white-brown grade for beer cases spread through the mill, giving added hope that Appleton Coated would be an attractive investment as a going concern. Workers were optimistic. "The management team were convinced that they had demonstrated enough viability with their new products," Swanningson says, "that somebody was going to come to the auction to buy us and keep us running. My union board and I, we were seeing the good brown paper grades we were trialing, and management said customers liked them and were putting in orders."

But time was running out. And beneath the surface, workers were feeling a growing tension. Mike Rask, a Virtus Holdings partner and the longtime head of mill operations, recalls:

> One day after the receivership filing, I was in the control room of the Number 1 machine with eight or nine of the guys.* One of them said vehemently, "All you folks in upper management who bought into the business, you're gonna walk away with big piles of cash in your pockets." I understood he was worried about his job and supporting his family, but I got mad that he would think that. I said, "No, the receivership wiped out our ownership stakes. We're in the same boat as you guys. All we've ever taken out of the mill is our paychecks, and the only thing we're walking away with is our pensions."

In hindsight, Rask wonders if management's announcement of the receivership should have included this information. "But, you know, Doug didn't want to put any focus on our personal losses, rather than the impact on the workforce as a whole."

At the suggestion of consultant Michael Compton, Appleton Coated had chosen Michael Polsky as receiver, a decision PNC

---

* At paper mills, machines are numbered in the order they were built. When machines are shut down, the numbers do not reshuffle but remain the same.

enthusiastically backed. Presented with Polsky's credentials, mill management assumed he was the best choice for all the company's stakeholders, including their valuable high-margin customers. Compton was well informed on the mill's current situation, and they reckoned that his motivations were aligned with their own desire to find a going-concern buyer who would pay more than an industrial scrap dealer. So Appleton Coated retained Compton and his firm, Silverman Consulting, to market the mill.

Meanwhile, Doug Osterberg, Marianne Sterr, Ed Bush, Ann Whalen, and sales director John Mazuroski reached out to the mill's customers and strove to assure them that they would fill existing and new orders at their normal high standard—or even better than before. Management did everything possible to preserve the mill's great customer base for its next owner, and show visiting going-concern appraisers that the mill had a thriving future.

On Thursday, August 31, 2017, receiver Michael Polsky filed a motion to auction the mill's assets "free and clear of all liens, claims, and encumbrances" on Tuesday, September 19. (The precise language would play a significant role in determining the mill's fate.) For the workers of Appleton Coated, their families, and other community members dependent on the mill, the time of reckoning had arrived. The coming Labor Day weekend would not be a celebration but a bedside vigil for a best friend, praying for a miraculous recovery.

On September 14, Tim Nixon shared his objection idea with me.

And at nine a.m. on Tuesday, September 19, the auction for Appleton Coated began in a small conference room at the Milwaukee Athletic Club. Depending on the bidding, the auction could run until nine p.m. that night.

Representing Appleton Coated management were CEO Doug Osterberg, COO Ann Whalen, CFO Marianne Sterr, general counsel Ed Bush, and sales director John Mazuroski. On hand for the USW were local 2-144 international representative Denny Lauer and Sara Geenen, partner at Milwaukee's Previant Law Firm, who was serving as the union's outside counsel along with senior partner Frederick "Fred" Perillo, a Midwestern labor law icon.

Sara's father was Jon Geenen, the Kaukauna native who was the USW's international vice-president. His life's work had been building the paper workers' union and strengthening the paper industry; Appleton Coated neighbored his hometown, and it employed several cousins and friends "whose very existence depended on the mill," as he put it. Since the receivership announcement on August 17, Geenen had hit the phones hard, cold-calling contacts in the industry—private equity firms, random investors, distressed-asset managers—to find someone who might be interested.

Geenen's pitch was solid—he'd had a lot of practice—but he was handicapped by the plant's lack of a pulp mill. On August 18, he had emailed me, "I am reaching out to the CEO of a major company about seeing if they could make this work. But the lack of a pulp mill exposes any buyer to volatility in input costs against the integrated producers. The only hope is a buyer who buys assets cheap to convert [the mill to make] packaging" for Amazon and other e-commerce companies. His assessment was the same as Doug Osterberg's. If Appleton Coated survived, brown grades would be their meal ticket. Now that the auction day had arrived, we'd see whether Jon's efforts had borne any fruit.

When the auction began, three interested parties arrived at the club in quick succession within the first half hour: California-based Industrial Assets Corporation (IAC), represented by CEO Steve Mattes; Big Shoulders Capital (BSC), a family investment office based in the Chicago area and represented by its president, Todd DiBenedetto; and Hilco Receivables, a division of HilcoGlobal, a large offerer of liquidation and restructuring services also based in the Chicago area. The representatives of the interested companies were ushered into separate rooms down the hall from the conference room. Receiver Michael Polsky also had a room next to the conference room. During the auction, the bidders would each communicate with Polsky privately via telephone.

The day before, Mike Rask had given Steve Mattes a tour of the mill. At the end of the tour, Mattes said, "This place is so spick-and-span. The workers are friendly and obviously take great pride in their work. It's going to be a shame to have to shut it down. I am not into running businesses. I scrap them. We take the metal and away we go."

Mike couldn't hold back the tears that came into his eyes. Mattes saw that and muttered, "It's just so sad," at a loss for further words.

The day of the auction, Mike Rask retired from Appleton Coated after thirty-three years of service, and Steve Mattes seemed to have gotten over his sentimentality from the previous day. Passing through the conference room at the Milwaukee Athletic Club, Steve Mattes pulled Marianne Sterr aside and asked, "How good are the accounts receivable?"

"Solid," she told him, knowing they were all collectible from Appleton Coated's high-end customers.

The action proceeded behind closed doors. It was impossible to know which bidders, if any, might be on the phone with Polsky to lodge a bid or discuss the parameters of one. Finally, at eleven a.m., Michael Polsky announced that he had accepted a stalking horse, or floor, bid of $21.5 million from IAC and that new bids would have to come in at least $500,000 increments.

The stalking horse bid not only set a dollar floor, it also set the parameters of every subsequent bid. In a receivership auction, bidders often want to offer only on individual lots rather than the entire enterprise. Polsky had let IAC exclude two pieces of Appleton Coated: the Farm House, as it was formally known, where a flamboyant mid-twentieth-century owner had stayed and entertained when he visited from Chicago, and a nearby landfill on the same acreage, about a mile from the mill. Any subsequent bidder had to make an offer on the same basis, for all of Appleton Coated except the Farm House and landfill. No other divisions of the mill and its assets, and no other exclusions, were acceptable—in other words, no apples-to-oranges counterbids that could lead to disputed outcomes.

Hilco responded by exiting the auction. It wanted to bid only on the accounts receivable. Not long after that, Todd DiBenedetto went back to Chicago in a huff after failing to persuade Polsky to allow an additional exclusion in BSC's bid (BSC may have wanted to exclude the mill's other landfill, this one right in Combined Locks). The remainder of the afternoon dragged on with no other bidders arriving.

When Marianne Sterr heard IAC's $21.5 million bid, she thought, "Mattes is smart. He knows the accounts receivable and other assets will guarantee him a solid return at that price, even if the mill shuts down tomorrow and never fills another order." But IAC's bid made Denny Lauer and Sara Geenen nervous, because the scuttlebutt was that the company had recently bought and shut two Verso paper mills. Throughout the auction, Sara Geenen updated both her father at USW headquarters in Pittsburgh and Michael Bolton, director of USW District 2 (Wisconsin and Michigan), at district headquarters in Menasha, Wisconsin. As the clock ticked with no other bidders, it became increasingly likely that IAC would win the auction. Despite Jon Geenen's efforts, no going-concern buyers were bidding in the auction.

Jon could feel the mill slipping away. He was furious and needed an outlet. He chose me. At 1:30 p.m., he put his thoughts down in writing and fired off an email to me just minutes after his daughter reported that BSC had left the auction:

> The governor and state lawmakers threw $3 billion dollars at a company [Foxconn] that will never pay the average worker anywhere near what workers are paid in the paper industry. Today, there will be an auction for a paper company based in the

Fox Valley. There will be no state government support for them, despite what the paper industry has done for Wisconsin for 100 years—although the county has certainly tried to help and other local officials as well.

Instead, the industry buyers who want to run the mill will be competing with no state help whatsoever against scrappers who want to buy the mill and strip it down, and export the machinery to countries that will use it to compete against our mills and our workers. The scrappers have learned that when an industry is ignored and no one stands up for it, the sum of the parts is greater than the whole. Of course, the only way to make that math work is to ignore the $300 million contribution the mill makes to the local economy.

Hoping today for a judge that weighs the interest of the community; a bidder who can see that investing in the hard-working employees at that mill is a winning strategy; and that our state officials wake up and begin to see the paper industry as the modern industry it is.

At 1:44 p.m., Sara reported to her father that IAC was still the only bidder. Moreover, she told him, "This morning, their CEO (Steven Mattes) said that they intended to immediately go dark and retain 25–30 [USW] members to do maintenance, etc., while they market and work with their potential operators. Mattes highlighted he has no interest in running a paper company or even holding it very long." Mattes had given no indication whether the skeleton crew would fill orders in hand; put the mill on a "hot idle," so that it could restart easily; or shutter it. But he made it clear that he would not pay the rest of the workforce while he and his associates were sorting out the mill's future, if any. Most troubling, Mattes told Sara Geenen he had a "major problem" with the successor clause of the USW's collective bargaining agreement (CBA) with Appleton Coated. The successor clause was the most important part of the CBA, because it obligated future owners to abide by the union contract.

The auction officially closed at 4:16 p.m., and a few minutes later Jon Geenen forwarded me Sara's final dispatch, which she'd sent to a collection of union officials. "The auction just concluded," Sara wrote. "The receiver is in a meeting with Appleton Coated and the bank. We are waiting to get additional information from them."

Reading the email was like reading an eviction notice. Despite everything I had tried to do, I felt I had failed hundreds of workers and their families, some of them from my childhood neighborhood across the river in Little Chute. Helping my neighbors was the reason I'd run for office in the first place. It made me think of a talk with my Lutheran pastor dad shortly after I graduated from college.

"Where have all the best and brightest gone? What about their hometowns? This is where they are needed," my father said.

He didn't have to cite chapter and verse. I knew exactly what he was thinking about: "Speak up for those who cannot speak for themselves; ensure justice for those being crushed" (Proverbs 31:8).

The sale of Appleton Coated to an industrial scrap dealer was the outcome that everyone associated with the mill had feared. Marianne Sterr recalls, "It was awful to have Mr. Polsky stand in front of us and tell us that by the close of business the next day, we had to shut down the mill and lay off almost all the employees, except for a caretaker crew of about fifty people."

Before he left the Milwaukee Athletic Club, Steve Mattes approached representatives from the union, offering the proverbial handshake after a tough loss. Sharing few details, Mattes said only that he would be at the mill the following week and that there was little chance that someone would eventually run it. The union was stuck on an island with no rescue boat in sight.

When the auction ended, Denny Lauer called union local president Tony Swanningson from Milwaukee. It was 4:30 in the afternoon, and Tony was at home on his day off. Tony recalls, "Denny told me I needed to go down to the mill and tell everybody that within two days we would be shut down. We had been purchased by an asset buyer and he had no interest in running the mill."

Swanningson drove across town and walked through the mill, speaking to workers one by one and in small groups. He did so again after the six p.m. shift change (the mill was on twelve-hour shifts). "People on the floor were in total disbelief," he remembers. Despite the receivership, the workers had clung to hope that a productive mill would not be shut.

Mack MacDonald walked the mill floor, too. He and Tony had 440 union members to care for, and they had a paper mill to wind down and close. MacDonald says:

> It was probably one of the hardest days of my life. Because most of these people I've worked with for thirty years. I know their families. I know who has kids and grandkids. Some people had daughters getting married, sons getting married. They're building their lives. A lot are planning for retirement. All of a sudden, they're told they are out of a job. The average age was fifty. They had done one thing their entire life and were thinking, "What the hell am I going to do now?"

AFTER WALKING THROUGH THE MILL, Tony, Mack, and a few others huddled with Denny Lauer, who had just made the one-hundred-mile drive from Milwaukee. There seemed to be no options left, but Tony felt a grim determination to do something, anything, to keep the mill alive. The look in his union brothers' eyes told him they had the same feeling. Appleton Coated was in a kind of purgatory, but not completely without options.

"Suppose we don't shut down," Tony said. "Suppose we stay in the facility and keep the machines going, keep making paper. Let's create a media sensation. Maybe that will attract a going-concern buyer. Heck, what's the worst that can happen? I mean, what are they going to do, fire us?" The others laughed, but their laughter had a bitter edge to it.

Denny Lauer liked Tony's idea and called USW headquarters to pitch it. From top to bottom—international vice-president for paper Jon Geenen, district director Mike Bolton—they all approved. Local 2-144 had the green light.

If ever there was a moment for the workers to take control of the facility, this was the time. It would be a reverse strike, with the workers continuing to make paper until ownership came to the bargaining table with an acceptable deal.

The okay from the union executives was necessary but not sufficient. The members of the union local would also have to endorse the reverse strike. Denny Lauer left the mill, and Tony Swanningson, Mack MacDonald, and the others in the huddle went through the mill from the shipping area to the roll line. Within an hour, they had covered the entire mill. The response was universal and overwhelming: the workers said "Do it!" in no uncertain terms. In keeping with their union motto, "One day longer, one day stronger," if it kept the mill going only for one more day, it was worth it. Tony called Denny to tell him everyone was on board.

There was enough pulp in the mill to run the Number 7 machine for another eight hours. After that, they'd need to open locked railcars to get more pulp. The workers' reverse strike was going to need the cooperation of management, albeit outgoing management.

By this point, Doug Osterberg was back in his office with its 1970s plastic-wood paneling and asbestos tiling—more like the office of a car repair shop operator than one occupied by the CEO of a company with $300 million in annual sales. The auction result was beginning to sink in, and Doug had seller's remorse. There had really been no alternative to filing for receivership, but he had made the decision to file and he owned it. He was kicking himself over the most regrettable decision of his career. But it was too late. They had to make the best of it, whatever that was.

A knock on his open door brought his head up. Tony Swanningson was standing in the doorway. When Tony revealed the scheme to keep the mill running, Doug was stunned for a moment. But figuring there was nothing to lose, he said, "Go for it." Tony shot out of the office and back down to the shop floor, sharing the good news like Saint Paul himself, lifting spirits and restoring hope.

Around this time, a few minutes before seven p.m., I was climbing into my car in my driveway, late to deliver a speech at a VFW auxiliary meeting on the other side of the county, when I took a call from Denny Lauer. Almost a decade before, Denny and I had stood shoulder to shoulder in the fight to save the NewPage mill just down the road in Kimberly. NewPage had made similar products to Appleton Coated and faced similar challenges: imports, electronic substitution, and declining consumer demand. It was nine years to the month since the NewPage mill had closed in 2008.

"Tom, I want to give you a heads up," Denny told me, his voice quavering a bit. "Stuff is going down at Coated. People may go to jail. I can't get too much into things. Call Bolton or Geenen, if you want to know more."

Flashbacks from NewPage filled my mind, not because of what Denny said but how he said it. It sounded like he was phoning in an on-the-scene report of a tornado or natural disaster. A knot twisted in the pit of my stomach. A part of me didn't want to know anything more, so I did not ask. Besides, I had work to do.

The auction having been won by a scrap dealer, the USW was ready for me to file an objection to the sale in my capacity as county executive. As soon as the meeting at the VFW auxiliary was over, I feverishly drafted my objection to the mill's sale for scrap, highlighting the economic damage to the community. At nine p.m., I sent it around to USW leaders, who saw it as a good complement to their legal objections. Jon Geenen and Mike Bolton told me it was important for an elected leader to speak out on the local economic effects of a shuttered mill, just as I'd done for Kimberly-NewPage in 2008.

All the objections had to be filed the next day, September 20, in the state circuit court of Judge Gregory B. Gill Jr. On Friday, September 22, Judge Gill would hold a hearing about the proposed sale of Appleton Coated to IAC. Receiver Michael Polsky and IAC CEO Steve Mattes expected the USW's objections, but past experience assured them that the hearing would be a mere formality. It was unheard-of for a state court to intervene in a receivership that had gone strictly according to the rules.

Back at the mill, as I learned later, the situation had changed again. While I was writing my objection, Doug Osterberg took a call from Steve Mattes. Doug didn't know whether to trust what Mattes said or not, but he couldn't ignore it.

Doug called Tony Swanningson back to his office and told him, "I was just on the phone with Mr. Mattes. He said there is a possibility that we can start back up next week. We need that pulp fiber in the cars." That meant the idea of continuing to run the mill would have to be abandoned.

Although he hated to stifle the workers' rising euphoria over taking control of the mill and their fate, Tony agreed with Doug. If there was any chance of Mattes's restarting the mill, they had to safeguard that possibility. Infuriating the new boss by disobeying the order to stop running the machines no longer made sense. They would shut down the mill safely, putting it on a hot idle to make a restart straightforward. No one was going to jail that night. But Tony still felt proud of the solidarity among the workers, knowing they all had each other's backs.

Rumors spread quickly that night among both unionized and nonunionized employees. When mill management arrived Wednesday morning, almost everyone already knew the auction result. The managers quickly had to decide who in the office and on the mill floor was going to be laid off and who was going to be kept on. Then the managers had to fan out through their respective departments and inform everyone individually, an especially difficult task given how long they'd all been working together and their great mutual respect for each other. The hope was that IAC would restart the mill within a few weeks. But no one could count on that. COO Ann Whalen urged those being laid off to begin pursuing other job opportunities immediately, because the future was so uncertain.

As the USW and I filed our respective objections that day, we recognized that we needed a parallel public relations campaign and a good spokesperson. They nominated me. My thirteen years in public life had prepared me for crises like these. The team agreed on four message points which I would hammer home in advance of the court hearing:

- A closure of the Appleton Coated mill would devastate the local economy.
- The mill must restart immediately.
- A new auction must be scheduled to give all interested buyers a fair shake and enough time to make bids.
- Governor Walker and other state officials needed to get their act together and help.

On Thursday, September 21, I did interviews with Fox Valley television, radio, and newspaper reporters. The state and national media weren't interested, but the story led the local television and radio news that evening. Next to the usual Green Bay Packers coverage, it was the top story for that day and the rest of the fall.

As our message got out, the responses started flooding in. In addition to complimentary Facebook posts and emails, my office took calls from investors and paper companies around the country. Despite the lack of any attention in the national media, and only perfunctory notice in statewide news outlets, the paper industry was paying keen attention, and I had become the public face of the battle to save the mill. Jon Geenen and I were juggling multiple calls—up to four at a time.

We had to make snap decisions on which calls were real and which were not. About one caller, Jon told me, "Don't call them back. They're not real. They're like a Dunder Mifflin," referring to the fictional company in *The Office*. "They're a paper broker, not a producer. Tell them we'll be in touch or something."

Other calls were more fruitful. "Let me take this one," Geenen emailed me about another caller. "It's a Hail Mary pass, but they could buy it in 2-4 weeks. DO NOT call—I will." This was a concrete example of why we needed to delay the sale. Interested parties wanted to take a hard look at the mill, but they couldn't do it overnight. They needed time. We needed time.

Workers and family members asked us about rumors that IAC intended to run the mill. They worried that our objections could spoil a restart. I guessed the rumors were coming from someone close to Steve Mattes, the presumptive owner, who was likely furious over the objections. For a man who did a hundred deals a year and cleaned out mills like cluttered basements, the opposition to the receiver's actions must have been a shock. Gossip may also have originated with workers. In one instance, I fielded a call from an irate worker and constituent who was convinced that IAC was going to run the mill and that the USW objection would torpedo the plan. I put her through to Jon Geenen, who calmly explained the USW's objection strategy.

Meanwhile, the community was furious that Scott Walker and the area's representatives in the state legislature had abandoned Appleton Coated. "Walker, get involved in this fight to keep the jobs in the valley," read one Facebook post. "Where is our state government?" another asked. Others asserted, "They're union jobs so Walker could care less." "Gov. Walker needs to pull himself away from Foxconn deal for a second and see what's happening here. These are 600 good jobs that are already here and it looks like nobody in Madison gives a damn."

The public and many workers were caught off guard; they had just heard about the sale. "We didn't realize it was gonna happen this fast," said one worker. "We're kind of confused and kind of left out here to dry at the moment," said another. Even news outlets were in the dark. "It's unclear what company will buy Appleton Coated. The company is not named in court documents." The auction was not forty-eight hours old.

"This is one of the most harrowing experiences an entire community can go through," I told *Appleton Post Crescent* reporter Madeleine Behr. "This is a company that has been a fixture in Combined Locks and Outagamie County for over a hundred years. This is a world-class paper mill; they produce a product that is second to none, a workforce that is second to none. We need to do what we can to keep them going. This is about the workers, this is about the company, this is about Combined Locks."

In an interview for Fox television affiliate WLUK and sister radio stations WTAQ and WIXX in Green Bay, I explained why I was filing an objection to the proposed sale. "We want to make sure that all the bidders out there will have enough time to do their due diligence, to put forth proposals, and hopefully someone will come forward that will commit to continue running [the mill] at its current scale."

Along with talking to the media, I had a busy schedule of dinners, talks, and events that day. In the morning, I welcomed school groups to Conservation Field Days, a county-sponsored field trip in Greenville on the western side of the county. That evening, I spoke at the annual 4-H Recognition Dinner in Appleton, thanking volunteers and patrons of the county fair's animal auction. (In keeping with tradition, I had officially "pardoned" a broiler chicken that I'd won at the fair.) It felt ironic to celebrate an auction on the eve of the hearing on the receivership auction.

Afterward, I skipped the chicken dinner and drove across town to the old Atlas Mill to join community leaders honoring my friend Leota Ester for establishing a journalism scholarship at Wisconsin Public Radio. More irony: the long-shuttered mill had been Kimberly-Clark's first Appleton mill. It had been repurposed decades earlier as a mixed-use development. It housed the Paper Discovery Center, a hands-on museum for school children; the Paper Industry International Hall of Fame; a café; and a few business offices. The limestone-and-cement edifice was fully intact, but the changes inside were stark reminders of what happens to paper mills when they die. There was so much at stake.

What could be done was done. We were ready for the next stage of the fight—in the courtroom.

One day longer, one day stronger.

Part Two

A Troubled History

4.

Profits, People, and Planet: 150 Years of Papermaking in the Fox Valley

O NE MILLION YEARS AGO, most of what is now Wisconsin was under water. What would become the Fox River Valley and the village of Combined Locks was a vast but shallow sea. In the ice ages that followed, glaciers covered the region, grinding south ten inches a day like a slow-motion crash before coming to rest in the Kettle Moraine region, sixty miles south of Combined Locks. As the Earth's climate began to warm, the massive ice sheets retreated and gouged Wisconsin's lake and river basins. They are the reason for the Fox River's peculiar south-to-north flow.

Flash forward thousands of years, and we find the Fox River becoming a major North American trade route and the site of bloody conflagrations between the First Peoples and settlers from Europe, especially France. Among the First Peoples were the Outagamie

(European explorers called them the Fox Indians), who in defense of their land stymied French trade for two generations. Connecting Lake Winnebago to the Green Bay, the Fox River abounded in fish, feeding wildlife throughout the river valley. It was a treasured natural resource stewarded by the Winnebago, the Fox, and later relocated bands of the Iroquois (Oneida) and Mohican (Stockbridge-Munsee Band). Not until the mid-1800s was it mechanized by European settlers, with dams powering sawmills fed by surrounding swaths of pine forest, some trees as old as 400 years and as tall as 250 feet. These trees were a resource that would soon be expended without care or concern.

To settle on the land, the European newcomers had to remove and confine the First Peoples. In 1836, immediately across the Fox River from where the Kimberly-NewPage mill would be established 53 years later, Chief Oshkosh surrendered four million acres of Menominee land to newly appointed territorial governor Henry Dodge in what was called the Treaty of the Cedars. The price: seventeen cents per acre. Similar deals were consummated between the Europeans and Native Americans, including French-Canadian trader Dominique Ducharme's purchase of present-day Kaukauna for two barrels of rum. In other parts of Wisconsin, Native Americans were driven from their land by the U.S. military.

The pattern of economic success at the expense of human rights and the environment persists to this day.

Europeans settled present-day Combined Locks beginning in 1842 when just ten German families arrived. The Dutch followed in 1848 with a larger contingent, and the Irish arrived the following year. Before industry could take hold, the river had to be tamed. In 1846, based on a study of the river basin, the U.S. government "made a grant of land" to "improve and build a canal" between the Fox and Wisconsin rivers. Two years later, when Wisconsin became the nation's thirtieth state, the legislature "accepted the grant" at a price of $1.25 per acre ($40 per acre adjusted for inflation). They got a good deal. Today, farmland in Outagamie County sells for $9,000 an acre.

At this time, a new industry of papermaking was being born in Europe based on a humble natural model. The groundwood pulping process was hardly new; wasps had been doing it throughout the ages to make their nests. But it wasn't until the 1840s that humans figured out how to copy the insects' technique. Charles Fenerty of Nova Scotia and Friedrich Gottlob Keller of Germany developed the process independently in 1844.

Wisconsin's Fox Valley was perfect for papermaking. It featured a thirty-five-mile winding river dropping 170 feet from its source in Lake Winnebago to its mouth, the Green Bay; abundant forest in every direction; and ready-made mills. The river provided water, itself a central ingredient in papermaking, as well as mechanical and electrical power. Its current also carried the mill's toxic waste out of sight and mind, covering up papermaking's harmful costs to nature and society.

Wisconsin had originally been a wheat-producing state. Wheat had attracted brothers John R. and Harvey L. Kimberly to the then-village of Neenah. They built their first flour mill in 1850, adding several more mills in the following years. When the flour industry waned because of competition from the Plains States, dairy and paper took over. Wisconsin's wheat fields turned into pastures and hay fields; flour mills became paper mills. Flour millwrights and machine tenders took on similar roles in paper mills. The westward migration meant hungry mouths and eager hands seeking work. There were plenty of jobs for plenty of workers. It was a match made in heaven.

The year 1872 would prove a watershed. The Kimberlys began transitioning from flour to paper. They would team up with the Clark family and build their namesake business into an enduring corporate power that eventually spawned household brand names—Kleenex, Kotex, and Huggies.

In the fall of that year, the federal government sold the newly constructed Fox River canal system's waterpower and property rights to the privately held Green Bay and Mississippi Canal Company. With its power harnessed thanks to the combined efforts of Uncle Sam and private business, the river catapulted the Fox Valley into the industrial age.

The Kimberlys are generally accepted as the most important of the Fox Valley paper makers. A close second would be brothers William M. and John S. Van Nortwick and Henry Rogers.

The Van Nortwicks got into paper in 1867 in Batavia, Illinois. In 1873, they joined fellow entrepreneur Henry Rogers and inventor and manufacturer Gustavus Ames in building what would become the Appleton Paper and Pulp Company in Appleton, Wisconsin. They used Ames's wood pulping process, a patent-evading variation on Keller's process, to produce newsprint for major customers such as the *Chicago Tribune*, the *Chicago Daily News*, the *Denver Chronicle*, and the *San Francisco Chronicle*.

The Panic of 1873 followed the Paper Valley's birth; it would go down as America's first Great Depression, brought on by unregulated financial engineering and speculation in railroads as well as tight monetary policy. As in the Great Depression of the 1930s and Great Recession of 2008, workers bore the brunt of the downturn, financially and physically. Companies and compliant state and local militia leveled violence against striking workers. The depression seeded the rise of the so-called prairie populists of Kansas and Nebraska and later the Progressives of Wisconsin. But through it all, the Fox Valley's paper industry took root and grew, persevering and strengthening.

By 1888, the Van Nortwicks and Henry Rogers "controlled all power rights along the lower Fox River" from Lake Winnebago to the Green Bay. John S. Van Nortwick ultimately rose to be president of the Green Bay and Mississippi Canal Company, whose ownership would remain in the family until the 1950s.

The following year, the Kimberlys and Van Nortwicks built pulp and paper mills in present-day Kimberly and Combined Locks, respectively, and later mill towns to house the workers. The Kimberlys named their village The Cedars; the Van Nortwicks named theirs Combined Locks for the canal boat locks along its shoreline. The Cedars would soon be renamed Kimberly, but the name Combined Locks stuck.

Papermaking is highly toxic and generates a lot of pollution; wood chips are bathed in sulfuric acid to be ground into pulp. A Fox Valley mill first used this process in 1879; Combined Locks followed a decade later. If the by-product waste is not disposed of properly, it can cause immediate and long-term environmental damage. Throughout the Paper Valley, sludge was pumped into the river, whose strong currents carried it downstream and out of sight for future generations to deal with. However, during those early years of the Fox Valley paper industry, few people considered its environmental consequences. "Most people tolerated the blighted waters and foul odors of the stream as an unfortunate but necessary evil, part of the cost of making paper," in the words of environmental historian Gregory Summers.

The growth of the paper business also took a toll on the workers it employed. Workers toiled an average of seventy-two hours a week and got just one night off every fourteen days—a punishing schedule.

The roots of the labor movement in the American paper industry date back to 1893, when the paper workers of Holyoke, Massachusetts were chartered by the American Federation of Labor (AFL) in 1893 as the International Brotherhood of Paper Makers (IBPM) Local 1. In 1901, the IBPM dispatched an organizer to the Fox Valley, where he was welcomed with open arms. That same year, the valley's paper workers notched an early victory when Kimberly-Clark, Wisconsin's biggest paper company, agreed to end the Saturday night shift—with conditions. If competitors did not follow suit,

Kimberly-Clark would return to the longer schedule at their mills. Gilbert Paper of Menasha followed Kimberly-Clark's lead, but other mills did not. Workers were forced to strike the mills that did not eliminate the Saturday night shift.

In late winter and early spring 1902, four more mills ended the Saturday night shift, including Combined Locks. But less than a year later, most Fox Valley mill owners returned to the long-hour schedules. Workers did not give up; they prevailed upon owners at the Strange, Winnebago, and Neenah paper companies to keep the shorter hours. Kimberly-Clark also agreed to return to the shorter schedule.

In 1904, the IBPM sought union recognition in the Fox Valley—the crucial first step in organizing union locals. Rebuffed by the mill owners, workers struck the Fox River mills, including Combined Locks, whose superintendent had ordered employees to quit the union. Kimberly-Clark went all-in and hired replacement workers under protection of private security forces. At one point, an over-zealous guard fired three rounds into a crowd of strikers. Incredibly, no one was hurt. Neenah was beset with violence for days. Undeterred, Kimberly-Clark trucked in more replacement workers. The company's use of violence weakened workers' resolve throughout Fox Valley's mills. On August 13, 1904, strikers met and voted to accept the Saturday night shift.

It was the beginning of the end of organized labor's first efforts in the Fox Valley. Fewer and fewer workers attended labor lodge meetings, and, by 1905, the Kaukauna and Appleton lodges had closed. Two years later, there were no IBPM lodges anywhere in Wisconsin.

In 1909, a schism split the IBPM. From this date forward, the IBPM would cater to high-skill machine tenders and boiler engineers, while low-skill workers in the wood yard and converting shops would be organized as the International Brotherhood of Pulp, Sulphite and Paper Mill Workers (IBPSPMW).

Of course, the Wisconsin mill owners were determined to prevent either of these unions from getting an organizing foothold in the state. In April 1914, Kimberly-Clark executive Frank Sensenbrenner founded the Western Paper Makers Association (WPMA), a cartel that aimed to impose owner-friendly wage and work schedules. The WPMA also established a massive antistrike fund to overpower union strike funds.

The creation of the WPMA was a preemptive move against labor. Mill owners saw that workers would gain leverage as World War I tightened the U.S. labor market by significantly reducing immigration from Europe. Accordingly, in one labor historian's words, the WPMA "maintained a strict surveillance of employee unionism" and "effectively mobilized the wealth and power of some thirty paper corporations against the workers of any plant whenever they strove for union recognition."

The WPMA fought workers on two fronts in the summer and fall of 1916, first at the Interlake Pulp and Paper Company in Appleton and second on the Wisconsin/Michigan border at the Marinette and Menominee Paper Company. Workers at both sites struck for eight-hour days and union recognition. Thanks to the tighter labor market, workers got the shortened day schedule, although they did not earn recognition for their union—the holy grail of labor organizers. Nevertheless, securing shorter working hours ignited a spark. Later that year and into 1917, both international unions, the IBPM and IBPSPMW, organized and reactivated locals across the state.

The year 1917 was also when John Burke ascended to the top post of the IBPSMW, where he would serve as president for nearly fifty years. Burke is the most important labor leader you never heard of. His accomplishments rank among labor's greatest. He built a tiny union into the industry's largest. With his playful Irish bonhomie, Burke attracted a following that would go wherever he led them. "When he said, 'Go in this direction,' people would follow," according to one paper company CEO.

Burke was a labor leader in the truest sense of the word. He worked the countryside like a madman, organizing mills by the dozen, rallying laborites at parades, and stitching together a wide and diffuse membership unlike those in industries that are concentrated in particular cities or regions. Burke's steady hand guided his union through the country's changing economic fortunes from the 1920s into the 1960s. He successfully navigated strikes that nearly killed the union, and he helped achieve the summit of union power in the post–World War II era, when one-third of American workers were organized.

Thanks again to the tightening of the U.S. labor market, paper mill owners reluctantly raised wages during World War I. Looking for additional workers, many U.S. industries, largely concentrated in northern cities and towns, cast their eyes on rural African Americans, who were then mostly restricted to sharecropping and indentured servitude in the South. Industrial recruiters triggered the internal Great Migration, in which significant numbers of African Americans entered America's economic mainstream for the first time. Between 1915 and 1919, half a million African Americans moved to northern urban centers. Twice as many followed in the 1920s. As African American painter Jacob Lawrence wrote in a caption to one of his landmark Migration Series panels, "All other sources of labor having been exhausted, the migrants [from the South] were the last resource."

African Americans from the rural South endured continuing racism in the urban North, including among unionized workforces. In *Rising from the Rails: Pullman Porters and the Making of the Black Middle Class*, Larry Tye writes, "Pay scales were higher than on the farm . . . but they met unexpected hostility from their unionized white coworkers who resented Negroes." Yet although the Black workers who migrated to the cities earned considerably less than their white counterparts, their economic lot improved substantially. Increasing prosperity among African Americans dramatically expanded enrollment at America's historically Black colleges and universities, paving the way for new, much more numerous generations of Black doctors, lawyers, ministers, and other professionals. The participants in the Great Migration and their descendants transformed all of American society and culture in many ways, not least by leading the post–World War II civil rights movement. And the tighter labor market that benefited them also lifted the fortunes of all American workers during the World War I years.

DURING THE EARLY YEARS of the twentieth century, Fox Valley paper companies made huge strides in product development. Charles Boyd (1871-1952) was known as "Paper Bag Cholly" for his dogged pursuit of the perfect paper bag. But even more significant was Boyd's work in improving coated paper.

At the time, coated paper making was a two-part process: paper was made from base stock, then coated in a converting process. The first step was done in local mills, the second in converting operations along the East Coast. As a result, Fox Valley papermakers were missing out on economic opportunities.

Boyd used family and personal resources to found a paper mill in Kaukauna in 1905. There he experimented with base stock and special coatings to improve the writing surface of paper. In 1907, he founded a second mill, Appleton Coated, on what is now East Wisconsin Avenue in Appleton.* By 1911, Boyd's first coated paper product, White Porcelain Enamel Shelf and Lining Paper, was on the market. What made his coated paper unique was the use of casein—

---

* This is not to be confused with the mill in Combined Locks, known as Appleton Coated from 1999 to 2017; everywhere else in this book, "Appleton Coated" refers to the mill in Combined Locks.

a protein in cheese—to bind the traditional clay-water solution to the paper itself. This only-in-Wisconsin breakthrough helped make the Fox Valley a national hub of papermaking.

In 1916, Lewis Alsted, a man of humble roots who had married John S. Van Nortwick's daughter Mary in 1907, bought out the shares of the Van Nortwick family including those of his wife's siblings. In 1916 and 1917, labor strife was on the minds of Alsted and his fellow directors. The board minutes from their 1917 annual meeting are filled with references to "labor agitation," the "labor situation," and "labor conditions." To avoid unrest among the mill's workers, Alsted adopted eight-hour shifts and gave workers a raise and bonuses. Ultimately the entire Fox Valley paper industry adopted eight-hour shift schedules.

The Alsteds and other mill owners could afford to pay and treat their workers better. In 1916, the year Alsted took the throne, sales shot up twenty-five percent over the prior year. Not only did the Combined Locks mill survive, it thrived. Alsted rewarded his mill manager, Paul Smith, for his common touch with the workers with a grant of twenty-five shares of stock and a seat on the board of directors.

Early in his tenure, Alsted partnered with George Seaman, the nation's largest paper broker, who had as a customer Sears Roebuck, the nation's largest mail-order company. Sears needed six billion pages worth of newsprint-stock paper, an order Alsted was delighted to fill. To gain needed production capacity, he bought the Little Chute pulp mill and leased Kimberly-Clark's Lakeview mill in Neenah.

Another notable mill owner of this period was George W. Mead of Wisconsin Rapids' Consolidated Paper, who took an enlightened view of labor-management relations. In the wake of an employee walkout in 1919, he held a series of one-on-one meetings with his employees. Impressed by the importance they placed on the right to negotiate working conditions, he agreed to bargain with them, signing a one-year contract that both sides were happy with.

Mead discovered that a good union culture engendered cooperation. Having established good labor-management relations, Mead had credibility with workers and was able to secure wage cuts when necessary. He agreed to wage increases whenever possible and always bargained in good faith. Thus, in good times or bad, workers and management were there for each other. You couldn't ask for a better business model.

Unfortunately, the favorable conditions created by World War I didn't last. In 1920, industry slowed down and increased immigration from Europe again expanded the labor pool. Several rounds of wage cuts ensued, prompting strikes and touching off a five-year war of attrition between International Paper and Burke's IBPSPMW that would nearly break the union.

In the middle of the decade, the 1924 Immigration Act reduced immigration numbers and tightened the labor market. Workers had increased bargaining strength and won higher wages. However, the law's country-of-origin quotas were inherently racist and stained America—hardly a desirable trade-off.

THE BOOMING ECONOMY OF THE ROARING TWENTIES did not lift all boats equitably. Rampant financial speculation and unbridled capitalism funneled most economic gains to the top. The comparisons to today are uncanny: an underregulated financial services industry, rampant financial speculation, ill-conceived trade laws, gutted unions, and out-of-control economic inequality. "Large amounts of capital were beginning to accrue in few pockets," wrote historians William Bremer and Holly Lyon of Kaukauna's Thilmany mill. The laissez-faire system was reinforced by moneyed corporate interests who doled out campaign cash to obsequious legislators, governors, and members of Congress.

In the fall of 1929, the stock market crashed, triggering the Great Depression. But despite the economic calamity, the directors of the Combined Locks mill doled out dividends to each other in 1930, 1931, and 1932. At the same time, they cut wages for their workers. Alsted and his wife owned 18,000 shares, a ninety percent stake in the company. The workers would not forget, and in due time they would respond.

By 1931, Alsted was expressing concern about the company's "reduced production of paper due to general market conditions." The machines were operating at less than eighty percent capacity. Alsted made an adroit strategic move by leaving the newsprint business and turning to telephone-book paper. The mill invested in a process whereby used printed paper was cut up and washed with chemical solutions to remove the ink, known as de-inking recovery. The process generated highly toxic waste, but its immediate and long-term damage to the environment and public health was ignored.

Workers had little or no power to fight for economic justice until the advent of Franklin D. Roosevelt's New Deal. The National Industrial Recovery Act (NIRA) of 1933, followed by the Wagner Act of 1935, established limited but significant worker protections, though they fell short of leveling the bargaining field. The NIRA would be short-lived, struck down by the Supreme Court as its initial two-year authorization was about to expire. However, the Public Works Administration (PWA), which was part of the NIRA, survived. The PWA put hundreds of thousands of able-bodied Americans to work on infrastructure improvement projects. Those workers logged over a billion man-hours and created such national assets as the Hoover Dam and the Lincoln Tunnel (New York/New Jersey). They also built three planned communities, including Greendale, Wisconsin.

The NIRA was also foundational for its follow-on reform law, the National Labor Relations Act, known as the Wagner Act for its chief author, Senator Robert F. Wagner (D-NY). In addition to solidifying rights to organize, bargain and take collective action, the Wagner Act gave the National Labor Relations Board (NLRB) "powers of investigation, subpoena, and decision making."

The same year that the Wagner Act was adopted, ten industrial unions broke away from the American Federation of Labor (AFL) and established the Congress of Industrial Organizations (CIO). Industrial unions were upset over the AFL's refusal to organize semi- and low-skilled workers. CIO leaders Walter Reuther of the United Auto Workers (UAW) and John Lewis of the United Mine Workers (UMW) viewed unionism not just as a means to get workers their fair share but as a movement to achiever larger socioeconomic goals. Both the AFL and CIO began with radical agendas, helping to forge an all-too-brief era of worker-friendly tax and economic policy. By the mid-1950s, they boasted a membership of four million.

The impact of the Wagner Act was enormous. Before its passage, only two Wisconsin mills had union contracts. By the 1950s, the vast majority of Wisconsin paper mills were unionized, but only after many years of grueling organizing work.

Organizing mills was incredibly difficult. Organizers found the workers' support for unions sporadic, almost "manic depressive." According to Burke, they went from the exhilarating highs of strikes, job actions and epic management-labor battles to the lows and apathy of the daily grind of union work—meetings, dues collection, grievances. Worse, according to Burke, once workers got a good contract they often dropped out of the union.

In later years, paper workers began organizing on an industrial basis—company by company rather than by tradecraft. This meant organizing under the watchful eye of owners and supervisors. Most organizing was also done in small communities like Combined Locks, where locals looked askance at outsiders. Finally, paper workers were spread out across the country; at one point, there were paper mills in thirty-eight states, and Burke's IBPSPMW had locals in each of them. All these factors created the need for an expansive network of organizers, which cost a lot of money and required effective leadership.

The 1940s brought uncertainty to Combined Locks. In 1938, Alsted passed away. Until the end of World War II, ownership of the mill was vested in his estate, whose trustees included his widow, Mary Alsted, his brother-in-law Francis Bacon, and board member L. A. Lecher. A steady hand was provided by G. D. Muggleton, who succeeded Paul Smith and served as vice president and general manager. Under Muggleton's leadership, Combined Locks acquired worldwide recognition for its de-inking process and its leadership in the production of coated paper. Paper makers around the globe visited Combined Locks to learn about these new techniques and purchase licenses to employ them.

Following the Japanese attack on Pearl Harbor on December 7, 1941, patriotic fever swept the shop floor. More than ninety mill workers enlisted in the service. Those who stayed behind converted the machine shop to produce parts for tanks and other vehicles. While the mill contributed greatly to the war effort and gained handsomely in new business, three of its enlistees were killed in action in Italy, at sea, and at Guadalcanal.

In 1946, John Cuneo, a printing magnate from Chicago, bought the mill. Continuity was maintained as G. D. Muggleton stayed on board. But for the first time since its founding, neither a Van Nortwick nor Alsted was in charge. Cuneo owned and ran Cuneo Press, the second-largest press in Chicago. Cuneo also purchased the D. M. Bare Paper Company mill at Roaring Spring, Pennsylvania, to expand production, a mill that remains in the old Appleton Papers family today.

MEANWHILE, THE BATTLE OVER the societal impact of the paper industry in Wisconsin was being opened on a second front.

By the mid-1920s, a nascent environmental movement had begun to emerge in the Fox Valley, as in the rest of America. Local people began saying that the Fox River should be a source of beauty and recreation, not simply a sewer line for mill waste. In 1927, the state legislature created the Committee on Water Pollution with authority to investigate pollution and establish rules and regulations to control it. Still, the environmental damage caused by the paper industry remained largely unchecked.

In August of 1946, the state Committee on Water Pollution (CWP) announced a "major breakthrough in combating pollution along the beleaguered Fox River."

Researchers had developed ways to extract yeast and other "marketable by-products" left over from sulphite liquor from the pulp-making process. They discovered a way of not only cutting down waste but making money and even creating jobs.

Two years later, the state ordered thirteen paper companies to reduce the waste they pumped into the river. It marked a revolution in the environmental movement that had begun just two decades earlier, but it also ushered in an epic battle between environmental and community interests and industry that rages to this day.

Both labor and business interests lined up against environmental groups with a simple but, for many people, persuasive message: "Fish or Factories!" It wasn't easy to form a durable blue-green alliance that wedded two key progressive issues and constituencies—labor activists and environmentalists. Today's emerging Green New Deal is the best hope in a long time to forge a lasting progressive alliance.

But in the 1940s, no such alliance existed. In 1949, the paper industry prevailed on the state to rescind the order, claiming the necessary technology was not available, despite the development of the sulphite waste recovery process three years earlier. Like the tobacco industry and the fossil fuel industry, the paper industry used its collective financial and political clout to dispute scientific facts, deny harms, and disparage the opposition.

In 1953, one year after the passing of Charles Boyd, the developer of Fox Valley coated paper, his mill in Appleton began making carbonless paper, which automatically transferred written contents from a top page to a bottom page. Using a process invented in 1938 by chemists from National Cash Register (NCR) that employed polychlorinated biphenyl (PCB) as a coating agent, engineers at the mill in Appleton figured out how to make carbonless paper on an industrial scale.

Thanks to carbonless paper, NCR had become an important force in the paper business. In 1969, John Cuneo sold his mills to NCR for $32 million. Cuneo had just capped his own investments in papermaking with the construction of the largest papermaking unit in the Fox Valley—the Number 6 machine at Appleton Coated. A 500-foot building had to be built to house the mammoth paper machine, which was 245 inches wide and could run up to 2,500 feet per minute, producing 400,000 pounds of paper in one day. Soon after buying the mills, NCR installed a stand-alone coating machine to apply the PCB-based microencapsulated coating and expand production of carbonless paper. The base stock would be trucked down the road to the Appleton plant where the other sheets of the three-sheet paper grade were made. One year later, NCR purchased Charles Boyd's mill in Appleton, putting all U.S. carbonless paper production under one parent company. In 1971, NCR merged Cuneo's mills with Boyd's under the name of Appleton Papers, Inc. Subsequently, Appleton Papers became the "global leader in carbonless paper production."

In 1978, NCR sold Appleton Papers to British American Tobacco (BAT) for $280 million. BAT also owned Wiggins Teape, a European firm that made carbonless paper for the rest of the world. Together, the two operations controlled eighty to ninety percent of the world market. BAT would escape antitrust violations and maintain a stranglehold on the carbonless paper market for two decades, benefiting Appleton Papers and the local economy.

The expansion of the carbonless paper business was an economic boom for the Fox Valley companies. But the human cost was tragic. Research shows that PCB is a toxic chemical that poisons fish, contaminates water supplies, and is considered a "probable human carcinogen." Scientists at agribusiness giant Monsanto invented PCBs and began selling them to paper companies for use in carbonless production. Monsanto claimed it was not aware of PCB's detrimental effects until the early 1970s. Yet the record suggests that Monsanto knew from studies dating back to the 1930s that PCBs were dangerous. The paper companies stopped using PCBs in 1971. Future generations would be left with the cost of repairing the damage to human health and the environment.

In 1970, Wisconsin's Senator Gaylord Nelson founded Earth Day, cementing his legacy as one of the country's most important environmental leaders. At the end of the year, President Richard Nixon signed the Clean Air Act of 1970, which Nelson had a hand in crafting. The law enabled regulation of car emissions—the provision which Nelson wrote—as well as of stationary sources of pollution, including factories like the Fox Valley paper mills. The U.S. Senate adopted the bill on a unanimous vote, a fact which becomes ever more astonishing in hindsight.

In 1976, Nelson helped shepherd through Congress the Clean Water Act, a second law affecting the paper industry. That same year, PCBs were banned under a federal law that Nelson authored, though the law would not take effect until 1979, thanks to a frustrating rule-making process and intensive lobbying by industry. By then, 125 tons of PCBs had accumulated on the bottom of the Fox River. Tightly bound to the riverbed sediment, the PCBs were pulled by the river's current downstream, closer to the Green Bay, the entry point into the

Great Lakes. The country was still a decade away from a serious evaluation of the effect of PCBs on animals, plant life, and humans, let alone concrete solutions and plans for a cleanup.

IN THE EARLY 1980S, the economic future of Wisconsin paper continued to appear bright. In 1980, the Combined Locks mill rebuilt its Number 5 paper machine. Counting on continued rising demand for paper, BAT invested millions in the papermaking process, including a new coating preparation plant for its increasingly popular high-end paper grades, an upgraded boiler facility to power the growing operation, and a five-year mill-wide expansion and modernization program. Taken together, the capital campaign had the size and scope of a major public works program for a small country. BAT's investment signaled a bullish market for paper. It also reflected the self-confidence of a company that had cornered the market and could dictate price and quantity.

As the Combined Locks mill grew, jobs multiplied. By 1988, employment reached 600. The neighboring and larger Kimberly mill had 1,400 union and management employees on the payroll. Total employment at both mills equaled the population of the village of Combined Locks.

Jobs were plentiful and local economies strong. School districts were flush with cash, and a strong union culture in the schools, mills, trade crafts, and local governments made sure teachers were well compensated. The Fox Valley boasted some of the best schools in the state and attracted excellent teachers, who gave the kids of mill workers and others a solid education to reach their full potential. This was my childhood. This was the American Dream.

But all the while, a storm was gathering.

The 1970s had brought some unprecedented shocks to American industry. The decade hit harder and hurt longer than any other. The U.S. economy was pounded by two successive oil crises—first the Organization of Petroleum Exporting Countries embargo on sales to Israel's allies in the 1973 Yom Kippur War, then a second crisis following the 1978 Iranian Revolution. The combined impact of these two crises sent the U.S. economy into a tailspin.

The Democratic Party retook the White House in 1976, but Jimmy Carter was not a New Deal Democrat like Lyndon Johnson. In economic policy, Carter was more of a Republican in Democratic clothing—in this sense, a precursor to Bill Clinton—and the aggressive deregulation we associate with the Reagan years actually began in Carter's administration. Michael Lind has observed, "It was Carter, not Reagan, who brought the religious right into national politics. . . . Carter, not Reagan, pioneered the role of the fiscally conservative governor who runs against the mess in Washington, promising to shrink the bureaucracy and balance the budget. . . . Carter, not Reagan, presided over the dismantling of the New Deal regulatory system in airlines, railroads and trucking."

Most striking of all is that Carter, not Reagan, nominated Paul Volcker as chairman of the Federal Reserve and backed Volcker's aggressive hiking of interest rates to combat inflation, a policy that triggered a brutal recession that badly harmed working people. And Carter, not Reagan, initiated a turn to supply-side economics. The Democratic chairman of the Joint Economic Committee of Congress, Senator Lloyd Bentsen, who would become treasury secretary under Bill Clinton, said in the committee's annual report for 1980 that "the Committee recommends a comprehensive set of policies . . . to enhance . . . the supply side of the economy."

Carter's abandonment of New Deal policies helps explain the political tectonic shift of the 1980 election, which made Ronald Reagan president and gave Republicans the majority in the U.S. Senate. Northeast Wisconsin was a bellwether for the 1980 election. Two years earlier, Republican Toby Roth had toppled the incumbent Democratic congressman, Father Robert Cornell. (You know you have problems when a Catholic priest loses re-election in one of the nation's most Catholic districts.) In 1980, former congressman Bob Kasten captured the Senate seat of liberal icon Gaylord Nelson while Reagan took the state's eleven electoral votes.

Angry at the Carter administration's hostility to labor unions, many UAW members embraced Reagan, although the UAW leadership stuck with the Democratic Party. A few labor unions, including the Professional Air Traffic Controllers Organization (PATCO), endorsed Reagan and took pride in picking the right horse. They would soon come to regret their choice, as Reagan amped up Carter's economic policies. Reagan used a strike by PATCO workers to justify firing the strikers, and two months later the National Labor Relations Authority decertified PATCO. Reagan had sent a message to corporate America loud and clear: break unions. It was the start of an era of aggressive attacks on workers' rights that would set the labor movement back decades.

Meanwhile, the fortunes of U.S. manufacturing and its employees began to spiral downward. Steel mills, smelters, mines, and auto plants by the dozen were shuttered. Working men and women who had made the mills hum and given their best in good times and bad times were now shown the door. From 1973 to 1990, union manufacturing jobs plummeted from forty percent of the workforce to twenty percent.

In the tumult of the seventies, the two remaining paper workers' unions, UPP and IBPSPMW, combined in 1972 to form the United Paperworkers International Union (UPIU). While UPP leader Joseph Tonelli became the first president, he was turned out of office six years later after he pleaded guilty to embezzling $360,000 from the union's treasury. His vice president, Wayne Glenn, who'd come up through the ranks of the IBPSPMW, took the helm of the UPIU. He would complete Tonelli's term and be elected in his own right in 1980. (He died in January, 2021.)

As weakened unions sought strength in mergers and industry hollowed, financialization filled the void. Reagan's agenda of hyper-deregulation, tax cuts, and supply-side economics shifted the focus away from a manufacturing-based economy to a paper economy, setting the stage for the savings and loan crisis of the 1980s and more severe financial meltdowns to come. For the first time in decades, the paper industry would be caught up in labor turmoil. It was a radical departure from the status quo. Few strikes or work stoppages had occurred since the New Deal. Under the conservative leadership of John Burke and later Wayne Glenn, the paper workers' union had avoided major confrontations with management. This would no longer be possible, thanks to an aggressive new strategy by the paper companies.

In 1986, John Georges, the president and CEO of International Paper (IP), convened a secret meeting in Atlanta with the heads of five other leading paper companies—Champion, Stone Container, Georgia-Pacific, Scott, and James River. The objective was to settle on a "concessionary bargaining" strategy. Their goal was to remake industrial relations, restore managerial power, emasculate unions, cut wages and compensation, and, above all, make a ton of money. CEOs salivated. (I have sought out Georges for comment numerous times without success.)

The plan was put into effect immediately. Georges and other industry leaders completed customer orders at non-union IP facilities and took advantage of a 1938 Supreme Court decision, *NLRB v. Mackay Radio & Telegraph Co.*, which had given managers the right to hire strikebreakers. The NLRB, stocked with GOP appointees, issued new rulings that encouraged Georges and like-minded CEOs to keep undermining unions.

Wisconsin papermakers were caught up in the conflict. Bitter strikes at Thilmany in Kaukauna and Nicolet Paper in De Pere—both IP facilities—would rage for weeks. Nicolet Paper workers eventually crossed the picket line, leaving the union behind. Thilmany hung in and got through the strike, union intact.

Throughout the Fox Valley, the fight against John Georges and International Paper spread from the bargaining table and the picket line to the kitchen table and backyard cook outs. As a ten-year-old in the summer of 1986, I had to break my habit of drinking Coca-Cola; any company represented on the International Paper board of directors, like Coca-Cola, was an enemy combatant. Animosity between dads in management and dads in the union poisoned their children's friendships and prompted bullying and fights on the playground.

Though not part of the IP consortium, Combined Locks was not immune to the issues roiling the paper industry and did not escape the 1986 strike season. Unlike Thilmany or Nicolet Paper, however, the Combined Locks mill was not the target of an industry-wide conspiracy to destroy unions. The strike lasted just a month before the two sides settled, with workers taking a lump-sum payout and a minor wage increase.

Meanwhile, the game of musical chairs regarding ownership of the Appleton paper mills continued. In 1989, BAT separately spun off Appleton Papers, Inc.—which included the Combined Locks and Appleton mills—and their London-based papermaking operations. The next year, the two combined to form Wiggins Teape Appleton (WTA). Then, in 1991, WTA merged with Arjomari-Prioux of France to form Arjo Wiggins Appleton.

In 1989, George H. W. Bush took office. Reagan's vice president, whose powerful family historically owed its wealth to Wall Street, continued a laissez-faire agenda of deregulation and financial-ization. The country would maintain its rightward tilt for four more years. And as far as labor was concerned, even the return of a Democrat to the White House in 1992 didn't make much difference in the national trend.

Bill Clinton was not a favorite of labor. In his first term as president, Clinton picked up where Bush left off, pushing the North American Free Trade Agreement (NAFTA) through Congress. Precious attention and resources shifted away from the needs of the middle class to the wishes of Wall Street. At an early budget meeting, Clinton famously told staff including Wall Street veteran Robert Rubin, who proposed a deficit-reduction plan, "You mean to tell me that the success of the program and my reelection hinges on the Federal Reserve and a bunch of [expletive] bond traders?!" Fed chair and Bush appointee Alan Greenspan quickly endorsed the move. Clinton soon embraced the strategy and claimed it as a legacy.

Against this economic and political backdrop, Fox Valley paper continued to grow. In April 1994, Combined Locks started up the new Number 7, the first new facility in twenty-five years. It was a monster. As long as a football field, 300 feet, it produced 3,500 feet of paper every minute, fifty percent more than the next fastest machine. It cost $170 million ($300 million in 2019 dollars) and represented the plant's single largest capital investment to date. The following year, the company added a coater machine and expanded the workforce by 150 jobs. Company officials acknowledged that making popular coated products like high-end brochures and annual reports, books, catalogs, and direct mail pieces was a "tough market." But the Combined Locks mill still had confidence and moxie. "'We don't take anything for granted, but we think we bring some good things to this market,'" said one company official. It seemed to make sense then.

However, the Number 7 was installed just as the market for carbonless paper topped out. "Everyone who could be in carbonless was in carbonless. There was no growth potential," Ed Bush told me. "The early 1980s, that was the time to get into thermal and coated paper, not the 1990s." Noting BAT's core product line, Bush wryly explained the company's missed opportunity. "BAT made cigarettes, not paper."

Long-term economic trends continued to undermine the position of American workers, including those in the paper business. In 1965, Congress had repealed the Immigration Act of 1924, with its racist country-of-origin quotas, and replaced it with a new immigration law. Although the sponsors of the new law promised that it would not increase the total number of immigrants per year, a provision for extended family "chain migration" guaranteed that numbers would rise sharply after 1970. Organized labor protested in vain, fearing the use of immigration as a cheap labor supply, as did a number of Democratic Party stalwarts. In the following decades, immigration would become an ever more polarizing issue.

In 1994, the Democratic Congress established the U.S. Commission on Immigration Reform and selected as its chair the civil rights champion and former Texas congresswoman Barbara Jordan, the first Black woman elected to Congress from the South. The commission recommended returning to moderate immigration numbers that would still honor and maintain America's history of openness to the world. Clinton first endorsed the recommendations, then did a U-turn and shelved the report after Jordan died, aged 59, on January 17, 1996. Moderate and conservative-leaning voters would begin associating an open-borders agenda with the Democratic Party.

Other blows to American workers would follow. In 1997, the Asian financial crisis hit, one of the worst since the stock market crash of 1987. Rampant speculation, specifically "attacks" on the Thai baht, precipitated the debacle and triggered a global financial meltdown. For the year 1997 alone, total multilateral and bilateral aid packages designed to control the financial "contagion," including those from the United States, totaled $110 billion. The United States also opened its markets to southeast Asia, allowing cheap imports to flood the country. The U.S. began shedding manufacturing jobs at a dizzying rate. In November 1999, Bill Clinton and the U.S. Congress repealed the Glass-Steagall Act, which since the New Deal had restrained Wall Street speculators by separating commercial and retail banking from investment banking. Large investment houses like Goldman Sachs, Lehman Brothers, and Bear Sterns were granted easier access to bank deposits, the big retail banks went full tilt into investment banking speculation, and depositors had fewer protections.

For Columbia University economist Joseph Stiglitz, it was mind-boggling. According to the 2001 Nobel laureate, the U.S. was totally ignoring the lessons of the 1997 and 1998 financial crises, which showed why regulation was necessary to rein in "capital market liberalization." This latest round of financialization set the stage for the Great Recession of 2008-09. Under President George W. Bush, the nation's economic policy became even more Wall Street–driven. Bush slashed taxes for the rich and floated plans to eviscerate Social Security and Medicare. Meanwhile, the country bled manufacturing jobs. By the end of Bush's first term, the nation had lost three million such jobs.

As America's manufacturing base eroded, so too did union ranks. They consolidated to bolster their collective strength. In 1999, Glenn's United Paperworkers International Union (UPIU) merged with the Oil, Chemical and Atomic Workers International Union, creating the Paper, Allied-Industrial, Chemical and Energy union (PACE). On January 11, 2005, the paper workers found yet another new home, the United Steelworkers (USW), North America's second-largest industrial union. While the union would continue to be known as the USW, its full official name would be United Steel, Paper and Forestry, Rubber, Manufacturing, Energy, Allied Industrial and Service Workers International Union.

At the end of 1999, the Combined Locks mill was reorganized as a Delaware limited liability company and rechristened Appleton Coated, LLC. The next year, Worms & Cie of France, former parent of Arjomari-Prioux, acquired all of Arjo Wiggins Appleton (AWA). In 2007, Worms & Cie was renamed Sequana. This is the firm that would own Appleton Coated until it was sold to the company management consortium in December 2014.

The steady stream of ownership shuffles—another symptom of the financialization of the U.S. economy—could do nothing to protect the paper mills from the continuing decline of American manufacturing. In 1999, five years after the Number 7 had gone online at Combined Locks, Arjo Wiggins Appleton put $25 million into refitting the aging Number 6 to make even more white-paper grades. It seemed a safe move at the time. But management was missing the signs that coated and carbonless paper would both face significant challenges in the coming decade.

From 2000 to 2008, more paper mills closed, taking more jobs with them. Industrial job losses would accelerate when the Great Recession hit in 2008 and 2009, including in the Paper Valley. Unbridled speculation on Wall Street was responsible for the near-collapse of the global economy. Congress would step in to bail out the most endangered banks with $700 billion, but attempts under President Obama to enact an economic stimulus package commensurate with the disaster were stymied by the Republicans. After spending eight years rubber-stamping President George W. Bush's reckless, debt-building budgets, now they were all for "responsible budgeting."

THROUGHOUT THIS ERA OF FINANCIALIZATION and the damage it caused to American industry, the long struggle to control the damaging effects of pollution caused by the paper industry also continued. In 1988, almost ten years after the PCB ban had gone into effect, a "groundbreaking five-year, $12 million study commenced" on the "sources and behavior" of PCBs in and around the Green Bay. According to the Wisconsin Sea Grant, it was "the first attempt anywhere on the globe to account fully for every source, all modes of transport and the various fates of a toxic industrial chemical contaminant in an ecosystem." Progress was slow, but it was beginning to pick up.

The next year, the United States Fish and Wildlife Services (USFWS), the federal agency in charge of the nation's waterways, called a meeting with the Wisconsin Department of Natural Resources (DNR) to plan a cleanup strategy for the Fox River. The DNR had been dragging its feet. According to a 2003 study by University of Wisconsin-Eau Claire researcher Valeri Andrews et al., "DNR officials expressed reluctance to endanger their 'good working relationship' with the paper industry." The USFWS was growing impatient.

In 1996, the USFWS initiated a pre-assessment of PCBs in the Fox River and its tributaries, including the several creeks in the Oneida Nation. The Menominee and Oneida were part of the study because federal law required the involvement of affected tribes. Both tribes had a lot at stake. Among the Oneida, fish are considered "transition food" connecting the winter diet of meat to the summer diet of vegetables. In the tributaries on Oneida land, the PCB concentration was off the charts—fifty parts per million, fifty times the allowable limit.

Not surprisingly, the pre-assessment found a "reasonable probability of making a successful claim for damages" under the federal code of regulations. There were five main findings: (1) a substantial PCB discharge had occurred, (2) natural resources were likely to have been adversely affected, (3) concentrations of the chemical were high enough to "potentially injure," (4) an assessment could be done at a "reasonable cost," and (5) there were no planned responses that would adequately remedy the problems. This prompted a full assessment that began shortly thereafter.

Thus began what turned into a twenty-four-year PCB cleanup project. In 1997, local mills pooled their resources to conduct a few pilot projects to prove the cleanup could be done with local resources and leadership and to settle the scientific dispute as to whether PCB hot spots should be capped (left on the riverbed but covered with impervious material) or dredged. It was hoped that the pilot projects would dislodge the log jam and get the project underway. The federal Environmental Protection Agency (EPA) had thrown down the gauntlet: get your stuff together or become a Superfund site. The Fox Valley did not want to be in the same company as Love Canal, the notorious neighborhood in Niagara Falls in the 1970s that had been polluted so badly the residents had to evacuate the town. Further, local leaders wanted to drive the project since the companies and cities like Appleton that treated the PCB wastewater would have to foot the bill. Where possible, they would use local contractors and construction firms. The DNR and EPA would monitor closely, but locals would do the actual work. The city of Appleton concurred, and adopted a resolution on July 1, 1998, affirming the local and state-based cleanup strategy.

The pilot projects produced the desired results. By 2004, the effort was finally up and running—a land-speed record for a large-scale environmental cleanup. Initial estimates put the total project cost between $154.5 million and $728.3 million, depending on the combination of dredging or capping techniques, but the final tab would run well ahead of the projections.

By 2014, everyone involved in the cleanup was eager for the last barge to leave and the last platform to be disassembled. They were proud, too. Dave Ullrich, who helped oversee the project for the EPA, described it this way: "This is probably one of the most successful cleanups across the United States and Canada and probably one of the most successful in the world as well."

The celebration was short lived, however. Up the river, mills were set up like dominoes—ready to fall at any moment. The industry confronted a threat unlike anything it had seen in the previous century—worse than the Great Depression or the Great Recession. This time, however, the danger came from within.

5.

The Ghosts of Kimberly-NewPage

I RECEIVED MY FIRST LETTER from a constituent about the closure of the Kimberly-NewPage mill on July 30, 2008, the very day the news broke. The constituent saw through the smokescreen of excuses—rising pulp prices, excess capacity, worsening economy—and called out the news for what it was, a result of uncontrolled corporate greed:

> The announcement today by NewPage Corp of their intention to shutter their plant at Kimberly is a shameless demonstration of greed over the public good. NewPage is owned by the investment group Cerberus. They have never made a sheet of paper, sold a bag of groceries, operated a restaurant, or provided logistical support for the U.S. military. They are a bottom-line company that creates nothing and leaves broken lives and communities in its wake.

From day one, the people of Kimberly, Wisconsin had NewPage's number. No amount of spin by the paper giant or private equity parent Cerberus Capital Management—appropriately named after Greek mythology's three-headed hound from hell—would convince them otherwise. They never bought it, always fought it. The community—the workers, their families, a handful of politicians, and most important, their union, the United Steelworkers (USW)—understood the monumental task they faced in trying to fight the plant closure. They were undeterred.

My constituent's email ended with a challenge for me and my fellow politicians: "We can only turn to you for assurance that, as representatives of the people, you will take steps to make these moneyed interests understand that dignity also has its price. Please, it is time for you to act."

It was an election year for me, one that seemed to hold enormous promise for me and my allies in Wisconsin state politics. I was running for re-election to the state assembly and hoping to position myself to become majority leader in the coming session. Our Democratic caucus was within striking distance of taking over the assembly. The prevailing political winds were at our back, and every Democratic assemblyman and woman was on the hustings, knocking on doors and raising money, all the while angling for leadership positions or seats on the coveted Joint Finance Committee.

But I immediately realized that the assault on the Kimberly-NewPage mill was more important than my personal political fortunes. I suspended my re-election campaign. A planned vacation tour of Midwest baseball parks with my dad would also have to wait. And I had to figure out how to get through a painful breakup with a longtime girlfriend. It would be a long three months until election day.

The Kimberly mill had been established in 1889, the same year the Appleton Coated mill in Combined Locks was founded. Like

Appleton Coated, the Kimberly mill made newsprint in its early years before shifting into coated paper in 1926. Except for a few specialty grades like soup can labels, the mill had maintained the same product line—white grades, namely high gloss and fine papers—ever since. It was a profitable line and fueled expansion, including mill renovations, equipment upgrades, and machine rebuilds.

Thanks to this productivity and effective union representation, the mill also provided workers with good wages and benefits. Kimberly's workers had had an independent union until the mid-2000s, when they were reorganized by Jon Geenen and the late Vern Bowers on behalf of the Paper, Allied-Industrial, Chemical and Energy Workers International Union (PACE). Over the course of union local president Andy Nirschl's twenty-eight-year career at Kimberly, there were no work stoppages, strikes, or other episodes of labor strife. Contracts were negotiated and implemented on time. Wages and benefits kept up with those of other Paper Valley mills.

This was how a mill should be run.

Jobs were good not just because they paid well, but because management and labor worked together well, creating and fostering a healthy, productive work environment. Dubbed "the redesign," the labor-management program at Kimberly encouraged workers to share ideas and work through problems. Both labor and management viewed the program favorably. Former co-owner and operations manager Pat Maley, one of the four-person owner-manager team that ran the mill from 1976 to 1997, prided himself on good relations with workers. Every quarter, he took one of five crews, each with about 200 union workers, out to a supper club, the common man's social club in Wisconsin. In this case, it was the Starlite Club on the outskirts of neighboring Kaukauna. Its expansive banquet hall was big enough to accommodate everyone, all the workers and their spouses.

Head boiler engineer Ned Wittman (1972–2011) fondly recalled those quarterly dinners: "It was great. I'm talking good half-inch pork chops. And you'd get two drinks, and they'd even invite the retirees back."

The mill workers took immense pride in being Kimberly paper makers. When Andy Nirschl talks about how paper was made in Kimberly, you can hear the excitement in his voice. For Andy, everything about papermaking sings:

> How paper is refined, how different grades of paper are made with different types of wood. The pulping process, the chemicals that are added. Just watching it go from a log or a bale of pulp into the final product that's coming out on the drier side of these huge machines. I would be up on the paper machine and any little change you made could make the paper better or worse. And you'd run your tests on it and see the consistency and the freeness [the rate at which water drains from a fiber-raw material blend]. And you could see what little changes you made, how they were reacting, and you'd see it go on to the wire from the white end and then go to the other end and see it come out on a huge roll of paper.

For longtime Kimberly-NewPage employee Mark Van Stappen, the process had a spiritual dimension: "If you live near a flowing river, that river is the essence of life. It's always moving and flowing. That's what you have with paper mills. It's been there for a long, long time. It's part of the landscape. People have unknowingly built it into their psyche. It is calming, reassuring. No matter if it is cold or hot, rain or shine. It's always there."

But things began to change when Consolidated Paper bought the mill from Maley and his partners in 1997. The company promptly began liquidating or moving key assets to the company's flagship plant in Wisconsin Rapids. Finland-based Stora-Enso acquired Consolidated in 2000 and continued the pillaging. NewPage, owned by Cerberus, acquired both the Kimberly and Rapids mills from

Stora-Enso in 2007. NewPage would complete the destructive process.

Sally Feistel, who represented several NewPage facilities including Kimberly for the USW, was unconcerned about the NewPage purchase at first:

> I didn't think much of it when they bought us. I remember telling my husband, "I don't think they are the worst company that could buy you." That was my first thought process. You're always worried about private equity coming in for five years and then flipping it. NewPage seemed to be interested in making paper, running it as an actual paper company.

Ned Wittman had the same instincts. When NewPage bought the mill, he was convinced it was a good omen. First, they were Americans, not foreign buyers. Kimberly was the all-American town: good jobs, safe streets, and great schools, with a solid football program to boot. Based in Ohio, another Rust Belt enclave, NewPage seemed to be a good match. Wittman thought if anyone would appreciate the importance of a good Midwestern town and its people, NewPage would.

But if NewPage was "an actual paper company" headquartered in small-town Ohio, New York City-based Cerberus was still calling the shots.

Van Stappen is still upset about the resources that kept being stripped from the Kimberly mill by NewPage: "All the cutters, trimmers, packagers, all that converting machinery. It's like we were slitting our wrists." Making matters worse, management decreed the abandonment of the highly profitable, value-added products that Kimberly had been making. In Van Stappen's words:

> We went from heavy grades of paper that we were converting ourselves—which made a lot more money—to very light grades

of paper in a wet roll form that didn't. The problem you get is your tonnage goes way down. You are creating a lot less basis weight. You are putting out less tons of paper of less value with no integrated pulp mill. If NewPage or anyone else was looking to reduce the volume of paper in the market, you wouldn't run Kimberly and shut down part of Wisconsin Rapids, you'd run Rapids full [of product]. Plus, they had all the pulp there and didn't have the cost of shipping.

The strategy echoed that of the robber barons of the late nineteenth century, such as Andrew Carnegie and John D. Rockefeller, and their Wall Street backers, especially J. P. Morgan. According to Morgan biographer Jean Strouse, "In different ways, Andrew Carnegie and John D. Rockefeller took command of ... wildly competitive industries . . . creating huge, low-cost, high-volume enterprises organized to take advantage of technological innovations, administrative rationalization, and tremendous economies of scale." In Carnegie's case, this business model included "relentlessly underselling less efficient [steel] mills and . . . running his mills at full blast to maintain high production volumes even if it wore out the mills in the process."

The final nail in the Kimberly mill's coffin was moving its pulper to Rapids. This put Kimberly at the mercy of erratic prices for pulp, the biggest and most consequential input in papermaking. NewPage CEO Mark Suwyn would later cite shipping pulp as a "monster cost" that doomed the Kimberly mill.

According to University of Southern Maine professor Michael Hillard, a leading expert on the paper industry, buying instead of producing key inputs like pulp jeopardizes a mill's long-term viability. In fact, this was a crucial part of the reason for the closing of mills and overall decline of the industry in Maine. "Mills were always at some risk in not fully controlling wood production, and at times the system would go into crisis, creating great suspense and providing impetus for major restructuring," Hillard says.

NewPage supposedly had a logical reason for the plan. "The agreement was when they moved the pulper to Rapids, that they would make the pulp and ship it to us and we would be the only [other] users of the pulp," Nirschl recalled. The two mills were only 85 miles apart, and pulp mills don't come cheap. It made financial sense to invest and upgrade one, rather than two, facilities.

But then came the July 2008 announcement of the plan to shut Kimberly.

Desperate, union leader Nirschl offered generous concessions, including a $5 per hour, across-the-board wage cut to keep the mill running. Designed to offset the cost of shipping the pulp to Kimberly, this offer was akin to cooks at the Starlite Club offering to buy the perch and beer batter for the club's signature dish with their own money. NewPage didn't care. "When they said we were shutting down, they had no interest in bargaining," Nirschl said, his contempt simmering.

It was hard for an outsider to understand NewPage's motivation. In 2008, Kimberly-NewPage was North America's largest coated paper producer. With $54 million in earnings before interest, taxes, depreciation, and amortization (EBITDA) in 2007, it was in sound financial and operational condition. So why shut down the plant? Nirschl thinks he knows what NewPage had in mind: "Taking the biggest producer off the market was going to start their little process—or whatever they were thinking—to drive up the price of paper. Shortly after that, the recession hit and that all went to hell for them." The recession only accelerated NewPage's plans: shut down operations, wring supply from the market, and increase profits.

USW representative Sally Feistel recalls an early meeting with NewPage top brass that implied such a strategy. "They were talking about achieving a thirteen percent return on investment," Feistel said, her eyebrows arching up. It was a lofty, perhaps impossible goal for an industry with tight margins. "That's why they wanted to shut Kimberly. Obviously, you shut down big producers and you don't have as much paper on the market, and then you can raise prices. Plus, you've slashed your costs. That's how they make the numbers work."

Nothing the union leaders said would shake NewPage's determination to shut down the plant. NewPage was determined— but so were we.

Rereading my constituent's email, I got an idea. I took to heart the appeal to "representatives of the people." In Wisconsin, the state assembly is the lower house, with ninety-nine seats compared to thirty-three in the state senate. I considered the assembly the "People's House" because each district was one third the size of an upper chamber district, putting the occupant of an assembly seat closer to individual constituents. If you worked hard enough— knocking doors, conducting regular listening sessions, attending public events—you could develop a personal relationship with the people of the district, to say nothing of insulating yourself from serious challenges to the seat. (In testing the waters for a possible state senate run that year, I learned that my name recognition was eighty-three percent, higher than that of the incumbent.) I beat the odds when I moved a solid red GOP seat into the blue Democratic column. With a little luck, I felt we could beat the odds for Kimberly, too.

I realized that we needed a message vehicle to generate awareness, build community support, and buy time to save a mill's community-sustaining jobs.

Imagine the damage control NewPage would have to undertake, I reasoned, if all ninety-nine representatives in the state assembly, including those from the districts with the company's nine other Wisconsin facilities, spoke with one voice for the Kimberly mill and its workers. That kind of pressure, and the media attention it would garner, could bring NewPage to the bargaining table for some serious talks.

On August 11, just twelve days after the announcement, NewPage shut down the first machine (Number 6). The next day, I introduced a resolution in the assembly calling on NewPage to run the mill or sell to a buyer that would. A worker soon coined the slogan, "Run It or Sell It," which became a rally and yard-sign staple. The state legislature was out of session for the year, so I called for an extraordinary session, pumping extra octane into my resolution. The USW boosted the call, firing off their own press release demanding the assembly act.

While my call drew praise from the USW, workers and community, it was derided by the state's Republican politicians, including Kimberly's representative in the state assembly, Republican Al Ott. (I did not represent the village but neighboring communities Kaukauna and part of Little Chute.) Ott circulated a letter among local legislators addressed to NewPage CEO Mark Suwyn. The letter made a backhanded reference to me: "We feel that contacting company leadership directly . . . is a more sensible, productive and timely approach for addressing the matter rather than the introduction of an Assembly Resolution as the Legislature stands in recess."

Given that the GOP held the majority and could easily have reconvened the assembly, their refusal to do so was downright bewildering. A deteriorating political and economic environment jeopardized their control of the state house, with jobs and the economy far and away the biggest issue. They had a golden opportunity to shore up their bona fides with working families and help save a mill, if they cared to do so. Sadly, however, it was corporate campaign money that called the Republican Party's tune.

Ott's letter asked for a meeting with Suwyn, who promptly took up the offer. Republican legislators reluctantly included me as a lone Democrat. On August 20, we crammed into a side room of the village community center, one better suited for a Cub Scout meeting than a showdown with a corporate CEO who held the fate of a mill in his hands.

In the meeting, Suwyn simply repeated NewPage's public rationale for closing the mill: unexpected spikes in costs well beyond what was planned, including and especially pulp prices, and a steep drop in market demand for coated paper. NewPage would either shut the mill down and "maybe bring back workers in six months or nine months," or shut it down and hand out severance packages to allow workers to "get on with their lives," the latter being a "better" option, according to Suwyn.

GOP legislators swallowed Suwyn's glib condescension for the mill's workers as if it was holy gospel. I was the only one to ask critical questions. Why close this facility when it was the most efficient producer in the region? Why shut down a huge asset when the parent company (Cerberus) had issued an initial public offering that generated $800 million in new capital for NewPage three months earlier? Why close when sales were strong and the company's EBITDA was in good shape?

Before Suwyn had to answer, the longtime GOP state senator Mike Ellis jumped in. "That's just Nelson, don't listen to him. Any profits are plowed back into the corporate infrastructure, right?" Ellis said, tossing Suwyn a softball while the latter glared at me. Fellow Republican Rob Cowles, who represented Kaukauna and Little Chute in the state senate, said the state was a "minimal player" and asked Suwyn for talking points that could be shared with constituents. Suwyn obligingly encouraged the Republican caucus to "lobby federal legislators," causing the pliable legislators to nod in appreciation and relief—after all, that would make it someone else's problem.

Finally, Ott paternalistically claimed workers "aren't aware of the real reasons" behind the decision. He was dead wrong about that. A talk with any of the affected workers would have proven that they perfectly understood how they were being thrown under the bus to serve corporate profiteering.

Throughout the fight to save NewPage, my office took GOP flak directed at my resolution. One GOP staffer wrote, "It's unfortunate that much has been made of this resolution in the media, with seemingly little meaningful action to move it forward. Its ultimate purpose is now pretty transparent," suggesting it was all just a stunt.

Ott tried to muddy the waters by issuing a public statement supporting my resolution. "Representative Nelson is delighted that Representative Ott has signed on to the Resolution," my able staff director, Ben Nerad, parried. "However, Representative Ott's failure to call on the Assembly leadership to move his resolution forward is a pretty transparent attempt to have it both ways. You would think that with 22 years of seniority, Representative Ott would have greater influence in his own caucus."

Of course, representing people is more than just legislating. I worked with my allies to apply all the tools at my disposal—statecraft, tradecraft, and stagecraft—to try to move key issues forward. That included direct and creative public engagement—sit-ins, press conferences, rallies, petitions—to address urgent problems like the NewPage mill closure.

In late August, workers held a vigil across the street from the mill. It was a calm, cool late summer evening, but the group was far from calm. They stood at the precipice; everyone was fully aware that at any time the last machine at the Kimberly plant could be shut down. It was torture. Congregants held candles close to their chins, the flames glittering, illuminating faces eerily while the comforting rumble of semi-engines pulled in and out of the mill behind us, perhaps for the last time. Sally Feistel delivered a rousing speech, while heads nodded rhythmically to each point she made: "Afford insurance . . . pay for our kids' college . . . take pride in our work . . . make families proud." Her powerful remarks were overshadowed only by the painful words of a little girl, no older than six, whose quavering voice drew tears and applause: "I need everyone's help to save this mill so my dad can keep his job." It was heartbreaking, but inspiring.

On the same patch of grass ten days later on September 6, workers and families gathered at a USW-organized rally that attracted 3,000 people including Congressman Neil Abercrombie of Hawaii, a close friend and representative of Illinois's senator Barack Obama, then running for president. Unfortunately, Governor Jim Doyle did not attend, despite my repeated attempts to persuade him to do so. When I reached out to the governor and his staff, I was brushed off each time. Eventually his legislative liaison told my office to rein me in: "I don't think the governor wants to talk to him about NewPage." It was bewildering, but to the governor's credit, he was working behind the scenes with NewPage, urging them to reverse course and making us a good cop, bad cop tandem.

The rally was the venue where I shared my vision on the paper industry and what it meant for the economy, the community, and even my own family:

Growing up, I passed this mill at least twice a week—every week on the way to church. My dad brought our family to this great community thirty years ago to start a church just down the road. Crossing the Shopko Bridge every Sunday morning was a constant reminder that this mill was as much a part of this community as our church, the grocery store, or the ball diamond. That's what this mill means.

Last month we closed a chapter, today we write a new chapter in earnest, a chapter that now reads: we will do everything in our power, we will utilize every resource at our disposal and we will ensure this plant remains in our community. The fight we wage is bigger than Kimberly. If we can't keep a profitable and successful mill open, how can we keep any mill open? As Kimberly goes, so goes the nation.

On September 8, just two days after the rally, the day we hoped would never come arrived. NewPage ordered the second and last machine shut down.

I was at the mill when Andy Nirschl trudged up the incline from the Number 7 with the last roll of paper in his hands. Nirschl unfurled the poster-size roll while reporters snapped pictures and cameramen rolled film. In the background, the Number 7 unwound and then stopped. It was a few minutes before dawn—the darkest time of the day.

If you want to get people's attention, grab their checkbook. On September 10, I picked up my pen and drafted legislation that would suspend key tax breaks for paper companies, including NewPage, that shut down plants and refused to restart or sell. You may have the right to do with your property as you wish, but you do not have the right to claim tax breaks and take public money. Since the early 1970s, Wisconsin has offered a generous tax exemption for manufacturers' personal property (i.e., any movable property not attached to the building) like paper machines and related equipment such as rewinders, finishers, and cutters. As a result, almost nothing inside of the mill was taxed. This tax break hit local governments exclusively, because schools, municipalities, counties, and technical colleges are the sole recipients of property tax revenue.

One week later on September 17, I drafted another bill designed to hurt the owners of NewPage in their pocketbooks. Wisconsin was one of just two states with a fully funded pension fund, a source of pride for all. My new bill directed the state pension fund board to divest all Cerberus holdings. We were out of session, but I was now on pace to draft more prospective legislation than any other assembly member. The Kimberly fight was so important to me I was willing to break an unwritten rule and tangle up a sacred cow in a high-profile political battle. For me, everything was on the table. Resolutions, legislation, vigils, press conferences, and rallies. We were "building the résumé," as Jon Geenen said, ratcheting up pressure on NewPage, burning into their skull the message that we would not go down without a fight. And if we did succumb, then they would pay a price—a massive headache and a tarnished reputation.

That same day, Mark Van Stappen and other workers traveled to NewPage headquarters in Miamisburg, Ohio. Kimberly workers walked a tight closed-loop picket line, with "Run It or Sell It" signs sticking up on medians and patches of grass in the parking lot. Sadly, corporate employees entering and leaving the building pointed fingers and laughed at the Kimberly workers. Van Stappen shook his head as he recalled that episode. "When you get rid of the union, you get rid of a way of life, not just for the union workers," he said, recalling the advice he'd gotten from his Teamster dad years ago. Instead of scowls and laughs, those employees should have thanked Mark and the others.

We dominated news coverage throughout northeast Wisconsin, some weeks even beating out sports coverage of the beloved Green Bay Packers. Our message was also gaining traction statewide and popped up on the radar of Obama's presidential campaign. Andy Nirschl had introduced Obama at his Labor Day rally in Milwaukee, the official kickoff of the fall campaign. At a rally in Green Bay a few weeks later, NewPage figured prominently in the future president's remarks. We were accomplishing our goals of generating as much attention as possible and being a royal pain in the back end to NewPage.

On October 2, we held a press conference outside the doors of the "people's house." Several NewPage workers spoke, including Andy Nirschl and Jim Dercks. A few of my Democratic colleagues joined us, including former Madison representative Spencer Black, a renowned authority on environmental issues who well understood the vital economic role manufacturing played in our state. To some, manufacturing and environmental interests were opposed, but not in Black's mind. His support meant a lot to the workers. Unfortunately, aside from a handful of legislative and campaign staff and a few curious tourists and school groups passing by, the press conference garnered little attention. Undeterred, the workers soldiered on.

By October, national reporters were describing NewPage as a "potent symbol" of the global economic meltdown's impact on working people and families. It was also a keystone issue for the presidential race, one that could help decide what had been a tight contest. Before Barack Obama shifted his post–Labor Day campaign to focus on Wall Street's responsibility for the recession, he was running neck and neck with John McCain. At a luncheon hosted by Wispolitics.com—the state version of *Politico* or the *National Journal*—Democratic pollster Paul Maslin argued that an Obama double-digit win was possible because of the "dominating issue of the economy." Maslin predicted, "If that happens, battleground Assembly seats that might have been close go to Dems."

He was right.

On election day, Obama won Wisconsin by fourteen points, and the Democrats picked up five seats in the state assembly, giving us a three-seat majority. I won my re-election campaign by twenty-eight points, and my fellow Democrats in the assembly selected me majority leader, one of the youngest in Wisconsin's history at thirty-two years of age.

It was a bittersweet victory, one I attributed to the NewPage workers. The challenges they faced were the issues so many others across the country were confronting: job loss, cynical corporations, apathetic politicians, bad trade deals. Thanks to the Kimberly-NewPage workers, economic issues would figure prominently in the new legislative session. And once again, the NewPage workers would take the national stage and find themselves front and center in a debate that went much further than Wisconsin.

Throughout the fight to save the Kimberly mill, Jon Geenen pumped out creative solutions, proposing deals, seeking out investors, and facilitating back-channel talks with NewPage. Yet

NewPage never budged. They were hell-bent on shutting down the plant. No amount of worker concessions or state incentives would change their mind. Geenen and other union leaders realized that the only viable path would be a new owner and a new product.

Late in the fall and into the new year, Geenen, along with USW district director Mike Bolton and other union officials, held on-again-off-again talks with Germany's Koehler Paper Group. When I met with Geenen on January 9, 2009, a deal seemed possible. The day before, Geenen had spoken with his German counterparts and members of the global union federation IndustriALL, who promised to "facilitate anything that helps USW reopen any part of the Kimberly mill." A preliminary meeting was being set up for January 21 or 22 in Karlsruhe, Germany, and the union had secured a translator. According to Mark Van Stappen, the USW was inches away from a deal to save the Kimberly mill. Geenen went so far as to tell him. "It may be a done deal."

But just one week later, and one week before the scheduled meeting in Germany, the deal was "in peril," Geenen emailed me. The main problems, he said, were "new market data on Lightweight Coated paper (LWC), credit availability and the cost to retrofit some machines." "We may need a state incentive package," he added. I contacted Wisconsin's Commerce Department, and Geenen got back in touch with the German company. (The governor's office was returning my phone calls now.) It was all in vain. By the next day, January 16, Koehler had suspended its offer.

Like Geenen, Van Stappen felt the "downturn in the economy and general aftermarket effects from the recession caused Koehler to rethink things." But, in hindsight, he believes, "The sticking point was the Number 6 [Paper Machine]. NewPage wanted to retain the rights, but Koehler would have none of that." In other words, NewPage refused to sell the mill outright to a competitor. This made sense only if the whole point of the shutdown was to take product off the market to boost prices. Why enable another firm to maintain production and compete on price?

At the same time, NewPage wanted the ability to restart production should prices stabilize and the market rebound. As CEO Mark Suwyn told the closed-door session with Republican legislators the previous summer: "Keep the plant warm and turn it back on when the economy turns around." NewPage wanted both a brake and a gas pedal—while retaining the lucrative tax breaks.

Geenen continued working his national labor and industry network, trying to cobble together public and private financing for a buyout of the mill. He had spent his career traveling the country building a national labor network; many of the local leaders he met in the 1980s were now holding important international posts. Those connections were invaluable and indispensable. At the same time, the USW was moving NewPage to the center of their 2009 legislative agenda. In Geenen's words at the time:

> The need for a true economic renewal program should be the U.S. Congress's first priority after learning that prospects of a sale of assets and restart of the Kimberly Mill have been at least temporarily halted. When highly productive, efficient workers and equipment like those in Kimberly remain idled, it underscores the urgent need for an economic renewal program that creates an industrial policy to rein in unfair trade and recognize the importance of manufacturing as a pillar of the economy.

NewPage had moved from a local economic problem to a plank in Obama's campaign platform and finally the centerpiece of a major international union's legislative agenda. Despite the setbacks and disappointment, the Kimberly workers would not throw in the towel. But they couldn't catch a break.

In May, a skeletal crew of seventeen at the Kimberly plant was reduced further. In an email to Nirschl and USW officials, newly installed NewPage CEO Rick Willett was bearish on the economic and market outlook for paper: "The harsh reality is that we see very little in our current order rates that can provide us much optimism that we would need Kimberly's capacity in the next 12 to 18 months or if ever." In the same email, Willett reported that NewPage had supposedly been seeking out "a buyer for the whole mill or even a portion of the mill for well over six months." But Willett disclosed few other details. He characterized "the likelihood of success of someone restarting the mill as 'low' or 'very low,'" and capped it off with tone-deaf paternalistic advice not unlike that of Suwyn the previous summer: "I think it is more appropriate for us all to assist our former employees in moving on to other opportunities than to keep them hoping and waiting for Kimberly to restart."

True to form, Geenen would not quit. As late as the summer of 2009, Geenen was still working his national networks, seeking out financiers and investors. Geenen's analysis of the issues surrounding a potential sale of the mill was sound. The problem was not NewPage per se but the troubled economy and few signs of near-term recovery. At best, it would be a "jobless recovery," as GOP leaders around the country endlessly declaimed.

Imported paper remained a big problem, too. Geenen cited "intense new pressure from imports." According to Geenen, in July 2009 the U.S. paper industry was getting hit hard by tissue imports. In an email to USW officials, Geenen noted that "tissue could hold the keys to a restart of Kimberly-NewPage or another mill." However, Geenen observed critically, "No one will invest when they think our government is going to let them get put out of business by cheap imports." The unbending political commitment to free trade policies, which had dominated Washington since the 1970s, was now victimizing yet another industry.

On September 23, 2009, the USW set aside its differences with NewPage and filed a trade case alongside Appleton Coated with the International Trade Commission (ITC), citing unfair trade practices by China. The complaint alleged that Chinese producers were subsidizing or dumping coated paper on the U.S. market. The USW, NewPage, and Appleton Coated would have to wait an entire year to get justice. In October 2010 the ITC voted unanimously in favor of the USW and the paper companies, "finding that imports of coated paper from China and Indonesia [were] causing material injury to US producers and workers."

It was too late for the Kimberly workers. For many, the shutdown stayed with them the rest of their lives. They found it hard to adjust to the stress of leaving the only jobs they knew and trying to find new, almost always inferior ones. "There's many that aren't with us anymore," Andy Nirschl recalled in 2019. He attributes many of the deaths to "the stress and everything else and all the change—these guys were in their fifties and sixties. They struggled." Wittman counted "a dozen or so" who died of cancer, alcoholism, or heart failure—literally and figuratively.

One of those who died early was Jim Dercks, an outspoken advocate for the mill and one of Andy's close friends. When Andy couldn't take a TV interview, Jim was there. To northeast Wisconsin, he was one of the faces of NewPage. "It was a big part of his life. He could be a pain at times," Andy said with a wry smile. "But his heart was true. He fought hard."

Long-time worker Ned Wittman recalled five or six other workers who died because of alcoholism: "It's well known that the Fox Valley has a hard-drinking culture. Every place in the valley has some type of problem with alcohol." The stability of a good mill job mitigated such problems. And for those who suffered addiction to alcohol or other drugs, help was available and usually free. "The mill provided things where you could get help for yourself; help for drugs or alcohol." Such programs went away when the mill closed. Three of my close friends from my high school graduating class, none of whom graduated from college, have died of substance abuse; as far as I know, none of my friends from college or graduate school have suffered the same fate.

Kimberly was emblematic of a troubling national phenomenon—a huge spike in mortality rates among non-Hispanic whites between 1999 and 2013. It was a trend not seen in other countries, according to Princeton University economists Anne Case and her husband, Nobel laureate Angus Deaton in their 2020 book, *Deaths of Despair and the Future of Capitalism.* (I took Anne Case's class in 2004 as a student at the Princeton School of International and Public Affairs; she deserved her own Nobel Prize for both her research and her heroic efforts to teach a small-town Wisconsin boy to understand the difference between the elasticity of supply and demand, a concept I still struggle to apply.) Case and Deaton found that those deaths were attributed to alcohol and drug abuse, suicide, and liver disease, while their sample population self-reported a number of stresses in their day-to-day lives including "inability to work." Most remarkable, however, the rate of early death was much higher than among similar demographic groups in other developed countries like those in Western Europe. Unemployment itself was less an issue, Case and Deaton argue, than America's callous lack of concern, support, and respect for workers, signalized above all by the absence of a national health care system and adequate social safety net.

In 2020, ELEVEN YEARS AFTER Kimberly-NewPage closed, I met up with Mark Van Stappen. The hyperkinetic native of Little Chute, Wisconsin bounded into Seth's Coffee with a long white tube under his left arm. It contained one of the last rolls of paper to come off the Number 7 machine. For over a decade it had been stowed away in a corner of Van Stappen's home overlooking the Fox River and the Appleton Coated mill. I was honored that he wanted to give it to me.

As we sat in a corner booth, Van Stappen shared a memory from a happier time, his wedding day thirty years earlier. The ceremony was held in a small country church, built in the 1200s, outside his bride's hometown in Denmark. Van Stappen had never seen anything that old, and it fascinated him. How could anything 800 years old still exist? Mark dug into church archives and went into town to talk to the locals. What he discovered amazed him. It explained who the Danes were—and who we Americans were not.

"Cultures that really grab and hold onto their history; they are not so easy to move," Mark said. "Traditions mean so much. Paper was a part of ours. I don't know if the NewPages of this country can appreciate that. The Danes are considered progressive, but at the same time they value tradition. There is really no reason why we can't have it both ways, too."

Kimberly-NewPage wasn't just about enabling workers to feed their families. It reflected our values and what was important to us: good, meaningful work that you could be proud of, that enabled you to raise a family and pass on the American dream to your children. It wasn't just a concept or a formula—it was real. And in the Paper Valley, it was engrained into our psyche, as Van Stappen put it. Wherever you went there were reminders: powerful machines roaring alive, making hundreds of thousands of tons of paper each year; massive boilers belching out steam. To Mark it was "sweet music": "Not only was it this song, but it had this very slow, steady presence. The thing was always running. It had this reassuring presence."

Mark opened the tube, and the roll of paper fell out across the table. It was filled with hundreds of signatures and notes in many colors—red, blue, yellow, green, black, orange, purple—from workers, families, and friends. Raw emotion spilling out onto the canvas:

"My grandfather worked here 90 years ago."

"Save my dad's job."

"NewPage, why are you doing this to us? When other countries owned us, we kept running. Now a city in Ohio—USA—owns us and you shut us down!! Why?"

"You're not just taking jobs away, you're taking lifestyles, security, health insurance, and family stability."

"You're taking away my Papa's job and taking away my favorite backyard to play in when he can no longer afford his house."

The Kimberly fight ended in defeat. But other battles lay ahead. It wasn't too late to avenge the ghosts of Kimberly-NewPage.

"Papermaking was part of our culture," Mark told me. "Appleton Coated is one of those last stands of the ability to keep multigenerational papermaking culture alive. How long has papermaking been happening? Where would the world be without paper?"

Where would Wisconsin be without paper?

Part Three

Turning the Tide

6.

The Voice of God

MILL WORKERS AND THEIR FAMILIES lined the narrow halls of the second floor of the Outagamie County justice building. It was tight, and I had to walk sideways through the throng. Squeezing past USW-blue shirts emblazoned with the union slogan, "One Day Longer, One Day Stronger," I could feel the pressure on the workers. They were nervous and emotionally exhausted. Within minutes and with one fell swoop of the gavel, a judge could approve the sale of the mill to a scrap dealer, California-based Industrial Assets Corporation (IAC)—and that would be it. It would be the end of Appleton Coated, one of the state's oldest paper mills and still a major economic engine for the Paper Valley.

It was Friday, September 22, 2017, a few minutes past the appointed time of 10:30 a.m. for Judge Gregory B. Gill Jr.'s hearing about the proposed sale. Less than twenty-four hours earlier, the last paper machine had ground to a halt. Inside the courtroom, folks were packed in shoulder to shoulder on four rows of benches with even less breathing room than in the crowded hall. Tucked into one corner stood four TV cameras with camera operators and reporters.

I found my place in the row behind the lawyers' tables. I was sandwiched between two USW leaders, Jon Geenen and Michael Bolton. In front of us sat the attorneys for the USW, Sara Geenen, Jon's daughter, and her senior partner from Milwaukee law firm Previant, Fred Perillo. At a table to their right sat receiver Michael Polsky and stone-faced attorneys for the creditors, the bank, and the buyer, including Mark Freedlander from Pittsburgh-based firm McGuireWoods (representing Industrial Assets), John Lucian of Philadelphia's Blank Rome (PNC outside counsel), and Bret Roge of Michael Best and Friedrich, the old firm of former White House chief of staff Reince Priebus (representing Appleton Coated).

The case had drawn an impressive share of the state's and the country's top insolvency and labor lawyers. Their presence alone underscored the gravity of the case and its community- and industry-wide implications.

A hush swept over the packed room as Judge Gill entered from behind a wood panel divider. Trailing the amateur electric bass player and former All-American decathlete at the University of Wisconsin-Madison was Justice, his light-golden retriever. The dog would remain by the judge's side for the entire proceeding.

Gill had originally been appointed by Scott Walker, the state's Republican governor who was staunchly antilabor, so the steelworkers expected the worst. But the judge would need to face the voters in the spring. With the filing deadline for candidates just three months away, any potential opponents would be watching the proceedings actively, looking for missteps or misjudgments. The faces of voters in the courtroom, perhaps the largest gathering ever in his six years on the bench, must have reminded Gill of that fact.

I was hopeful that Gill might turn out to be a pleasant surprise. Gill and I were contemporaries. But we came from opposite ends of the political spectrum, Republican and Democratic. He hailed from the country club set of Appleton; I was from blue-collar Little Chute. Still, we had a lot in common. This was our home; these were our neighbors; and as public servants, we had a responsibility to them.

I had gotten to know Gill since his appointment to the bench shortly after I became county executive in 2011. He was deliberate, thoughtful, and above all sympathetic. He helped run the county's Veterans Court where he worked closely with ex-servicemen and women who had fallen on hard times but were willing to work a program to get their life back together. Perhaps he would see some of the struggles that his veterans went through in the mill workers and their families; not a few were veterans themselves, including union local secretary-treasurer Mack MacDonald.

With cameras clicking and reporters scribbling notes, Gill opened the day's hearing. "I understand that these are proceedings of great significance and interest to everyone," he began. "So I'm going to spend the time we need to. We're going to take this very seriously." Those words lifted the workers' spirits—and mine. Was there a chance we could pull this off?

The judge began summarizing the objections to a sale with no option of reviving the mill as a going concern, dividing them into three categories. There were "substantive and legal-based" objections (creditors might not get paid); those which were "emotional and not necessarily based on law" (a sale would hurt the local economy and overall community—my argument); and a "hybrid . . . this affects a lot of people, but there was also a legal basis" (workers would lose their jobs and the terms of their contract would be abrogated—the USW's objection).

I didn't agree that my objection was a purely emotional one. After all, it was based squarely on Chapter 128, Wisconsin's receivership statute. I caught the judge's eye, frowning to let him know I wasn't pleased. As if in response, he added an apparent concession: "It affects many of these fine people in this courtroom." I nodded my head.

The USW's objection revolved around the voiding of its collective bargaining agreement (CBA) with Appleton Coated, specifically the CBA's successorship clause, which bound future owners to the terms of the mill's labor contract. Although the prospective new owner was buying the mill's assets from the receiver "free and clear of all liens, claims, and encumbrances," the union held that this could not cancel the CBA. Rather, in the union's view, the CBA constituted an enduring asset. Second, the sale helped just one creditor, PNC Bank, at the expense of all others, including the USW members, who were owed over $1 million for "earned, unused but deferred vacation or paid time-off."

My objection centered on the potential loss of $300 million of annual economic activity and 620 jobs. I also cited $90 million in IOUs to local businesses that could go unpaid.

Michael Polsky, the receiver, had the first opportunity to present evidence relevant to the various objections. He called Appleton Coated's business consultant, Michael Compton of Silverman Consulting, to the witness stand. While writing his report for PNC, Compton had turned a deaf ear to Doug Osterberg and his fellow owner-managers when they tried to explain why the mill had a future as a going concern. After the receivership process began, Compton did little to identify prospective going-concern buyers, except to offer what Doug described as "an archaic database" listing many paper companies that "no longer existed or had merged with others." In the view of those of us trying to save the mill, Compton's initial job had been to help PNC justify shutting it down. Now he was in court to continue that work.

In his testimony, Compton made several points. First, Appleton Coated had burned through $2 million in cash each month for six months and would soon be out of money. Second, the mill's business model was weak at best; it was months away from getting its first orders for a new line of brown-paper grades. (CEO Osterberg disagreed vehemently with this contention.) Third, the market was against the mill; pulp prices were going up. Fourth, time was not on the mill's side. Prospective owner-operators had streamed through the plant for months, including the time before the receivership when Osterberg and his co-owners were seeking a buyer. All were "good buyers," including paper companies, private equity investors, and small investor groups—and yet there were no takers. Fifth, Compton claimed Appleton Coated had bad credit; no new lenders were willing to refinance, and the mill carried a pension liability, which any going-concern buyer would have to shoulder. (When the federal Pension Benefit Guarantee Corporation assumed the liability as part of the sale transaction, it was granted a $750,000 priority claim and allowed a $61 million unsecured claim—none of which would ever get paid because of "legal priorities" and the simple fact that sale proceeds of $21.5 million fell well short of the claim.)

Polsky asked his witness to define a stalking-horse bidder, the entity that establishes the baseline bid price that others must top. Steve Mattes's IAC had bid $21.5 million, and no one had bid higher, so Mattes got the mill at that price. Compton gave a crisp answer to the straightforward question, just the way Polsky wanted it. But Compton did not stop there. He continued, "So, we had one bidder that was a going-concern bidder early on. It was trying to negotiate an Asset Purchase Agreement (APA), the term sheet of the sale, but it was a value $3 to $3.1 million less than what this current offer is."

A smart witness never says more than is necessary. Compton had nudged a door ajar, and the judge kicked it open. The bidder in question was H.I.G. Capital, based in Miami, Florida; among the manufacturing companies in its portfolio was De Pere, Wisconsin's Fox River Fiber, a recycled paper and packaging company that sold fiber to Appleton Coated.

Gill interjected, "There was a buyer that would come in and allow for the company to continue to operate?" He was beside himself. Why had the mill been sold to a scrap dealer if there was a going-concern buyer?

Compton backtracked. "That was undetermined at the time, as we never got through a successful negotiation of the APA. That was their intent, I believe, but the value was $18 million to start," he responded.

Polsky resumed his questioning: "Do you think that if the bidders had more time there would be a different result?"

Compton: "That can't be answered. I don't know that it will."

Polsky: "Will the delay and approval of the sale lead a buyer to offer at least as much as Industrial Assets and that will hire substantially all of its employees?"

Compton: "No."

Now it was Fred Perillo's turn to question the witness. First, he cast doubt on Compton's expertise. Appleton Coated was the first paper mill he had ever been involved in. He was not the best man for the job.

Second, he questioned Compton's performance: "During the period when you acted as a turnaround consultant, the company's fortunes declined rather than improved; is that correct?" Perillo asked.

"They were out of money when I got there, so I don't know how you could say it declined," said Compton, sounding defensive. True, Perillo admitted. But after three and a half weeks, the company's balance sheet was still at zero.

Perillo paused to let that sink in before asking his next question: "What was your explanation for why the company was able to be so successful less than one year ago in 2016?"

Compton: "Probably better pulp pricing, better product mix. Pulp pricing had gone up significantly and none of that had been passed on to the customer, and then the volume was down significantly. The volume during the profitable years were significantly higher than this. So volume and mix."

Perillo: "Do you know why the company did not pass on its price increases to the customer?"

Compton: "They felt obligated to the pricing that they had set, and that's what they wanted to do."

Perillo: "As the result of long-term contracts?"

Compton: "I don't know that there were that many contracts, there were commitments though, verbal and otherwise."

Perillo: "Isn't that by definition a temporary problem that will cycle out as those commitments are fulfilled?"

Compton: "Possibly."

Perillo had planted an important seed of doubt. Perhaps it was true that Compton didn't really understand the business model for paper mills. Compton began shifting noticeably in the witness stand.

Perillo: "And you said that there was at least one bidder in the $18 million range that would have run the company as a going concern?"

Compton: "Correct."

Perillo: "It's your belief that if they had done that, it would have saved the jobs of the 600 or so employees at Appleton Coated?"

Compton hedged: "In theory."

Perillo had scored a crucial victory. Judge Gill was wide open to the community benefit argument. The fact that Polsky's star witness demonstrated little expertise in the paper industry and relegated the business model argument to secondary status opened wide the door to a strong community effects argument by the USW.

Next, Perillo turned to the bank. PNC had converted Appleton Coated into a cash machine, he suggested, pulling out $50,000 in penalties from the mill every day. No wonder the bank wanted to string along the mill as long as possible. Why would anyone want to stop that gravy train? Compton did not dispute the $50,000-per-day figure. Instead he quibbled: the payments were not penalties, they were fees.

Perillo continued to pound away at Compton's credibility, extracting key facts that cast Appleton Coated's future in a different light. Prices were improving, and the mill had $28 million in standing orders. A new going-concern buyer would be making money on day one.

Next came the APA, which had been talked about, but never cited. It seemed odd. This was the blueprint Polsky and IAC planned to follow. Then again, the receiver and the scrap dealer knew the APA forwards and backwards—but not the judge or the USW.

To get at this issue, Perillo stated, "We don't believe you can approve the sale without conditioning the purchase upon the assumption of the collective bargaining agreement. In other words, the group [Industrial Assets] that has purchased the assets would have to assume the labor agreement." He had just summed up the legal foundation for the USW's case.

"I haven't even, at least last I checked—" Gill looked down at his desk. He tapped the keys on his computer keyboard before looking up with arched eyebrows. "I don't even have the asset purchase agreement, so I—"

"We also don't have a copy of the APA," Perillo interjected.

"I don't know what's in it, so I don't know how I can very well approve it today," Gill said, appearing relieved. "It seems that at a minimum I should probably look at it. Am I—am I missing something?" said the judge in passive-aggressive style, a well-honed trait of a true Midwesterner. He suggested that he would need a few days to review the document.

Perillo said, "Your Honor, we would be agreeable to your suggestion to moving the hearing to next week Wednesday [three business days] in order to permit the parties to read the asset purchase agreement, give the receiver the opportunity to upload it to the system or deliver it to us in another way, and to present our testimony and argument on that day. And perhaps in the meantime that will give the parties an opportunity to discuss other solutions."

Like a well-timed kettledrum ending an orchestral crescendo, a voice from the intercom loudspeaker boomed, "There you go!" Dumbfounded faces turned upward, and a couple of onlookers chuckled. The TV reporters shook their heads in disbelief—what a weird twist to an already compelling story. We never did find out whose voice that was and how it made it to the loudspeaker. But whenever I recall that day, I think of it as "the voice of God," encouraging us to keep working on finding a way to save Appleton Coated.

Attorney Mark Freedlander represented IAC, the billion-dollar scrap dealer. At the mention of a possible delay, he looked frustrated. And if Freedlander was frustrated, his client Steve Mattes, IAC's CEO and president, was furious. It was later learned that Mattes had been sending a steady stream of angry text messages and emails to Freedlander's smart phone.

"I just can't assure the court at all that my client is willing to go beyond today in incurring expenses if an agreement is not filed or approved," Freedlander told the court.

I looked at Jon Geenen and whispered, "This is good, right? They're going to walk away."

"Ah, just hold on, it ain't that simple," Jon replied.

Freedlander continued. "I'm not trying to leverage the court, but I do need to—"

"You're doing a good job of it," Judge Gill interrupted.

"I get paid to do something," Freedlander punched back. With a furrowed brow, the judge shook his head. "The balls on that lawyer," his expression read. But he let it go.

Freedlander continued, "My client is not prepared to stay in the process where all he does is incur money with no understanding that there is really an end date, so—"

"Well, there is—regardless, counsel, there is an answer Wednesday," the judge responded.

"Maybe," Freedlander said, dismissing the judge's observation—and crossing the line.

"Pretty certain I'm the one who can say there is an answer Wednesday, unless there's someone over my shoulder." Gill was holding his own.

Rocking back and forth on his heels, Freedlander was losing his cool. "If we're not approved today, that guarantees two things," he declared. "One, my client won't be at the table, and two, there is no opportunity whatsoever for my client to potentially have some form of operations. And I say that telling you again that my client is a liquidator. That's what they do for a living," he emphasized.

IAC was going to scrap the mill. Freedlander had just proclaimed that if the purchase proceeded on the terms agreed with Polsky, the mill would never again be a going concern.

John Lucian, PNC's attorney, raised his hand. When Judge Gill recognized him, he said, "The bank is not prepared to consent, I just need to be clear on the record, to any sort of extension that I think the union is suggesting. There is no funding. We're going to instruct the receiver to begin the liquidation process at this point. We have no other alternative. We have gotten to the end of our line, your honor, with one foot dangling over the cliff. If we lose the offer on the table, it's a pretty dreary outlook."

This was a pretty nervy statement coming from a lawyer representing a $67 billion bank with $445 billion in assets under management. As Tim Nixon later commented, "It is difficult in a court to argue that the court should dismiss a case and receiver that [the bank] requested to be appointed because [the bank] is now unhappy with the way things are going. The receiver is an officer of the court and will do whatever the judge tells him to do."

Under the circumstances, I was distressed when Judge Gill replied, "Mr. Lucian, I don't know that there was anything that you've just said that I disagree with."

I turned to Geenen and then to Bolton. Both were speechless. Sara shifted her head just enough to read my what's-up-with-that? expression. She arched her brows as if to say, "Don't ask me."

The exchange left me wondering what to think about Judge Gill. Would he fold, cowed by all the expensive legal talent on one side of his courtroom? Or would he hold fast? Was he Governor Walker's boy or his own man?

BEFORE GOING TO BED Friday night, I opened my computer. There sat the APA, top of my inbox. My fingers froze. I couldn't bear to open the document. I powered down the computer and went to bed.

In the morning, I emailed co-counsel Sara Geenen. "I think the buyer made a couple of big mistakes yesterday," I wrote. "He basically showed his hand. I think we have two strategies. One, we can show the business model going forward that will attract a buyer. Two, we can get some sort of delay, because that means Industrial Assets will walk away." She never replied.

After procrastinating for most of the day, I finally opened and read the APA. It was clear IAC had no intention of running the mill. We needed a new APA or a new buyer, because straight-up approval would be a death sentence. If it wasn't clear before the hearing, it was crystal clear now.

Before heading to work on Monday, I did some dialing for dollars, campaign slang for fundraising. My re-election campaign for county executive was still eighteen months away, but I was under enormous pressure. I had gotten smoked by twenty-five points a year earlier in an ill-fated run for Congress. Now, several viable candidates were mulling a run for my county job, including two members of the state assembly and the longtime sheriff.

Thumbing through call sheets, a few cards from donors from the year before fell out of the binder. One note really stood out:

I can't imagine how you and the other really great candidates we fielded must feel. I can appreciate the "strong headwinds" you ran into and can only applaud your effort and courage in such a venture . . . I know you gave your campaign every ounce of effort you had. I hope our state can continue to have the benefit of your leadership in the future.

Those words really bucked me up—"courage," "every ounce of effort," and "leadership." The reminder was just what I needed.

When court reconvened on Monday morning, everyone looked tired. The bags under the judge's eyes said he'd devoted most of the weekend to understanding the APA and boning up on the relevant case law. Sara Geenen had also scoured the APA and she'd filed another objection—the reason she'd never replied to my email. Her hands discreetly jittered as if she'd consumed nothing but coffee over the weekend. Attorney Mark Freedlander looked as if he'd been run over by a bus. The workers were bone-tired and shifted nervously in their seats. As for me, my adrenaline was slowly building the way it does when a crucial campaign event is starting. I live for this kind of stuff.

The judge started by summarizing the pluses and minuses of Appleton Coated's condition. On the one hand, the company was facing a $500,000-per-week burn rate. On the other hand, although 2017 had been a bad year so far, the previous two had been good—so good that Appleton Coated's relationship manager at PNC Chicago had told Marianne Sterr that the mill was a "prize account" for the bank in 2015 and 2016. The past few months had been difficult, but the company had weathered so many storms before. Why should this time be any different? That was the argument that the workers and I were making.

Following a brief recess, Fred Perillo reported to the court that the USW had made a written offer to IAC—a modified APA of sorts, called an "interim running agreement." If it was accepted, the union would withdraw its objection to the sale. In addition, Perillo announced that there was a new buyer in the courtroom prepared to make a competing bid.

Big Shoulders Capital was a boutique Chicago private equity firm that specialized in helping small to mid-size companies like Appleton Coated. Their portfolio ran the gamut: transport companies, fabricators, food processors, and niche manufacturers. While most of their investments were under $10 million, here they offered $18 million and a promise to run the mill for thirty to forty-five days. This could be the win-win solution Judge Gill had asked for.

Freedlander was not impressed. Big Shoulders Capital had attended the auction but had not bid, a fact Freedlander kept repeating. "My client showed up at an auction, it bid pursuant to court-approved auction terms and procedures," he declared. What Freedlander missed was that Big Shoulders had left the auction after the stalking horse bid from IAC was accepted, which meant all subsequent bids had to be made within the same parameters.

Judge Gill had a different view. Two issues were at hand, he said. First, the successorship clause: could the state court invalidate a CBA? This was the foundation of the USW's legal argument. If it cracked, it would take the union's entire legal strategy with it. Second, the fate of the mill: what were Industrial Assets' intentions? By now, it should have been crystal clear that IAC intended to shut the mill down and sell off the pieces. But Freedlander was reticent and would not disclose his client's intentions, if he even knew what they were.

Gill insisted on a clearer answer. If he ruled in favor of the buyer, the parties would soon be back in court—a federal district court—to litigate the successorship clause, something the USW did not want. (In northeast Wisconsin, the eastern district was led by Judge William Griesbach, a George W. Bush appointee and a reliable conservative.) It was also "exactly what we don't want for our creditors," Gill noted, to the relief of the USW. "But that doesn't mean we can't be creative." This was a not-so-subtle invitation for the parties to break new ground and achieve his win-win goal. Big Shoulders was the only viable buyer other than IAC, but they were shy by $3.5 million of IAC's $21.5 million bid.

"I'd say, Mr. Perillo," Judge Gill said, "if you had that number at $21 million, it probably becomes a lot easier to say that's a pretty good deal . . . and if you need a few minutes to talk about it, I'll let you."

Big Shoulders Capital president Todd DiBenedetto took the witness stand to make the case for his company's bid—in effect, the USW case for keeping the mill running. His stout frame and broad shoulders filled the stand like a thickly padded goalie blocking a hockey net. Big Shoulders had made a good offer, and, if it failed, they were content to pick up and return to the Windy City. "We're here today responding to your request on Friday to provide an alternative," DiBenedetto told the court. "We are not here to circumvent or top the existing bid." Perillo tried to assuage the judge's concerns, asserting that the mill had $28 million in orders, and prices were coming their way. They could make up the $3 million difference in weeks, if not days.

Gill pushed back. If the buyers would recoup the additional $3 million or $3.5 million in short order, why not come up with the money now? DiBenedetto claimed they didn't have an extra $3 million lying around.

Industrial Assets, PNC Bank, and the receiver all opposed the union's proposal. They wanted an unconditional sale. No strings attached, no court hearings, no appeals, no nothing. Yet John Lucian, PNC's outside lawyer, insisted, "This isn't just about money, it's about time."

DiBenedetto's ears perked up. "Can I add one more piece to our offer?" DiBenedetto cleverly interjected. "If we would be willing to buy the PNC loan at par within the same period of next Monday when the current offer is supposed to close, so that they get paid in full within the same time period they otherwise would have got paid in full, does that solve their concerns?"

"The answer to that is obvious," Lucian told the court. "If my client gets the money by the date on the proposed stalking horse bid, it doesn't matter who the source is, Your Honor."

Judge: "So it is about money, gotcha."

Lucian: "We are a financial institution, Your Honor."

Judge: "Understandable. Well, you get my $900 at some point this month," he said, referring to his home mortgage.

Lucian responded with a straight face. "Your Honor, for the record, this is PNC business credit, you're dealing with a separate entity—or separate division."

Judge: "Even if I make an adverse ruling, I still get to keep my house." Still no chuckle or even a smile from Lucian.

If you can't win on substance, you argue process. That's the route that C. J. Murray took, standing in for the receiver, Michael Polsky. Never imagining that Judge Gill's hearing would be more than a formality and extend beyond Friday, Polsky had made plans to be in Chippewa County on the other side of the state that Monday for a receivership case involving a twenty-four-store supermarket chain.

"Mr. DiBenedetto came into the receiver's room, they decided not to make a bid," Murray said. "They're here today essentially trying to retrade and reoffer things, upsetting and really avoiding the competitive bidding process that the receiver has set up." This was "really cheating Industrial Assets out of a chance to make a higher bid" and violating "the sanctity of the auction process."

Process arguments are important to most judges, and Gill was no exception. But he was torn. "I think if you had a 25—20 million 500 offer with similar terms to what's in the [Asset Purchase Agreement], I would be hard pressed not to say that I'm going to support that," the judge said. He wanted a job-saving deal badly.

A jolt of electricity ran through the courtroom. Workers whispered to one another, "Could this be the answer?"

The judge delivered an ultimatum to Perillo: "If you want another five, ten minutes to see if you can get there, I'll do it. I want terms similar to what's in the asset purchase agreement. We have to have something done today." The court recessed.

Fred Perillo, Doug Osterberg, and Ed Bush and I gathered around the empty jury box. Looking to get a deal done, we started with Michael Bolton and Jon Geenen. The easiest source of cash, as usual, was the workers—an unfortunate but inescapable reality. We signaled to union local president Tony Swanningson in the gallery to join our huddle in a corner of the still-packed courtroom.

Osterberg, Bush, Perillo, Bolton, and Geenen all looked at each other. Who was going to ask Tony for the money?

"Tony, we need a million dollars," Geenen finally said.

Dead silence. You could hear Tony's labored breathing, even above the surrounding din.

"There really is no other choice, Tony," Jon Geenen said. "I know it sucks, I wish it wasn't so." He sounded like a big brother breaking bad news that only a parent should deliver.

Tony walked back to the crowded benches. He leaned across the bar in front of the first row of seats and whispered to a smaller huddle of union members. His head nodded up and down ever so slightly, as they whispered back. He tapped the bar and returned to us.

"Go ahead, use it," Tony said. It was done. The union would contribute $1 million in deferred vacation and other benefits. One million down; two million to go.

Now it was my turn to contribute what I could.

The county had a revolving loan fund (RLF) worth $800,000, an unusually high sum for a county our size. At the time, credit was widely available and cheap, and there was little demand for government-funded loans. Also, the RLF committee was especially careful about approving loan applicants. Unlike banks like PNC in the subprime mortgage market, we invested in companies that were successful and faithfully paid back their loans.

I phoned my planning director, Kara Homan, pulling her out of a meeting. If I could count on one person to get a job done, it was

Kara. She snapped into action, calling a few of her colleagues to decide whether it would be possible to issue a loan under these circumstances for the purpose of leveraging the acquisition of a paper mill.

Kara got back to me within the hour and gave me the okay.

Meanwhile, Big Shoulders had upped its bid by $2 million, seemingly impressed by the union's willingness to kick in. Mr. DiBenedetto apparently figured that, if the workers were willing to put that kind of cash on the table, it might be a good investment after all. We had cleared the threshold, giving the judge his number without having to use any of the county's loan fund.

Gill called the court back into session. We were cautiously optimistic. Perillo revealed the terms of Big Shoulders' offer: $20 million from Big Shoulders and $1 million from USW workers in vacation pay claims. The total matched the price set down by the judge. If Gill was true to his word, it should be open and shut. If only it were that simple.

Gill explained that he needed one more thing from Perillo and Big Shoulders—indemnification, a guarantee that if the deal did not work out, the bank and other secured creditors would get paid. That was the sole responsibility of the receiver, one he could not abdicate, and one the judge could not look past. Gill had the right idea, but it was a bridge too far.

Attorney Perillo said, "In response to the suggestion that the court made that a $20-and-a-half-million offer would—with everything else being equal and assurances that the plant would run, I believe I have presented that. I believe that Big Shoulders is willing to put $20 million of that amount subject to—"

Gill: "And the indemnification on the loss for the next 30 days which keeps things running."

Perillo: "That I do not believe is possible, Your Honor. I mean, you know, terrorists could blow up the plant and we would be indemnifying against any number of completely unforeseen and unforeseeable circumstances."

Gill: "Pretty sure that you're not tops on North Korea's list. But I could be wrong."

Perillo: "There could be any number of contingencies that would cause the company to lose money. And the United Steel Workers is not management. We are here and we believe management will represent to the court that they have a way to run better than cost neutral, that they will actually make money during that period and not lose money, but that's not something that's in the control of the United Steel Workers."

Judge Gill needed good people making a good faith effort.

"What I'm looking at is a million-dollar difference. A million-dollar difference to continue versus a million-dollar difference that we don't know," Gill instructed the parties. It was getting late. Nerves were frayed and stomachs were growling.

Still, the judge pushed on. After a brief recess, it was Perillo's turn to try to close the deal. He called his first witness, Doug Osterberg, the mill's CEO.

"Mr. Osterberg, can you explain to the court how it is possible that in one month you will turn from a $2 million loss to a cost-neutral or profit position?" Perillo asked with a bit of incredulity for effect. This is what it all boiled down to: could the mill run successfully?

Quiet and reserved to a fault, Osterberg had to reposition the microphone a few times so the judge only a few feet away could hear him. Looks were deceiving, though—Osterberg was more than prepared. Armed with Marianne Sterr's calculations of the company's profitability, Osterberg systematically dismantled the receiver's case. He started by attacking the myth that the mill was losing $2 million. "First of all, from a cash standpoint, we're not talking about $2 million. That was a net income statement which would include depreciation and amortization."

Second, Osterberg drilled into the operational details. The mill could restart with one-third of the current workforce, approximately 180 men and women, running just two of the three machines (Number 6 and Number 7), with limited long-term maintenance, enough infrastructure, and overhead to fill out the current and new orders in the queue.

Third, his projections were a worst-case scenario, the probable outcome if they only ran white commodity grades, which had hair-thin margins. Plans were in the hopper to do more, much more.

Fourth and most important, Osterberg emphasized the future of brown grades, a market the mill was well positioned to enter. Global online sales for this product sat at $2.3 trillion in 2017 and were expected to double by 2021. Appleton Coated had completed successful trials and lined up a good customer base for brown grades with additional orders in the queue, Osterberg said, directly contradicting Compton's testimony. Machines were tuned up and ready to go.

Osterberg's testimony overwhelmed the receiver, Freedlander, the bank, and the judge. Gill tried poking holes in his presentation. "Why didn't you do all this before?" Gill asked.

Osterberg explained that they'd simply run out of time. Appleton Coated had been working on moving into packaging for all of 2016 and the first half of 2017. They had been close to fully transitioning that spring, when they'd hit two of their worst months in years. Now things were looking up. "We have not only run trials, we've run a large order for a customer. They were very satisfied with it . . . They gave us another order for 300 tons of corrugated medium [cardboard box material] and they asked us how fast we could ramp up to 3 to 4,000 tons a month. We're trying to bridge from where we were to a model that includes that business. If we can get to that business and get the mill full and operating, even on traditional grades, if we are full, we can run profitably." Osterberg's testimony included a lot of ifs and other qualifiers, but it offered a plausible a path to profitability.

That wasn't all. Osterberg also pulled back the curtain slightly on his secret skunkworks project code-named Mountain Top. Osterberg, his research and development team, and a few millwrights had been laminating brown and white grades on an off-machine coater. The outside was glossy white, the inside was a light brown grade. This was an important and quite possibly lucrative innovation, a far superior product for beer and soda cases that could also be made faster and cheaper than traditional methods allowed.

The name Mountain Top referenced a potential customer and one of the country's biggest beer companies, Coors, with its Rocky Mountains-themed marketing. According to one worker, there was "talk around the mill" that another new customer could have been Kimberly-Clark with its adult undergarment line, Depends. Ironically, the Depends facility in nearby Fox Crossing would find itself on the chopping block four months later. The synergies between the two were obvious, to say nothing of the chance to save both plants.

Next, Judge Gill brought to the witness box Big Shoulders' Tony DiBenedetto, whose name he struggled with

"Mr. Dee-BEN-uh-det-toe," Perillo carefully sounded out.

"DEE-ben-ud-det-TOE," Gill replied like a front-row student struggling to please the teacher. "I'll get it right by the end of the day," he promised. He didn't.

DiBenedetto used his testimony to describe a plan that delivered exactly what the judge wanted—details and all.

DiBenedetto guaranteed that Big Shoulders would make the bank and the secured creditors whole. In financial terms, they would buy out the bank note and step into the credit facility. Those who were owed money would get it. DiBenedetto and his team would commit to keeping the lights on and the machines rolling for at least forty-five days. If there was enough business, they would keep going.

DiBenedetto stressed to the judge that this was a temporary arrangement, a stopgap to establish "proof of concept" so a larger private equity firm or investor group would have more confidence in the business model and be more likely to buy the mill and run it as a going concern. Repositioning businesses in this way was Big Shoulders' specialty. DiBenedetto told the court that, in addition to H.I.G. Capital, other firms had expressed interest in buying the mill, although he would not divulge names.

Gill liked what he heard. "It's adding a great deal of clarity to the landscape," he said. The proposal interested him so much he was willing to entertain a lower offer.

Freedlander saw the writing on the wall and gave up on the original APA. His client had to match the Big Shoulders offer or come close. If he did, the judge would likely go with him, because he could then have it both ways, adhering to the receivership process while keeping the mill open and running. With a tinge of sarcasm, Freedlander said, "If you are conducting what amounts to an alternative approach auction today, that may be something that my client is prepared to participate in."

Perillo stayed a step ahead of Freedlander. He took full advantage of the moment, hammering home two points: a sale to Big Shoulders would preserve large-scale economic development and jobs, and it would do so with zero risk to the mill's creditors.

Tim Nixon would later say that the way the receivership law operated that day took on the flavor of European insolvency law. "In the United States," he explained, "labor does not usually play a legal role in insolvency proceedings. You as a community don't have any standing in the United States to raise the social fabric community issues." By contrast, in Germany and other European countries, insolvency procedures include workers, community, government, and owners, as well as creditors. The legal systems recognize that insolvency hurts more entities and people than the bank or other creditors, and that sooner or later the collateral damage will be felt and must be addressed. That is why European countries would do all they could to keep a mill like Appleton Coated open and make layoffs a last resort, not the first option.

"Technically speaking," Tim said, the mill "should have been shut down the moment [Steve Mattes] wanted it shut down. But you all showed up, and you created the space in which to put a deal together. So, you functionally converted this into a European process."

The only way we were able to put the receivership law to work in this way was with Judge Gill's assent and his openness to the community-interest provisions of the law. He was willing to consider all aspects and ramifications of the receivership, to the chagrin of the bank and the purchaser and to the delight of the workers and me.

The judge had gotten the kind of win-win deal he'd asked for. However, he couldn't rule without giving Freedlander's client a shot at matching the new proposal. So he pulled Freedlander to the table. "Would you be willing to talk to your client to entertain [running the mill for a limited time] and possibly just close this?"

"When a judge asks me a question like that," Freedlander replied, "the answer is absolutely positively and always yes. Of course, I'll talk to my client about that."

It was well past dinnertime. The vending machines in the basement had been emptied out. Patience was running out. The judge was determined as ever to hammer out a deal, even if it took all night. Meanwhile, no one had left: the gallery and the narrow hallways were as crowded as they were at 2:30 p.m. The spectators, too, wanted a deal as well as closure to this torturous roller-coaster ride.

The court recessed.

Standing in the corner of Gill's jury room, I watched attorneys, management, and labor representatives settle around a conference table. I looked at the pale white walls, standard in all county rooms, including my office. But this room was different. How many capital cases had been decided here? How many murderers sent to prison? How many innocent men and women vindicated—or wrongly convicted? The room's history weighed heavily on mind.

We had to get this case right. That meant getting the hot-tempered Steve Mattes on board. Next to Freedlander, he was the proceeding's most colorful character, even though most had never laid eyes on him. Freedlander picked up his cell phone and called him.

Mattes came on the line and immediately unloaded on Freedlander, loud enough so that others in the room could hear him. "What do they want now?" he demanded. "Why isn't this fixed?" To say he had a temper was an understatement. Freedlander tried to get a word in through brief interruptions: "But . . . now . . . yeah . . . wait." It wasn't until Mattes stopped to catch his breath that Freedlander was able to explain that he wasn't alone and that others had heard at least some of the rant.

"Who is there with you?" Mattes asked.

"Well, everyone except the judge," Freedlander said.

Freedlander outlined the judge's request. Playing to his boss, he dismissed Sterr's calculations as notes "on the back of an envelope," even though she was sitting right next to him. He was pissed off and wanted everyone to know it, especially his boss.

Slowing, reality began to sink in with Mattes. If he wanted to buy the mill, he would have to show some flexibility. One way or another, there was still a lot of money to be made from Appleton Coated. No one knew that better than Mattes, "one of the sharpest assessors of economic value and opportunity that there is," in Tim Nixon's words. What about matching what Big Shoulders promised to do? "Well, I can live with that," Mattes said grudgingly. "I guess I have no choice."

We filed back into the courtroom, and the judge gaveled us into session. All eyes focused on Freedlander, whose disposition had brightened considerably. He was close to wrapping up the case and completing the sale. Soon he could get out of this backwater town.

Industrial Assets was "prepared to do what Big Shoulders has suggested," Freedlander began. Gill's eyes widened and his head jerked up. This was it, his face said.

But Freedlander wasn't ready to concede gracefully. He slammed the proceedings and criticized Big Shoulders with righteous indignation. "It still remains somewhat amorphous to me and to my client exactly what it is that they're prepared to do, because we have a written asset purchase agreement on one hand, and, again, something that in fairness I've tried to describe—so we'll do whatever it is that they suggest they're going to do."

The judge wanted a straightforward yes. Would IAC match Big Shoulders or not?

"They will do that, provided that we—"

Gill cut him off. It looked as if he was about to tomahawk his gavel across the room. "Attorney Freedlander could have made it very easy on me and said, 'Judge, the asset purchase agreement plus two weeks,' and it would have been pretty easy for me to decide."

Freedlander relented. "What we can do today is do our very best to work through a term sheet. I don't know what else to say."

Gill responded blithely, "I think worst case scenario we can always then fall back to the APA, if all of a sudden this blows up in our face." He suggested reconvening in the morning, dragging things out one more day. That snapped Freedlander awake.

"We're coming back again?" Freedlander asked.

"Do you want to?" Gill responded.

"No, emphatically, no. As great as you are, I have not enjoyed this even a little bit. I mean it," Freedlander answered. He offered to put together a final proposal in writing, pull an all-nighter, and file it in the morning. The judge had a better idea: a lightning round. Go through the agreement line by line and answer all remaining questions, hash out any differences, and tie everything up with a nice bow.

Gill and Freedlander began to take it from the top.

As Gill plowed through the proposal, he got giddy. Every problem solved, each line checked off, every page turned brought him closer to the finish line. He could taste victory. But he couldn't foul it up in the last turn. For Gill, this was second nature. Completing a decathlon requires strength, speed, and endurance. Fortunately for the mill's workers, Gill was an all-rounder as a judge, too.

While the receiver and buyer and the union agreed on most terms of the new proposal, there remained the question of the labor agreement. As the receiver had earlier requested, would the union forgo its right to take a collective bargaining agreement claim to federal court?

"I thought earlier you said the way you were going to deal with the successorship obligation was to simply say that you were granting a sale free and clear to the maximum extent you had that authority," Freedlander said to the judge.

Gill acknowledged as much, which unnerved Perillo. "So [not ruling in favor or against on the successorship question] is meaningless if we are not then free to pursue those successorship claims someplace where we can get a ruling on them," Perillo told the judge.

Gill felt Perillo was getting ahead of himself. "Don't we need to see how this fleshes out a little bit before we get to that point?" Gill asked. "Why would I lift the injunction [against pursing litigation in federal court] when the purchase hasn't even been consummated? If I lift it right now, I'm just prematurely encouraging litigation." Gill didn't want to jinx the deal. Nothing was going to get in his way of getting the deal done, especially a hypothetical, however important, that might never come to fruition.

The parties would need to convene one more time to hash out the labor agreement and ensure full agreement to a proposal. Before he called a recess, Judge Gill wanted to make sure everyone was on the same page and clearly understood what was expected. He asked DiBenedetto to take the stand one more time and clearly spell out the terms of his proposal.

DiBenedetto reluctantly did so. It appeared Freedlander would take the deal and this was just wasting DiBenedetto's time, although you just didn't know with Freedlander. An exasperated DiBenedetto said:

> Let me reiterate one more time. We will buy the PNC credit facility in its current form and agree to fund the receivership for 45 days. No less than 45 days. If we don't successfully get H.I.G. or one of the other "strategics" [going-concern owners] to the finish line in that time, we'll make a decision then: does it make sense to continue receivership operations, are they breaking even, are they earning a profit, are there strategics in the world hovering? If not, we will have a backup asset purchase offer under the same APA at $20 million that we will close then.

The court recessed.

The coda was uneventful. The parties returned to the court room around nine p.m.—all except for DiBenedetto, who was on his way back to Chicago after being used and hung out to dry. It was a heck of a way to treat a fellow who was one of the biggest reasons they had gotten this far. "If Big Shoulders wouldn't have been in the courtroom to agree to run the business," Sterr later said. "It wouldn't have forced IAC's hand, and the mill likely would not have run."

We were beginning the eighth hour of the marathon proceeding. We would soon learn if it had been worth all the head- and heartache. The gallery was full; shifting bodies against hard wood seats sounded like low tide washing onto a beach.

Freedlander stood up and walked to the lectern. He was back in the driver's seat. "We have reached agreement in principle, Your Honor," Freedlander announced.

Looking back, it all came into focus. Once Freedlander figured out that his client could buy the bank's note and walk into the credit facility and assume the loan and its obligations, it was Freedlander's deal to lose. He knew Judge Gill wanted to stick to the usual receivership process as much as possible and not look like a hometown ref. Freedlander exploited that, seeking the best possible terms for his client. In the end, really nothing much had changed from the original APA, except that his client got it for a lot less. Freedlander wasn't crazy; he was a master of his profession.

Freedlander presented a modified purchase agreement that sounded a lot like that of Big Shoulders. The receiver would knock $1.5 million off the purchase price so it was an even $20 million—a discount that would cover Freedlander's legal fees with a lot left over. IAC would market the facility as a going concern for forty-five days and submit an operating budget that mimicked Osterberg's plan, including running Machines 6 and 7 and calling back 195 union and salaried workers. PNC would get paid in full, albeit a day later, Monday, October 2, 2017, than the originally scheduled closing, and IAC would "step into the shoes of the PNC facility."

Freedlander made it clear that, if his client could not find a going-concern buyer, the court would have to approve the original APA. This greatly unnerved the USW and management. Industrial Assets hadn't been excited about the deal in the first place, and now they had a clear path to return to court, buy the mill outright with no strings attached, and scrap it. Putting IAC in charge of the marketing made the scenario even more likely. However, the deal was not without incentives; IAC could keep any value or sale above the $20 million price.

The USW went along with the deal—with one reservation. "We do not agree with automatic approval of the APA, if we reach an impasse on Friday," Perillo warned the court. That would send them directly to federal court to protect the CBA, where, in all likelihood, the conservative Judge Griesbach would rule against them. The judge understood and confidently assured Perillo that the matter would be handled in due course. Gill was pushing his chest across the finish line.

"Let's hope we don't get there," he told the veteran labor lawyer with a slight nod of his head and a wink. "I think this is setting us up for the best possibility for a win-win situation for everybody," the judge continued, a smile arching up at the corners of his mouth. His joy seemed contagious; I felt it.

The judge had done his job and given the mill's workers a lifeline. Now they would have to haul themselves to safety.

"We're adjourned," Judge Gill said, banging his gavel.

7.

On Our Own

A S IN ANY GOOD COMPROMISE, each side in the receivership hearing had given a little, and no one had gotten all they wanted—except for me. I had gotten exactly what I had hoped would happen but never really considered possible. As I told the media, "We get a second chance. I cannot stress this enough. This is a good thing. We have forty-five days to market the Appleton Coated mill to a strategic buyer who will run it."

In convincing the judge to take seriously our community-economic argument against the receivership deal, we had accomplished something unprecedented. No wonder I was elated. I felt even better on October 5 when Judge Gill formally approved the sale, because he doubled the marketing period to ninety days, increasing the chances of finding a going-concern buyer.

True, the ruling could have been more favorable to the union. A loophole large enough for the Number 7 machine to fit through could allow IAC CEO Steve Mattes to run out the clock on the marketing period, return to the judge, and throw up his hands, saying, "I tried to make the mill profitable, but it couldn't be done. Now please get out of the way so I can scrap the mill like I planned." My big worry was that this would happen.

Thankfully, I knew we had a remarkable team and support network on our side. We'd seen them in action during the court hearing.

"Things in court would not have played out the way they did had Fred Perillo not performed as he did," said CEO Doug Osterberg. He was right. The USW's outside counsel had deftly elicited crucial testimony from Osterberg and opposing witness Michael Compton, showing that the mill just might be able to continue as a going concern. Perillo had been ably assisted by his law partner Sara Geenen, who'd written effective briefs laying out the union's case, and CFO Marianne Sterr's financial analysis had provided additional crucial support.

Perhaps even more important, we had workers, 620 strong, and their families who'd refused to give up. An entire village built by the mill had our backs. And Appleton Coated had brilliant engineers, technicians, and millwrights on the cusp of proving once and for all they could make the elusive brown grades that would secure the mill's long-term viability. We'd won for this community a ninety-day reprieve on what had appeared to be their death sentence. In the months to come, we'd see whether this short-term opportunity could be converted into long-term survival.

ALTHOUGH THE APPLETON COATED CASE had dominated my days and nights, as a local government official I'd also been deeply engaged in following other matters of pressing importance to our state. Less than two weeks earlier, on the eve of the receivership auction, Governor Walker had signed into law the Foxconn bill, the controversial legislation that would dole out $3 billion in state

subsidies over fifteen years to the Taiwanese electronics manufacturer in exchange for a promised 13,000 jobs—a cost to Wisconsin
taxpayers of $230,000 per job. Each of these jobs would pay a lot less,
and have a much smaller multiplying effect, than a paper job. What's
more, the new law weakened wetland and waterway protections; it
would allow the right-leaning state supreme court to circumvent the
appeals process to take up Foxconn legal cases; it would redirect
millions into new state and county roads connected to the Foxconn
campus, and authorize additional bonding from the state's cash-
strapped transportation fund to expand the nearby interstate. It was
a classic boondoggle, one of Scott Walker's worst policy decisions—
and that is saying a lot.

The Foxconn deal formed the backdrop to the Appleton Coated
fight and the Fox Valley paper industry's struggles. The contrast
could not be clearer or more troubling. Our state's elected officials
afforded scant attention let alone resources to the paper workers.
Some didn't even return phone calls. Foxconn basked in the
limelight; Appleton Coated sat in the dark.

Appleton Coated wasn't the only troubled paper company being
ignored by the Walker administration and Republicans in the state
legislature. On October 2, 2017, Appvion, owner of Appleton Coated's
former sister mill just up the road from the courthouse on East
Wisconsin Avenue, had filed for bankruptcy. Founded by Charles
Boyd in 1907 and headquartered in Appleton, the company also had
facilities in Roaring Springs, Pennsylvania (a plant former Appleton
Coated owner John Cuneo had purchased in 1946), and West
Carrollton, Ohio.

In some respects, the Appvion bankruptcy was not a surprise.
After the employees bought Appvion in 2001 from Arjo-Wiggins
through an employee stock ownership plan (ESOP), the company's
three mills in Wisconsin, Ohio, and Pennsylvania were leveraged to
the hilt. The purchase price was $810 million. Employees ponied up
$107 million, and the ESOP took out the rest in loans. For the first five

years of the ESOP, things looked good, and the stock price tripled from $10 to around $33. But the stock declined after that, and in 2015 Appvion was still up to its eyeballs in debt and needed cash. Appvion sold off Encapsys, their micro-encapsulation research division, which in 1953 had developed the first viable, industrial-scale form of micro-encapsulation, the technology behind carbonless paper, to a group of local investors for $208 million. While the sale infused much-needed cash into the company, it severely compromised the firm's outlook by stripping the aging paper company of a key revenue-generating source. Said Appvion retiree Bob Corning, "Encapsys was supposed to be our future. When they sold that, to me, that was putting the closed sign on the door."

The news of Appvion's bankruptcy hit hard. Mayor Tim Hanna assured Appletonians this was not another Appleton Coated, a term that—despite Judge Gill's favorable ruling—was now a euphemism for defeat. "It seems logical to equate the two, as they're both paper mills," Hanna told the *Post Crescent*. "But it's two different scenarios."

Two red flags were now flapping in the autumn wind, and still no state officials were paying heed. While my counterpart in Racine County was heralding "the return of electronics manufacturing to the United States" because of Foxconn, our elected officials were ignoring the troubles of paper. As far as Walker and the GOP were concerned, Foxconn was the state's economic salvation and their political deliverance. Somehow the local and regional chambers of commerce, local politicians, and even a few labor unions convinced themselves to support Foxconn.

On October 4, the week after Appleton Coated won its reprieve in Judge Gill's courtroom, Foxconn officially announced its selection of a plant site in Mount Pleasant, Racine County. Louis Woo, special assistant to CEO Terry Gou, said it was the "people who won over the company." (Gou himself didn't attend this milestone event.) "They're not only hard-driving, hard-working people, but they are passionate, and they are determined," Woo told the *Racine Journal-Times*. The same could be said of the people of Appleton Coated.

When asked what Foxconn's first steps would be, Woo said the company would be "doing some testing assembly . . . we're renting a space to set up a training center and also an experimental center to make sure whatever we do two, three, four years down the line will be the most advanced that no one has done before." The same strategy had been applied at Appleton Coated when they were trialing new paper grades. The similarities were obvious. Both communities had good people; both were focused on innovation. The biggest difference was that the Taiwanese company was getting a cool $3 billion from the state's taxpayers, while Appleton Coated was getting nothing.

ON OCTOBER 5, 2017, JUDGE GILL formally approved the sale of Appleton Coated; five days later, the deal closed. Steve Mattes and IAC were now the proud owners of a paper mill. For the time being, the new owner would manufacture products to fill the pending orders on the sole-running Number 6 Machine, a veritable cash machine that would last several weeks. In the meantime, the rest of the facility went on a hot idle, like a running car engine stuck in park, with a skeletal crew of just thirty paper workers.

The news of this partial reopening did not sit well with local workers. A few began losing hope. Michael Young made up his mind quickly; he did not need to stick around any longer. "The mill is not going to restart. I'm looking for another job. I'm going on with my life," he told the *Appleton Post Crescent*. Others spoke in apocalyptic terms: "I think the end is near," Tim Somers said. Ann Shippy was more sanguine. She wanted to believe the mill would not be scrapped, but she wasn't so sure. "We're hoping for a buyer, but that's the most we can hope for."

On the other hand, Chris Bogan never lost hope. Seared into my memory is the image of Chris Bogan waving an American flag outside the courthouse during the receivership hearings. The slender back tender (dry-end) for the big Number 7 put all his weight into moving Old Glory side to side; against Chris's wiry frame, the flag appeared gargantuan. More than any other Appleton Coated worker, Chris embodied the spirit and determination to restart the mill. In his heart of hearts, he believed Appleton Coated would survive. How could it not? He would do what had to be done to get it up and running: "I wasn't going to give up the mill without a fight."

But Chris wasn't one of the thirty skeleton crew members, and he couldn't afford to wait to see if he would be called back to join them. He needed a decent job with good health insurance fast, because his severely disabled son, Henry, needed 24/7 care. Chris couldn't afford to extend the family health insurance that had been part of his compensation at the mill; the cost under the federally mandated COBRA program was a hefty $1,200 per month. While Mattes sprung for an extra month of health insurance (October), after that, Chris had to go on BadgerCare, the state's low-income Medicaid health insurance program.

In search of a new opportunity, Chris enrolled in a twelve-week truck driving course at Fox Valley Technical College. Throughout it all, he never abandoned his USW brothers and sisters. While taking the class, he sat at the bargaining table, helping to restart the mill and getting his old co-workers the best possible contract, a particularly important role because the APA had nullified the successor clause in the old contract.

On December 22, 2017, the day after Chris graduated, he landed a job at YRC, a local union transport company with salary and health insurance in line with his paper job. Chris appreciated the role the Teamsters had played in negotiating that deal. "It was important to have a union job," Chris told me. "I was union at the mill, and I wanted to stay union because I realized its importance, especially through the receivership fight." He'd gratefully become a Teamster, but in his heart he would always be a paper maker.

It was because of people like Chris that I remained hopeful.

Meanwhile, Combined Locks village administrator Raquel Shampo-Giese had a job to do. Within hours of the judge's ruling, she'd gotten to work helping new owner Steve Mattes with the task of marketing the mill. Shampo-Giese shared marketing websites to help advertise the mill. She also passed along helpful information from the Department of Revenue, including property valuation and tax information to back up the argument regarding the mill's overall value. Unfortunately, there wasn't much interest. The village did hear from a defense contractor looking for land that matched the mill footprint in order to build a $123 million factory that would create 350 new jobs. The idea didn't meet the goal of restarting the mill, but it was better than nothing.

Still, Shampo-Giese remained hopeful. The following Monday, she shared with the village trustees a phone conversation that she'd had with Mattes—one he'd initiated, she emphasized. Mattes had insisted that his company was not just a used equipment dealer, and it was "not unusual" for his company to flip mills. He'd cited a few examples, including a chemical company in South Bend, Indiana.

All in all, Shampo-Giese thought it was a "good conversation." "I did not 'drink the Kool-Aid,'" she wrote the trustees. "But I want to believe that his intention to find a going concern is genuine."

In early October, Appleton Coated advocates were opening a second, parallel track of activity, focused on getting important unemployment resources to the idled workers. The Bay Area Workforce Development Board, which I sat on and at the time served as chair, helped workers sign up for unemployment compensation and COBRA insurance. They also enrolled workers in job training programs at Fox Valley Technical College, where I also sat on the board as county executive from 2014 to 2017, and paired workers with new employers. The Bay Area Workforce Development Board organized a job fair at the end of the month just for the Appleton Coated workers, an event that attracted twenty-five to thirty employers offering jobs that matched the skill set and experience of a mill worker.

I had worked with Bay Area's executive director Jim Golembeski for years. He and his team were so good, I'd pulled Outagamie County out of the regional board we were originally assigned to so we could transfer to his organization. I couldn't imagine going through the ordeal with any other board. We were blessed.

In addition, Matt Valiquette of Bay Area Workforce Development helped the mill apply for Trade Adjustment Assistance (TAA) from the U.S. Department of Labor. If the application was approved, TAA, a more robust version of unemployment compensation and displaced worker resources, would extend unemployment benefits up to eighteen months and offer tuition-paid job training and course work, among other assistance.

Unfortunately, TAA isn't always what it is cracked up to be. In *Janesville: An American Story*, journalist Amy Goldstein followed former General Motors workers who were granted TAA benefits. Some enrolled in technical college programs, some did not. Goldstein discovered surprisingly little difference in the outcomes of the two groups. If anything, those without training did better. "Worse still," Goldstein wrote, "more of those who retrained were not earning any money at all." In 2010, the federal government spent $575 million on 100,000 displaced workers through the TAA program. According to Goldstein, one-half of trainees who received assistance in 2010 and one-third in 2011 "will not quickly find work."

WHILE THE APPLETON COATED MILL IDLED, concerned board members of the Wisconsin Economic Development Corporation (WEDC) were diligently combing through the proposed Foxconn contract. Many had sat on the board for years. They were well acquainted with the cynical approach to economic development taken by Governor Walker. He consistently favored campaign contributors over inventive entrepreneurs with promising business plans, and exercised little oversight on loans. No wonder Paul Jadin, the Green Bay native who'd been CEO of WEDC, had resigned early in Walker's first term in disgust over the governor's politicizing the department. He'd been replaced by Mark Hogan, who toed the Walker line all the way.

Lo and behold, the WEDC board members found significant holes in the Foxconn deal—not surprising, considering that the initial framework of the contract had been sketched out on a napkin when Walker and Foxxconn chairman Terry Gou first met. On October 18, it was reported that Democratic state senator and WEDC board member Tim Carpenter had found what he termed a "nuclear bomb" in the Foxconn contract. Scrupulously respecting official procedure, Carpenter did not describe the problem, saying only that, had it gone unnoticed or unresolved, the contract "would not have protected taxpayers whatsoever." Hogan delayed the scheduled board vote on the contract, no doubt while he negotiated new wording with Foxconn, and never disputed Carpenter's characterization of the problem.

One week later, a damning audit of WEDC was released by the state's Legislative Audit Bureau. While the WEDC had "improved" since the prior audit, "the corporation continue[d] to have issues in tracking the number of jobs created or retained by economic development job programs," which was the whole purpose of having an economic development agency in the first place. The report further identified problems of "accountability, transparency and accuracy."

The problems were not limited to contract procedure and oversight. It seemed Walker's WEDC lacked common sense and basic problem-solving skills. One recommendation made by the

Legislative Audit Bureau was that WEDC "use the [state] Department of Workforce Development (DWD) unemployment insurance data and compare it with jobs-related information submitted by tax credit recipients." That one state cabinet officer needed to be told to pick up the phone and call a fellow cabinet officer for appropriate assistance did not inspire confidence.

To shore up confidence in the Foxconn deal, Hogan said a third-party verifier would ensure that the company was meeting the contract's required benchmarks. Those concerned about good stewardship of the public's money could only hope that this would indeed occur.

MEANWHILE, YET ANOTHER FOX VALLEY paper company went under. On October 23, U.S. Paper Convertors of Grand Chute, a thirty-year-old family-owned and -operated company, announced they would shutter their doors at the end of the year. They were not going through a restructuring or working through insolvency, they were closing—period. More than fifty workers would lose their jobs within a week of Christmas. Could things get any worse?

In the Fox Valley, there had been no period in modern history when so many mills fell on hard times, laying off workers, struggling through insolvency or going out of business. The body count of lost jobs was closing in on 1,000. And yet the industry's trade association, the Wisconsin Paper Council, was curiously silent. The few times when the council did speak publicly, it had its head stuck in the sand. At no point did it reach out to the USW or me, even when we were resuscitating a dying mill that was a dues-paying member of the council. What's more, the council never came up in conversation with management or anyone else involved in the three mills.

The day after U.S. Paper Convertors announced their shutdown, Wisconsin Paper Council President Jeff Landin shared his thoughts on Wisconsin Public Radio. He broke no new ground, offered no new insights, and proposed no solutions. He seemed clueless, as he had in telling the *Appleton Post Crescent* earlier in the month, "It's an incredibly important industry in Wisconsin and I'd argue still incredibly vibrant. I'm not trying to take away from the struggles with Appvion and Appleton Coated, but the reality is that the paper industry is still a vibrant and important industry here in Wisconsin." His diagnosis of the problem during the public radio interview was straightforward. Appleton Coated was in receivership because they made a product that was not in high demand. Other paper mills were doing well because their products were in high demand. Thank you, Captain Obvious.

Landin did make one important observation: ninety percent of the paper products produced in the state were tissue, packaging, and specialty grades with promising long-term markets. But he didn't connect the dots and see the need for state funding to help a viable industry through a rough patch. Grants or loans to Appleton Coated would have assisted them in their transition to brown grades. Appvion could have benefited, too. When Appvion entered bankruptcy, it needed cash. Left with no choice, it took out an $85 million debtor-in-financing loan, applying $65 million of the loan to help pay for ongoing operations.

But my fiercest indignation was reserved for Governor Scott Walker. For ten years, he had been campaigning in the Fox Valley. Now he was nowhere to be found, literally and figuratively. He made few if any trips to Outagamie County in September or October of 2017. The self-proclaimed "jobs governor" refused to look the workers in the eye and see for himself the damage being done to the people of the Fox Valley. When Walker finally responded on November 22 to an October 26 letter I'd written in the Appleton Coated fight, he didn't even mention Appleton Coated, Appvion, U.S. Paper Convertors, or the industry in general. Instead he offered pabulum most likely from campaign material for his re-election announcement the first week in November:

> These targeted investments [in non-paper industry companies] combined with our reforms to reduce the tax and regulatory burden on individuals and employers are helping drive economic growth in Northeast Wisconsin and across our state. We remain committed to supporting economic development in Northeast Wisconsin and across our state through targeted investments and continued government reform.

One year out from election day, Walker was blowing off a crucial bellwether county. A recent poll showed him five points down against a generic Democratic opponent. Hubris unabated, on November 7, 2017, the governor held his Fox Valley re-election announcement at a paper convertor across the highway from the USW district office.

As Appleton Coated completed its last job order in early November, Doug Osterberg and Marianne Sterr proposed a business plan and budget to Appleton Coated's interim president, Kyle Putzstuck, who was beginning to take over the day-to-day operations of the mill. Only thirty-one years old, Putzstuck had a master's degree in accounting and was on loan to IAC from Chicago-based Morris Anderson, a financial and operational consulting firm Mattes had employed in previous projects. Getting buy-in from Putzstuck was crucial, because Mattes didn't trust Osterberg. The court proceedings had no doubt soured that relationship; Osterberg had been the key witness that persuaded the judge and others to give the mill a second chance, something Mattes never wanted.

So Osterberg alone could not persuade Mattes to keep the mill and run it. Thankfully, Marianne Sterr, who'd kept a low profile during the proceedings, seemed to earn Mattes's trust. Additionally, Osterberg was building a good rapport with Putzstuck, who was keeping an open mind and considering the brown-grade paper production model that Doug and Sterr had developed prior to the sale. Putzstuck collected the information and pitched it to Mattes.

The new business plan was straightforward. First, prove that the machines could make brown grades and that the company could fill orders quickly and reliably. Doug and the workers had proven the concept in midsummer with several successful trial runs—they'd filled a few orders, too—before the mill entered receivership. There was no reason why shifting to brown grades wouldn't work.

Next, collect enough orders—brown and white alike—to fill the Number 6, a dependable and versatile machine that could make a range of grades. Although the machine was nearing its fiftieth birthday, the mill had made plenty of upgrades to it over the years. It was battle-tested and more than able to get the mill through this crucial period.

Third, lock in a good source of pulp. The best solution was building a pulp mill. That would provide a steady source of base stock while controlling pulp prices, the biggest price variable in making paper.

Finally, make the necessary machine upgrades to boost the overall productivity of the mill—especially the Number 7. As one of the world's largest machines of its type, the Number 7 held great potential, but that promise could be only realized with real money and real upgrades. While a typical brown-grade mill utilized smaller machines, the market was moving in a direction that demanded larger machines and scaled-up operations. This was another reason why Appleton Coated was uniquely positioned to not just survive but thrive in this market. The cost of building a pulp mill and making equipment improvements would be around $30 million, according

to Osterberg, a pittance in comparison to the Number 7's price tag—
$300 million in 2020 dollars.

Unfortunately, while this new plan was waiting for approval
from Mattes, Doug Osterberg was being eased out of his job. He had
lived and breathed paper for thirty-five years, the great majority of
them at Appleton Coated. Now he would have to leave—and not on
his own terms.

On the payroll or not, Osterberg offered to help Putzstuck and
the rest of the management team work through the coming changes
to the plant, especially the upgrades and other investments.
Putzstuck and his team knew the overall cost, but they didn't know
how to spend it. With his decades of paper industry experience,
Osterberg knew where and how to get the best bang for the buck.
Whether Putzstuck and Mattes realized it or not, they were blessed
to have Doug on their team.

ON NOVEMBER 9, HAVING WORKED THROUGH all the kinks and
defused the "nuclear bomb," WEDC passed the amended Foxconn
contract. It was on its way to Governor Walker and Foxconn CEO
Terry Gou for their signatures.

That same day, Appvion's Wisconsin facility took another
punch to the gut. The company announced that three under-utilized
coating machines and related rewinding equipment would be shut
down at the Appleton plant, and 200 hourly and salaried jobs would
be eliminated. Carbonless manufacturing, once the company's bread
and butter, would go to the sister plant in Roaring Spring,
Pennsylvania, along with rewinding and sheeting. As Wisconsin lost,
Pennsylvania gained. The Paper Valley could not catch a break.

My frustration and anger boiled over. Since August, the entire
state had lost 3,000 paper jobs; Outagamie County alone had lost
1,000. Rather than give our do-nothing governor a pass, I released a

statement and took to the airwaves. "It's ironic that this latest gut-punch comes right before the signing of a $3 billion agreement with Foxconn," I said. "We're all wondering why Wisconsin residents—especially the workers and families hit by these layoffs—must spend their tax dollars on a foreign company, while we lose hundreds of good paying jobs right here in the Fox Valley. Don't rob Peter to pay Taiwan."

The next day, Walker and Gou signed the Foxconn contract. It was official: Wisconsin taxpayers were now on the hook for up to $3+ billion. Future governors, legislators, and generations would be bound by the deal and left to sort through all the fallout. Unlike a law that can be amended by majority vote, contracts cannot.

I continued to hammer the governor and the Foxconn boosters, including the local GOP legislators who'd all voted for and praised the contract. I was particularly upset with the regional economic development organization, the New North, Inc., which had previously done a pretty good job representing the area and supporting local industry. Until then I had looked forward to their annual conventions, which brought together business leaders, school administrators, technical college officials, and local economic development agencies. How the New North could support Foxconn and ignore the Fox Valley's paper mills was beyond me. Even if Foxconn was a resounding success, it carried an enormous price tag, and local businesses would reap little benefit, especially when measured against the costs. On the other hand, saving the paper mills would secure the region's short- and long-term prospects. I haven't been to a New North conference since 2017, but I'll gladly attend again if they refocus attention and resources onto the paper industry and the area's real needs and economic strengths.

Danger signs for the Foxconn deal were appearing even as the ink was drying on the contract signatures by Governor Walker and CEO Gou. On November 13, 2017, Wispolitics.com, the state's leading source for governmental news, reported on a disturbing review of the contract from Wisconsin's Legislative Fiscal Bureau (LFB), which provides policy analysis on legislation and related issues. Wispolitics said: "Estimates from the [LFB], as well as separate analyses from [auditors] Ernst and Young, [consulting firm] Baker Tilly and the WEDC, found it would take some 20 or 25 years before the boost in tax revenues and the jobs the project would create would exceed the state's $3 billion investment." That scenario assumed that the project would indeed boost tax revenues and create jobs as promised, which was by no means certain, and that cost overruns and other factors would not push Wisconsin's investment beyond $3 billion.

Wispolitics also highlighted three other weaknesses in the contract: "the potential for the project's start date to be impacted by the timing of property acquisition and negotiations with property owners, Foxconn's low profit margins compared to industry benchmarks and a Foxconn subsidiary's net loss in 2016."

Reports like these made it increasingly clear that anyone looking to Foxconn to fix Wisconsin's economic woes was sadly mistaken.

On November 29, Walker asked the Republican-controlled legislature to approve $6.8 million for an advertising campaign to attract new workers to the state. Early in the month, he'd signed the Foxconn deal ostensibly to create jobs for Wisconsinites. Now he was spending money to get out-of-state workers. Maybe he had eaten too much turkey over the intervening Thanksgiving holiday and an excess of tryptophan had made him lightheaded. It was impossible to tell whether he was totally oblivious to Wisconsinites' needs or intentionally antagonizing voters. The GOP legislators dutifully complied.

MEANWHILE, THE DEPARTMENT HEADS in my county government office were pitching in to help Combined Locks and Appleton

Coated. Following the mill's sale, county planning director Kara Homan helped Combined Locks draft a tough brownfield ordinance to protect the village if IAC ultimately scrapped the facility. Hope for the best, plan for the worst. Among other mandates, this ordinance provided that Industrial Assets would not be able to cherry-pick the most valuable equipment and metals and leave the rest to rot, creating a disaster area like the Kimberly-NewPage property. IAC would also be responsible for fully reclaiming the site to a grass-vegetative state available for fresh development.

Outagamie County solid waste director Brian Van Straten made accommodations to accept sludge waste from the mill. This wasn't easy. Of all the waste that a landfill can take, sludge is the worst. It's hard to unload, its viscosity gums up machines, and it's highly toxic. Landfills must get special certification to accept the material. It was a heavy lift, but my staff knew how important Appleton Coated was to the community.

Around this time, I officially called for the creation of what I dubbed the Papermaker Fund. The fund would have an initial value of $35 million, one percent of Foxconn's projected cost. Paper companies like Appleton Coated and Appvion could apply for grants or forgivable loans to get through rough business patches. The rationale was simple: paper is a major Wisconsin industry with a viable future as well as a productive past. It deserves our support much more than a foreign company with zero ties to the state and zero credibility in keeping promises.

"If the Papermaker Fund would have been around a year ago [2016]," Osterberg told me, "we could have invested in the capital needed to transition to brown paper grades that would sustain profitability and our overall operation. We would not have had to go into receivership."

Wisconsin's junior U.S. senator, Democrat Tammy Baldwin, was the only other elected official who tried to help Appleton Coated's workers. Baldwin hails from Madison, but she'd developed an affinity with paper workers and their industry as a congresswoman fighting the unfair trade practices of China and others that hurt Wisconsin manufacturing in general and paper in particular. Her 2012 U.S. Senate campaign's first ad had evoked that prior battle to safeguard Wisconsin's economic health.

Our senior U.S. senator, Republican Ron Johnson, who was nowhere to be found during the receivership, took a different tack, with a snide dismissal of the paper industry. When I asked him at a meeting of a regional planning commission about helping Appleton Coated and the rest of the Wisconsin paper industry, he replied, "Let me ask you this. Should the federal government, one hundred years ago, have bailed out, propped up, the buggy whip?"

The comment was breathtaking not just for its display of ignorance about a crucial industry that any Wisconsin elected official should be familiar with, but because it came from a politician who was a millionaire many times over because of the paper industry. (Senator Johnson had co-owned Pacur, a plastics manufacturer and subsidiary of his father-in-law's packaging business.) One hundred years ago, the buggy whip market was already shrinking to the vanishing point, and making automobiles was one of America's most important industries. By contrast, we not only still use paper in vast quantities in our daily lives, we also continue to find new, environmentally sustainable uses for paper in packaging and other applications.

Understanding paper's present and future viability, on November 16, 2017, Senator Baldwin wrote a letter to PNC's chairman, president, and CEO, William S. Demchak, asking fifteen important questions about the Appleton Coated case:

1. How much did Appleton Coated have outstanding on its loan to PNC when the firm entered receivership?
2. By how much did Appleton Coated miss the earnings (EBITDA) target established in the loan covenant? Did PNC

discuss the implications of the violation with anyone at Appleton Coated? Please describe those conversations.

3. Why did PNC Bank choose to enforce the $50,000 per day penalty for missing the EBITDA target?

4. How much in total did PNC collect from Appleton Coated in penalties due to the violation of the earnings covenant?

5. Is it correct that Appleton Coated never missed a payment on its loan to PNC Bank?

6. How frequently does PNC call loans in which the borrower has never missed a payment? Please provide the number of business loans that PNC has called this year in which the borrower has not missed a payment.

7. Did any other lenders offer to buy out PNC Bank's loan to Appleton Coated? If so, why were those offers rejected?

8. Did PNC, any employee of PNC, or any representative of PNC discourage Appleton Coated from entering Chapter 11 bankruptcy?

9. Did PNC, any employee of PNC, or any representative of PNC refuse to provide debtor-in-possession financing to Appleton Coated in the case of a Chapter 11 filing?

10. Did PNC, any employee of PNC, or any representative of PNC discourage other creditors from providing debtor-in-possession financing of Appleton Coated that would have allowed the mill to continue operating?

11. Please describe the nature of the relationship between PNC Bank's representatives in Milwaukee and Chicago and the advisors that the bank required Appleton Coated to hire.

12. How much in revenue did PNC Bank earn on its loan (including fees) to Appleton Coated? How much would PNC Bank have earned without the fees?

13. Does PNC Bank have a business relationship with any other paper producers in the region? If so, please describe the nature of those relationships.
14. Did PNC Bank consider the impact of its decision to call the loan on Appleton Coated's employees?
15. When did PNC Bank first inform Appleton Coated that it was considering calling the loan?

The questions were good ones and deserved detailed and thoughtful answers. Two weeks later, on November 30, PNC Bank responded to the letter—sort of. The bank answered just one question—Appleton Coated chose their consultants, not the bank—and danced around the other inquiries, hiding behind technicalities, deflecting blame, and generally defending their actions to the hilt. Worse, Mr. Demchak didn't respond to the letter himself. Rather, he kicked it down to the regional president to answer. At least Demchak didn't make the Appleton branch manager write it.

Senator Baldwin's seventh question was a particularly crucial one: "Did any other lenders offer to buy out PNC Bank's loan to Appleton Coated? If so, why were those offers rejected?" This had been Doug Osterberg's Plan B. There was enough in outstanding receivables to cover the note plus interest. It would have set the mill back, but it would have been a lot better than going through the receivership process, which they knew was a death sentence. PNC had refused to consider Doug's plan. Now they refused to answer the senator's question. PNC merely wrote, "We did not receive any other written offers to acquire the loan prior to the sale."

According to Osterberg, this was technically true but deeply misleading. An offer was made, and PNC knew about it. "I can tell you, they were notified," he told me. "Everybody involved with the loan was notified with about a dozen lawyers present." Infuriatingly, the offer was not memorialized in some manner. It was a technicality, but that was enough for PNC's attorneys to be able to dismiss the issue altogether—yet another example of how Appleton Coated's consultants failed them.

As for the penalty of $50,000 per day during the receivership, a total of $1.7 million, according to PNC's letter this was not a "penalty" but a funding "fee," because the bank continued to "fund" mill operations while they were in receivership. (Remember, the machines stopped two days after the auction, the eve of the first court hearing.) That, too, was misleading if not downright deceptive. Appleton Coated was still filling orders, getting paid and making money. And there were more orders in hand. Shouldering a $50,000 penalty/fee made it difficult if not impossible for the mill to get ahead. "PNC wanted us shut down and created a cash burn plan that couldn't allow time for another party to refinance," Osterberg told me. Under the circumstances, it was only a matter of time before Appleton Coated would fold.

The bank also notably evaded Baldwin's question about a possible conflict of interest by citing confidentiality clauses. However, as a well-trained lawyer, Baldwin had phrased her question so as not to require any confidential names or figures: "Does PNC Bank have business relationships with any other paper producers in the region?" A simple yes or no would have sufficed. The lack of a no, which would have instantly quashed the widely held suspicion that PNC was financing other paper makers, suggested the answer had to be yes.

Bottom line: PNC could have stuck it out. Appleton Coated was turning things around, and they were well positioned to succeed. PNC would have had a small but profitable investment in their portfolio, one emblematic of their supposed mission, proclaimed on the home page of their website: "We are proud of our longstanding history of supporting not only our customers but also our communities, employees and shareholders."

As far as Appleton Coated went, PNC's avowed mission was illusory. They showed no hesitation in withdrawing support and forcing the mill into receivership, destroying 620 jobs and cratering the local economy in the process.

As 2017 neared its close, Appleton Coated was overdue for some good news. On December 6, Christmas came early. On that day, fifty workers were called back, bringing total employment to eighty-eight. Machines idling since the remaining orders were filled in October were now ready to go.

Five days later, on December 11—Doug Osterberg's birthday— the Number 6 machine roared back to life. Appleton Coated was back in business.

MEANWHILE, THE PROBLEMS WITH FOXCONN kept piling up. On December 12, the American Transmission Company, a multistate transmission utility, announced they would need an extra $140 million from Wisconsin ratepayers to build powerlines to carry electricity to the Foxconn plant. A manufacturing facility the size of eleven football fields was going to need a lot of power. It was an obvious issue, yet it apparently had never come up in negotiations and was not part of the final contract. How could everyone have missed it?

Other costs continued to mount, and public confidence in the project continued to wane. Two days later, the final price tag for new state and county roads serving Foxconn came out: $134 million. That was on top of the $252.4 million already earmarked for interstate expansion. It meant less money for road projects around the state, including Outagamie County.

For home owners unfortunate enough to be in the way of Foxconn's bulldozers, the new year was not much better. In early January, eminent domain eviction notices flooded mailboxes of homeowners on the new footprint. They had thirty days to vacate. (A few days later, a kinder, gentler Foxconn expanded the deadline by ninety days.)

Wetlands and waterways were next. The first environmental exemption was made, paving the way for twenty-six acres of wetlands to be plowed under. These wetlands were within the basin of the Great Lakes, which constitute twenty percent of the world's surface fresh water. This, too, was a big deal. Forward-thinking legislation adopted in 2008 had partnered Wisconsin with seven other U.S. states and two Canadian provinces to protect the lakes and their surrounding watersheds. Many of the legislators who voted for Foxconn had supported the Great Lakes Compact. Now, they were standing aside and allowing a foreign company to degrade this precious resource. They ignored the concerns of the other parties to the compact, as well as the experiences of countries that had been burnt by Foxconn's empty promises in the past.

On January 17, 2018, the second shoe dropped. The cost of Foxconn had shot up fifty percent from the initial projection to $4.5 billion—a figure that made even the staunchest Walker allies blush.

Two weeks later, January 31, the fourth and fifth paper plants in the Fox Valley went down. The paper makers of Wisconsin were battling valiantly for survival, but the state's governor and his political allies couldn't be bothered to lift a finger. We were on our own.

8.

Foxconn for Kimberly-Clark

I T MADE MY BLOOD BOIL to watch Governor Walker and the GOP legislators completely ignore Appleton Coated, standing by and watching the workers suffer. There was a sociopathic quality to their apathy.

It was not as if the local GOP representatives were powerless. The number-two leaders in the state senate and assembly both lived in Outagamie County. I remember a comment from one, excusing their total disregard on the grounds that receivership took state help "off the table." Gimme a break. There were plenty of opportunities to do something.

Just one example: the second night of the receivership, when the USW and Outagamie were putting money on the table, we were a couple million shy of completing a package for a new buyer who would run the mill. That would have been a great time to help. State leaders could have swooped in and saved a productive mill with a viable path to profitability—for 0.01 percent of the Foxconn giveaway.

Since September 2017, I had been beating the drum about the need to adopt a statewide, industry-wide strategy to help Wisconsin's paper mills. I used a refrain that Jon Geenen had suggested: "If we can muster $3 billion for a foreign company like Foxconn, we can spare a fraction for a Wisconsin industry."

Most folks got it, especially the workers. "They spend money on Foxconn, but what about us? [Walker] doesn't care about us," one worker commented to me. Another added, "We have 620 well-paying, family-sustaining jobs. At the same time, you've got Foxconn, which the state has offered billions of dollars. They pay $10 an hour and aren't family-sustaining jobs. Our pleas go on deaf ears."

Still, the GOP-dominated state government refused to act. And meanwhile, the paper business continued to suffer.

On January 31, 2018, the Paper Valley took its fourth hit in as many months when paper giant Kimberly-Clark announced it would close two Winnebago-based facilities as part of a global restructuring plan—paid for by the recently enacted Trump tax cut. One facility was Neenah Non-Wovens (located in Neenah), which produced the base stock for the other facility, Kimberly-Clark Cold Spring (in Fox Crossing), which made Depends undergarments. According to officials, the corporation's global plan, which called for closing ten facilities and shedding 5,000 jobs, would save $500 million and improve the Fortune 500 company's stock price.

For a company often described as having a legacy of paternalistic and benevolent employee relations, it seemed a puzzling decision, especially in its hometown of Neenah. But history showed that, when push came to shove, Kimberly-Clark did not hesitate to throw workers out on the street. Kimberly-Clark was in the vanguard of anti-union practices for the first half of the twentieth century. In 1904, it trucked in replacement workers and Pinkertons when workers struck, unsuccessfully, to end Saturday night shifts. It's the same company whose private security forces opened fire that year on a gaggle of strikers. It led the way in creating the notorious Western Paper Manufacturers Association, a cartel of mill owners in the state to eliminate union activity at paper plants— a boon for unscrupulous mill owners.

So for Kimberly-Clark to boost its share price at the expense of workers wasn't as big a break from the company's past practices as some commentators seemed to think.

In response, Scott Walker threw up his hands, telling a local radio station that "there wasn't much the state could do" about the closure. Company officials quickly convinced Walker and others that there was "no way to save" the Non-Wovens plant. Besides, according to Walker, it wasn't that big of a deal; there were plenty of jobs to go around. "We have more jobs today than we have people to fill them," he told one TV station. According to Walker, this supposed bounty of jobs paid as much as union paper jobs. He claimed that the state could connect underemployed workers "with opportunities that are equal to or greater than the ones they have right now." It was an especially ignorant comment coming from him. If he had asked any laid-off Appleton Coated worker, he would have heard how few jobs match the pay and benefits of a paper mill job.

The WEDC, the state's flagship economic development agency, backed up Walker's talking points. A couple of days later, a spokesperson told another TV station that Wisconsin was "still the number one paper making state."

And GOP legislators parroted Walker's lines. In a canned statement, Roger Roth, the president of the state senate, said, "With the overall favorable economic climate in this state, Wisconsin's unemployment rate is 3 percent and people are getting jobs faster than ever before." The comment was breathtakingly ill-informed. Had he spoken to even a handful of constituents, he would know the numbers did not match reality. It is why jobs and the economy remained a top issue, even in supposedly good economic times.

Representative Mike Rohrkaste, who represented the district containing both the Neenah Non-Wovens and Cold Spring facilities, echoed Roth's comments and added vague promises of help: "I am committed to working with Kimberly-Clark, and both local and state agencies to ensure that those individuals and families affected by the recent announcement have the resources and assistance they need moving forward." Other local GOP legislators chimed in. Rarely was there any daylight between Walker and Republican legislators. They were like marionettes in his hands.

I had a different take. "When you look at the broader economic picture, continuing to lose paper jobs can be devastating to the regional economy. Each paper mill job supports about five other jobs," I told the *Milwaukee Journal Sentinel* the day of Kimberly-Clark's restructuring plan announcement.

"It goes beyond the economic [issues]," I told a local TV station a few days later. "Because it's so much about who we are historically. Our history, our culture."

The governor and the WEDC had, at best, a poor understanding of economic development. The Kimberly-Clark paper jobs were not interchangeable with any other jobs. They came from an industry that is the backbone of the local and state economy. If the paper industry goes away, so too will every other industry and business connected to it. And as far as Walker's "more jobs available than people to fill them," you can say good-bye to those, too.

This raises another issue: the GOP's cynical use of statistics to cloak real jobs numbers. The unemployment figures highlighted continually in the news don't count people who have become so discouraged that they've stopped looking for work. The statistic that matters is the percentage of working age people who would like full-time work but cannot get it, a trend that is reflected in the rarely discussed labor participation rate. Equally significant are the numbers of people who are underemployed, forced to take jobs that don't pay a living wage. Too many of today's businesses are based on models that assume low wages thanks to dysfunctional immigration policies and anti-union laws.

One underappreciated consequence of using immigration as a source of cheap labor has been a transfer of wealth from the bottom to the top of our economy on the order of $500 billion per year in depressed wages and excess profits. This big annual transfer surely ties into the trend I mentioned earlier, the huge spike in mortality rates among non-Hispanic working-class whites highlighted by Princeton professors Anne Case and Angus Deaton, which they attribute to America's threadbare social safety net and its general disregard for workers.

The Kimberly-Clark announcement made action to support Wisconsin's paper industry even more urgent. On February 5, I called a press conference to bring attention to our proposed Papermaker Fund, which would help struggling paper mills like Appleton Coated get through rough times by helping them invest in new equipment or job training.

I had invited former Republican representative and current Neenah mayor Dean Kaufert to join our press conference. Regretfully, I had disinvited Democratic gubernatorial candidate Dana Wachs from attending, despite the fact that Wachs was the only candidate for governor talking about paper jobs. But we didn't want our plan to appear partisan or political; we had been reaching out to Democrats, Republicans, and nonpartisan officer holders since the fall.

In the end, Mayor Kaufert couldn't make it, but we had Chris Britten, a Kimberly-Clark Neenah Non-Woven worker, join us. It took a lot for Chris to put himself out there; he came to the press conference straight from his night shift at the mill. But he wanted to speak up for his fellow workers and tell the community that paper jobs were important and needed to be saved—not just at Kimberly-Clark, but at Appleton Coated, Appvion, and U.S. Paper Convertors, too.

The press conference went well, but the fate of the bill was another matter. Consistent with its general conduct, the hyperpartisan GOP majority in the legislature quickly shelved the bill. Not only was the bill not brought up for a vote, but its authors, Representative Amanda Stuck (D-Appleton) and Senator Dave Hansen (D-Green Bay), weren't even given the courtesy of a committee hearing. Trying every possibility to help Wisconsin's workers, Stuck extended an olive branch to GOP legislators, suggesting the creation of a paper caucus in the legislature to improve communication with industry and labor leaders, and to develop policies to help pulp and paper mills. Legislative Republicans rejected her entreaties, and her caucus never materialized. (One year later, legislators from central and northern Wisconsin would form their own paper caucus. Fox Valley legislators were conspicuously absent.)

So thanks to Republican intransigence, our Papermaker Fund idea was dead on arrival. But perhaps the light we shone on the issue at least created some political pressure on party leaders. That would explain one of the more cynical maneuvers I've seen in my years in politics.

On February 5, just fifteen minutes before our Papermaker Fund press conference, Governor Scott Walker used a Tweet message to roll out what he called Foxconn for Kimberly-Clark—a transparent political gimmick to paper over Walker's neglect of the Fox Valley's economic backbone. It proposed an incentive plan that would apply the exact same terms of the Foxconn deal to Kimberly-Clark, giving the company a mammoth $117 million taxpayer subsidy. (It didn't escape my notice that the only troubled paper plant Walker wanted to help was *not* based in Outagamie County.)

Suddenly the problem that Walker had been pooh-poohing for weeks now demanded state action. Republican legislators followed the governor's lead. The state senate president and assembly majority leader had ignored the Outagamie County mills—Appleton Coated, Appvion, and U.S. Paper Convertors—despite the fact that they themselves lived in Outagamie. Now they were named the lead authors of Walker's proposed bill. Both were up for re-election in nine months, and they needed to shore up their credibility with the industry, its workers, and communities. State Senator Roger Roth tweeted, "Kimberly Clark has been a cornerstone of the Fox Valley for decades and we want to keep it here! Investing in our community and our state is a of [sic] top priority, which is why I'm encouraging @govwalker and @wedcnews to work with @kccorp to help them stay and grow," Roth even attached his tweet to Walker's statement.

Other Republican politicians also jumped on Walker's bandwagon. "We are talking about a real solution that will keep good paying jobs here in Wisconsin," said Mike Rohrkaste, sounding more like a corporate representative than a state representative. "This will give Kimberly-Clark the opportunity to improve their business plan and be here for the long run."

But as the Foxconn for Kimberly-Clark show unfolded, Walker floundered. The political environment for Republicans was deteriorating by the day. President Trump couldn't keep off Twitter, and Republicans found themselves always one tweet away from a scandal they'd have to defend. Democrats kept racking up victories across the country in special elections. State senate district 10 in the northwest corner of Wisconsin flipped blue after Walker, oblivious to everything going on around him, opened the seat up by appointing the sitting GOP senator as a cabinet secretary. Stunned by the special election loss, Walker hit the panic button with three words on his Twitter account: "WAKE UP CALL!"

With his career on the line, Walker became distracted and began losing control of the Kimberly-Clark legislation. The proposal was put together haphazardly, and the plan was introduced without any assurance that the company would even accept the incentives if the bill passed. Walker offered this half-hearted comment about his own proposal: "My sense was we wanted to make sure we weren't walking away from the situation without putting our best offer on the table and that is what we're doing." It sounded as if he was content to accept his constituents' job losses and move on. Given his indifference to Appleton Coated, Appvion, and U.S. Paper Convertors, that would not have been a surprise.

"That's exactly what I have been guessing," one union official emailed me. "He knows the numbers and just wants votes."

Nevertheless, I wanted to be optimistic, and I offered a qualified statement about Walker's plan: "I am encouraged that state leaders are beginning to pay attention, but I'm concerned that the bill does nothing for the plants in Outagamie County, nothing for future closures, bankruptcies and receiverships, and there is no industry-wide strategy."

MEANWHILE, SOME GOOD NEWS began to emerge for the beleaguered Fox Valley paper companies.

First, the Appleton Coated mill was approved for the federal Trade Adjustment Assistance (TAA) program, which would make additional retraining and education resources and benefits from job loss due to foreign trade available to the mill workers. The announcement wasn't on the same level as keeping a mill open, but it still was good news. And it came at just the right time; the Kimberly-Clark ordeal was making a lot of workers nervous. In any struggle, *esprit de corps* is essential; it is the fuel that powers perseverance. The TAA announcement helped.

Then, news broke that suggested that Appleton-based Appvion was beginning to inch its way out of insolvency. The company was highly leveraged. Seventeen years after the employee buyout and the formation of the employee stock ownership plan (ESOP), the company was still $745 million behind the eight ball, roughly the same amount they started with in 2001. But on February 8, four months after the insolvency announcement, a group of potential investors emerged. The stalking horse bid was for $325 million and the "assumption of substantial liabilities." Word of a potential buyer offered relief and some hope for the future.

I was happy for the workers and their families. "The initial news seems promising, but if we've learned anything in the past, restructuring is not always a good thing," I stated in an *Appleton Post Crescent* story on the potential sale. My comments were the only remarks in the story from an elected official.

However, Appvion's good news was short-lived. One week later, on Valentine's Day, current and former Appvion workers got a card from their CEO telling them their company stock was worthless. Those who had invested their pension funds solely in the ESOP lost everything. The workers were furious. At the time of the ESOP's creation, ninety percent of the company's workforce had chosen to throw in with it; some put all their life savings into the company's stock. The workers had total faith in their company, and they'd put their money where their heart was. They were true believers. Now their faith had been repaid with betrayal.

This is what people like Scott Walker never understood. Paper was more than a job, economic development, or even heritage. It was personal. It was family, literally and figuratively. Many paper workers followed in a parent or grandparent's footsteps; for a long time, that was the only way to get a job in the Fox Valley mills. For some, the mill was all they knew. Like their union brothers and sisters at Kimberly, Combined Locks, and Kaukauna, a lot of Appvion workers had just two lines on their resumes: high school and the paper mill. In the words of former Appleton Coated worker Chris Bogan, at Combined Locks "half of the workers didn't know anything else besides paper." Most had walked off the graduation stage and into the mill the next week. Many, like Jack DeKoch, met their spouses at the mill.

When Jessica Schiessl left Kimberly-Clark, it hurt because "it tore a bond" she had with her co-workers. Taking a job at Procter and Gamble's Green Bay mill wasn't an easy decision for her, even though she was landing on her feet, keeping a paper job, and, most important, remaining in a union. Her Kimberly-Clark union job had pulled her out of poverty, giving her enough money to provide for her son and gain custody. She bought a house and gave her son his own bedroom.

And Schiessl credits the USW with keeping the Kimberly-Clark plant operating. Punching out the words for emphasis, she told me, "My – Union – Kept – Our – Mill – Open."

TWO DAYS AFTER APPVION WORKERS had learned that their company stock was wiped out, U.S. Senator Baldwin met with USW members at the union's district office. She was incensed, which was unusual for the mild-mannered, Wisconsin-nice Democratic junior senator. But these were unusual times.

"Kimberly-Clark made $3.3 billion in profits last year, and this plant contributed mightily," she told workers. "I have a hard time understanding that this plant is meeting and exceeding its goals and that it's on the shutdown list."

The plan was especially strange given the massive windfall from the recently enacted Trump tax cuts. "The decisions are very puzzling to me," Baldwin said. "I've heard $100 million in incentives. But Kimberly-Clark just got major tax benefits from the recently passed tax bill in Congress. They could whittle back a little of the $900 million stock buyback they had this year and make it $800 million." The workers nodded in agreement.

When it came down to it, it was greed, plain and simple. Senator Baldwin declared, "These are decisions made to jack up the stock prices next quarter. [But] the community impact is enormous. It's absolutely enormous." Baldwin also shared a letter she'd penned to Kimberly-Clark executives demanding justification for their decision. "This is not right and it is not fair," Baldwin had written. "It is simply wrong for the company to use corporate tax cuts to reward the wealth of its executives and shareholders through increased dividends and more stock buybacks, while closing facilities and laying off workers."

The next week, on February 22, the state assembly convened in a special session to take up the Foxconn for Kimberly-Clark bill. Making the most of the state's gerrymandered districts and lax campaign finance rules, Republicans had built a 62 to 37 majority in the assembly. The bill passed easily and headed to the senate.

The assembly's vote pumped fresh blood into the Kimberly-Clark effort and raised expectations. For Kimberly-Clark workers, it was good news; for Scott Walker, it generated political pressure. Some of Walker's key political allies had jumped into the fray opposing the Kimberly-Clark aid package. Right-wing groups like the Wisconsin Institute for Law and Liberty (WILL), the Koch Brothers' FreedomWorks, the Bradley Foundation's MacIver Institute, and the conservative think-tank the Badger Institute were not happy. They hadn't liked the Foxconn deal from the get-go, considering it an abuse of taxpayer resources and an interference in the free enterprise system. They'd accepted it as a one-off, a necessary concession to guarantee Walker's re-election. But they wouldn't support any future deals of the kind.

Now the *Wall Street Journal*, the closest thing to an official mouthpiece of the country's movement conservatives, chimed in, even quoting me in their angry editorial:

And now local politicians and state legislators are demanding that the Governor provide equally generous treatment to Kimberly-Clark. "Surely, if we can muster $3 billion for a foreign company like Foxconn, we can spare a fraction for a Wisconsin industry," Outagamie County Executive Thomas Nelson, a Democrat, said this week.

Walker's cynical ploy aimed at placating the workers and families dependent on Kimberly-Clark looked as if it was backfiring politically. That didn't trouble me a bit.

AS THE WINTER OF 2017-2018 morphed into spring, the turnaround story of Appleton Coated began to emerge with startling clarity.

One of the milestones of the saga came on March 8, when the Midwest Paper Group—the new name for the company now running Appleton Coated—signed a two-year labor contract with USW Local 2-144. Pronounced dead six months earlier, ignored by the state's political establishment, and pitied by naysayers, the Combined Locks mill had now fully come back to life. It was "nothing short of a miracle," I told the *Post Crescent*. "Rarely has a company gone into receivership and come out to tell the story." (The good news of the mill's rebirth included Chris Bogan's return to work there.)

Although the new two-year contract gave both the workers and the company much-needed certainty, it didn't win over everybody. But on balance, it was a good deal, and most recognized it as such. Longtime worker Jim Weyenberg put things into perspective: he termed the mill a "start-up," which helped to explain the compromises that the union had had to accept. Wage schedules were maintained, although time-and-a-half overtime pay was nixed. Callbacks by seniority were reinstated, a sticking point during the early phases of the restart. Vacation schedules came back.

Perhaps most significant, a new profit-sharing system was put into place, one which actually put money in workers' pockets. Workers received payouts in the third quarter of 2018 and the first two quarters of 2019. In other words, it took just two quarters for Mattes's investment to start turning a profit. At that rate, Mattes would recover his initial investment of $21.5 million in two years, about the time the union contract would be up.

Don't tell me unions aren't good for business.

Complementing the new contract was the restart of the big Number 7 two weeks later (March 25). Now all the machines were up and running. The Number 7 was on a shortened schedule, just five days a week, but the machine was tuned up and ready to go 24/7 if need be. I asked Bob DeKoch, the former mill manager who'd overseen the construction of the Number 7, how he felt when he heard the news of its rebirth. He smiled: "I put a lot of heartbeats into that place."

There was plenty of praise to go around. Doug Osterberg and the mill workers singled out owner Steve Mattes, the industrial scrap dealer now turned mill owner. Having been maneuvered into running the company rather than selling it off in pieces, he'd embraced the challenge. He'd invested a considerable sum of money into the plant, "seven figures, maybe eight," according to Osterberg. The money had gone to build a de-inker, a DLK pulper, and related equipment essential to making brown grades. (DLK stands for Double Line Kraft, a thick and durable cardboard material that is crushed into base stock to feed the paper machines.) Now Mattes had a world-class mill and a workforce to go along with it.

Osterberg deserves a big pat on the back, too. He was the one who'd convinced Mattes and his team to keep the mill and run it. Village president John Neumeier and administrator Racquel Shampo-Giese considered Osterberg the "real hero," the one who "had the vision, the correct vision," to turn the mill around and give it a future. The *Appleton Post Crescent* named Osterberg a Person of the Year for 2018. That pissed off a lot of people, including owner Mattes. Osterberg would be out of a job a few weeks later.

Surprisingly, the one group most responsible for saving the mill—the workers—received few accolades. The *New York Times* article that chronicled the story under the appropriate headline "The

Great American Cardboard Comeback" gave passing reference to the USW and me—and only because the reporter interviewed me. When I plugged the USW to a local official following the mill's restart, he feigned disbelief: "That may be." And when Walker came to Appleton Coated in July 2018 to take a victory lap, neither his office nor the company included the USW or me.

But the history is clear. A highly productive unionized workforce was one of the mill's most important assets. The objections the USW and I raised to the sale during the receivership were what forced the court hearing, which, in turn, and thanks also to Judge Gill's focus on preserving jobs, made possible a brokered compromise that saved the mill. And the workers' great skill, expertise, and dedication ensured that the mill could restart efficiently and profitably.

Worker Chris Bogan was the first to tell the Appleton Coated story. He posted it on a national pro-union Facebook page, garnering 5,000 shares within twenty-four hours. He credited the union with making the difference that restored hope and put the mill on track to reopen. "If it wasn't for the union, Appleton Coated would never be running again today as Midwest Paper Group," Bogan told me. "There'd be no way. The steelworkers, they led the fight to keep the place running and worked with the new owner to find a way to keep it running."

Mattes needed the workers as much as they needed him. There isn't a button you can push to turn on and run a paper mill. You need experienced and talented workers who know the equipment and can run half-billion-dollar paper machines. Without such people to run the mill, even the best business plan in the world wouldn't matter. As former mill manager Bob DeKoch says, "We don't do anything or move anything forward without the support and hard work of our people."

WHILE APPLETON COATED WORKERS and their boosters were euphoric, their brothers and sisters at Kimberly-Clark–Cold Spring were dejected. March was an awful month for them. State senate president Roger Roth was unable to muster the votes for the Foxconn for Kimberly-Clark proposal before the senate ended its regular floor period on March 19. (By not gaveling out, the Republicans preserved the possibility that they could later gavel in for an extraordinary session, a technical though crucial parliamentary detail.) Roth had had almost three months to gather the needed votes, but he wasn't even close. Worse, high-profile Republicans were publicly announcing their opposition. They had parroted Walker's promise to their constituents that there would be "no more Foxconns," and they weren't about to break that promise, especially in an election year, and especially not for a bill that wouldn't even help their own districts. Democrats refused to lend any support. They had been shut out of the law-making process for seven years and weren't about to bail out Walker and their GOP colleagues, even if it hurt union workers. The bill was so unpopular no one aside from Roth praised it publicly.

Compounding the problem, Kimberly-Clark had still not signaled whether they would agree to the bill's terms. The *Appleton Post Crescent* reported that Roth's colleague, Senate Majority Leader Scott Fitzgerald, who schedules bills for a vote, believed "talks between the state and K-C weren't far enough along to have legislators sign off on a deal." Fitzgerald said, "Until they take a deal or until they give us the high sign that they're willing to take a deal, we don't know what we have before us.'" So he punted, handing the political football back to Walker and his economic development agency and leaving it to them to "monitor" the situation.

I couldn't tell whether Walker was relieved or upset by the bill's failure. He has one of the best poker faces in politics. His eyes are dark, black, and emotionless, scarily so. But it was clear that the entire Kimberly-Clark ordeal, on top of the three other mill closures, was a pain in the back end for Walker as he struggled through the election season.

It was shaping up to be a terrible election year for Walker and the GOP. As Roth returned home after a disappointing session, two Democratic challengers were awaiting him, one a top recruit by the senate Democratic caucus. By summer, it was clear that the contest could decide control of our upper house. It was emerging as one of the top ten state legislative races in the country—and the planets and stars were aligning against Roth.

As for me, I was pissed off. The Kimberly-Clark workers had been through a lot. They deserved an explanation; more important, they deserved action and results. If the governor wanted to get this done, he could. He did it for Foxconn, he could do it for the Fox Valley. I said all this, publicly and repeatedly. My goal was to make the fight as public as possible—to exert as much pressure on Walker and legislators as I could. (The best way to get a politician to do their duty is to threaten their job.) Reporters continued to come to me for comment and insights. It served as a good platform to get our message out, to keep the focus on the workers, and to turn the screws on Walker.

In response, Kimberly-Clark, Walker, and the senate GOP conspired to push the USW into a corner. The strategy of the corporate behemoth and their yes-men and -women was simple: if the union would accede to a string of draconian concessions, the senate would take up the rescue bill, and Kimberly-Clark would "consider" the package. Politically, it was the best and perhaps the only option Roth and the senate had. And unlike Appleton Coated and Appvion, Kimberly-Clark made consumer products—Huggies, Depends, and Kleenex—and had a brand to protect. So they took a page from their old playbook and tried blaming the workers.

But the union fought back. For three months, the USW had been quietly but diligently gathering information and meeting with company and state officials, staying far away from the limelight. But by mid-April, they had had enough. The USW unleashed a well-deserved attack on the state senate and Kimberly-Clark, calling the senate's inaction "unfair" and the company's behavior "disturbing." District 2 director Michael Bolton did not hold back:

> What is happening in the Senate is an indictment on what is wrong with politics in America. The GOP-controlled Senate is refusing to conduct a vote until the company approves the package and after they have used their Republican allies to help extract concessions from workers. It's time that these politicians remember that they represent the citizens of Wisconsin, not multi-billion-dollar corporations.

Meanwhile, support was building for the workers. I had been in the news off and on for seven months speaking out for the workers. Constituents were approaching me to thank me and to ask for updates on the prospects for the mills. The support extended well beyond the Fox Valley and the state. USW partner-unions around the globe joined their cause. Geneva-based IndustriALL got involved. A global union representing 50 million workers in mining, aerospace, textile, rubber, and pulp and paper, among other industries, IndustriALL was the same labor federation that had facilitated negotiations between the USW and August Koehler when the German firm was considering buying the Kimberly-NewPage mill in 2009. Now they joined Swiss-based UNI Global Union and the USW in condemning Kimberly-Clark's "unacceptable behavior," mentioning specifically its "heavy-handed tactics and threat[s] of closure."

On April 23, Kimberly-Clark released a much-delayed first quarter earnings report. Sales from the first three months of the year had risen five percent, year over year, beating expectations. The same report boasted of $500 million in dividends and stock buybacks, fulfilling Senator Baldwin's prediction that Kimberly-Clark would use its payoff from the Trump tax cut for short-term profiteering rather than long-term investment. Pleased with the report though cognizant of a potential $100 million windfall from the Kimberly-Clark deal, CEO Tom Falk tamped down expectations, intimating the numbers were not good enough. Falk planned to "take actions to increase net realized revenue and reduce costs." The good news, according to the report, was that Kimberly-Clark was on track to "execute" the restructuring program and looked forward to creating "long-term shareholder value." Nowhere in the report was there mention of the workers at the Neenah and Fox Crossing plants.

This felt like the final kick in the pants. Workers were apoplectic. So was I. I fired off a tweet: "Good news, right? @Kimberly-ClarkCorp beat 1Q profits and sales expectations. Should be enough $ to keep both @cityofneenah facilities open – w/o $100 M state subsidy."

As for the workers, they were ready to take matters into their own hands. They were the only adults in the room, demonstrating remarkable leadership and grace under immense pressure. What happened next would alter the course of the saga and demonstrate to the world the union difference.

9.

State of the Unions

B Y THE SPRING OF 2018, Appleton Coated had been rechristened Midwest Paper Group. Three giant paper-making machines were up and running, and over three hundred workers had been called back. They'd worked hard, they'd persevered, and they'd prevailed.

The same could not be said of their brethren at Kimberly-Clark–Cold Spring. For them, the journey had just begun. USW Local 2-482 president Dave Breckheimer and his members were slogging through the swamps of election-year politics. Midwest Paper Group union local president Mack MacDonald (Tony Swanningson's successor in that role) understood what they were going through. He told Breckheimer, "Look, we were there. We're struggling, but we're coming back. You let us know if there is anything we can do."

Four months after the unveiling of Foxconn for Kimberly-Clark, the bill that promised the company $100 million in incentives to stay open, the GOP senate was nowhere near passing the legislation—even though the assembly had signed off in February, and Governor Walker had pledged his full support. With pressure mounting, on April 18, the senate GOP, led by Roger Roth, shifted strategies: they would wait until the workers and Kimberly-Clark ratified a contract.

It sounded reasonable, but the underlying strategy was not. Taking a page from the manual of how to screw over a union, Roth was trying to set up the workers to fail. There was little progress being made at the bargaining table, and he calculated that the impasse would not break. Making a deal contingent on contract approval was designed to ensure that the union would take the blame—not Roth, the GOP-led senate, or Walker.

"We don't want to interject ourselves in the middle of the negotiation process," Roth said to the local ABC affiliate WBAY. "I'm not party to that. That's between the union and Kimberly-Clark." It was a well-crafted lie. They had been "interjecting" themselves in the process for two-and-a-half months by pushing the legislation while the union and company were in contract talks.

It was supposed to be the latest clever move by a state GOP that had ridden a remarkable wave of success. Roth was proud of the part he'd played. In a 2018 campaign speech to a packed room of supporters, he boasted, "Years from now they're going to be writing books about what's happening here in Wisconsin. There will be those intellectuals, those college types—political scientists—who can't even change a tire, who are going to be articulating what happened here between 2010 and now." Roth's mocking tone belied the fact that he himself had graduated college with a degree in political science. He went on to ask, "How did we go from a blue to a red state? One thing they're going to forget to mention, is that you all outworked our opposition."

Roth may have been right about the opposition. But this time, it would be the union that out-hustled Roth and his cohorts.

Tiring of all the election year politics, the Kimberly-Clark workers decided to take matters into their own hands. With a gentle nudge from the USW, Dave Breckheimer and a few of his co-workers, including shop steward Jessica Schiessl, traveled to Dallas, Texas, to attend the company's annual shareholder meeting in late April. (Kimberly-Clark had been born in the Fox Valley, but the company had moved its headquarters to Dallas in 1985, using a foil— Wisconsin's Democratic governor Tony Earl—to cloak the real reasons for their decision: their executives didn't want to pay state income taxes, and they didn't like the Wisconsin weather.)

The USW team piled into a van and drove all day and part of a night to the Lone Star state to plead their case to the company shareholders. It was a Hail Mary pass at best, but the workers were accustomed to being underdogs.

While the board afforded them "as much time as they needed," according to Schiessl, in the end, she didn't think it made a difference. "Nobody that mattered said anything," she told me later, her voice quivering. It broke her heart just to say those words and to relive that day. "But it was cool to see the support from the people who were at the meeting, including the other shareholders," she said. "They applauded our courage and were impressed with our fortitude that we would fight this hard. Some of the girls from the Dallas office were even crying during our speeches. They pulled us aside after and wished us well. They wished they could do something for us."

One of the members of the board of directors they spoke with was Neenah's John Bergstrom, paper scion and owner of the state's largest car dealership. (His family had founded its namesake mill in 1907. It was sold to Glatfelter in 1979, then torn down in 2006.) Bergstrom was the hometown board member and had held a seat for thirty years. If anyone could save the Neenah plants, it would be the Neenah board member.

"Didn't he care?" I asked her.

"Nobody cared," Schiessl answered, referring to the full board. "Because this was better for the shareholders, they told us. They were making the better business decision. They trusted [CEO] Tom [Falk] was making the best choice for the company." Later that fall, Bergstrom and I would work together on the Kimberly-Clark plant closure; I'd offered to serve as a conduit between Bergstrom and local union leadership.

Schiessl's experience was exhibit A on why corporate governance is broken. "They trusted Tom," she'd said. But a board is not a rubber stamp. It should serve as an important check on a company's major decisions. Boards exist for circumstances just like the one Kimberly-Clark now faced, in which the well-being of entire communities is at stake.

As a county executive, I know what a board is responsible for, and I encourage board members to do their job. I run the day-to-day operations of the county; the board makes decisions on policy. "Do we run one or two shifts at the recycling center?" "How many legal assistants should be afforded the district attorney?" "How far should setbacks be on a roadway?" We turn to the county board to vet our decisions on matters like the circumference of drainage pipes. Surely a decision as consequential as whether to close a paper plant should fall under the purview of a corporate board.

Breckheimer's take on the shareholders' meeting was more positive. "We connected well enough with the board that we made a positive impact," he told me. "I think that was the turning point as far as keeping the facility open."

His premonition proved correct. Shortly afterward, the company changed its negotiating team. Breckheimer described the change as an installation of higher-up officials, "who could actually work toward a contract" and not just lower-level human resources representatives who were there "to just go through the motions." "Once there was a serious chance that we could keep the facility open," Breckheimer said, "then they had different people at the bargaining table."

Dave Breckheimer adroitly held his own with the company's negotiating team. Back in February, he had pored through reams of memos and spreadsheets the company had released to the union. To his amazement, Dave found that this data dump contained an alternative company plan to keep the plant open, including installing new equipment and investing other assets.

Dave had been waiting for the most strategic moment to drop this bombshell. When he and his union colleagues returned from Dallas in late April, with negotiating momentum building but resolution still far off, Dave decided the time was right.

The company negotiating team was taken aback: "Why are you guys bringing this up? We never said anything about bringing assets or equipment here to Cold Spring."

Dave produced the company document outlining the alternative plan. He said the union wasn't working to win the Cold Spring mill a brief reprieve but "to make it a viable entity for the future."

Just a mill rat from the Fox Valley, Dave Breckheimer had been underestimated throughout his life. That day was no exception. He chuckled as he told me how his maneuver "slowed the bargaining process down." That slowing down was crucial, because it provided time to increase the pressure on both Kimberly-Clark and Scott Walker.

Negotiations over the fate of Kimberly's Cold Spring plant were at full tilt by summer. On June 8, President Trump was in Wisconsin for the groundbreaking at Foxconn's Mount Pleasant site. By this point, the total Wisconsin subsidy for Foxconn had swelled to $4.8 billion, "the largest giveaway to a foreign firm in U.S. history," according to the *Guardian*. A bit less than a month later, on July 5, Kimberly-Clark and the workers at its Cold Spring plant had hammered out a tentative agreement, and on July 24, the union ratified the contract.

The workers had done their part. Now the state senate had to live up to their end of the bargain and pass the Foxconn for Kimberly-Clark bill.

But rather than being pleased, Walker and the GOP were taken aback. They'd enjoyed the photo op with President Trump, House speaker Paul Ryan, and Foxconn CEO Terry Gou at the Mount Pleasant groundbreaking. A ratified contract with Kimberly-Clark's blessing and a promise to keep the plant open if the Foxconn-for-Kimberly-Clark bill passed was not what they expected. Now all eyes were on them. If they didn't pass the bill, it was squarely on them. The union and Kimberly-Clark had called their bluff.

One week after the contract ratification, Roth refused a TV interview. Instead he deflected responsibility, hiding behind a statement:

> I fully support Senator Fitzgerald in his efforts on this legislation. I am continuing to talk with members on how important this legislation is and continue to advocate for the Senate to come in as quick as possible to pass this legislation to save good, family-supporting union jobs in a bipartisan manner.

As for majority leader Scott Fitzgerald, his remarks were on message, but for Dave and the Kimberly-Clark workers, not encouraging:

> Senate Republicans had a productive discussion yesterday regarding Kimberly-Clark. Like anything else that comes before the senate, we will be deliberative in determining the best path forward to keep our paper industry strong.

To no one's surprise, the contract ratification flipped few if any state senators. The vote count was still well under the number needed to pass the bill.

The senate dithered for the rest of the summer, and, by fall, Walker had had enough. He ratcheted up the pressure on GOP senate leaders, declaring, "the only plan that can save jobs at

Kimberly-Clark is AB 963," citing the number of the Foxconn for Kimberly-Clark bill. The disarray in GOP ranks reflected poorly not only on Walker and the state's legislators; it made all of us look bad. A lot of people were watching. The senate's decision would affect other facilities, workers, and families. Fortune 500 companies were watching closely as well. Would other companies based in Wisconsin get their own Foxconn deals?

On October 2, Kimberly-Clark threw a life preserver to Walker and the senate by agreeing to extend its original deadline from September 30 until after the election. But in the end, it made no difference. On November 6, Democratic candidate Tony Evers was declared the new governor-elect. Within hours, the state legislature—still Republican-led—convened a lame duck session to strip Evers of basic governing powers, redefining the term "sore loser." The lame duck session sucked the oxygen out of the room, leaving Roth gasping for air. The Kimberly-Clark bill died a slow and painful death.

Walker took matters into his own hands, commencing backroom negotiations with Kimberly-Clark officials to hash out a new deal. One month after his defeat, on December 13, Walker announced a deal to provide funds from the WEDC to keep the Kimberly-Clark plant open.

True to form, Walker took all the credit, largely overlooking the sacrifices made by the workers. All told, workers' concessions would exceed $40 million over a five-year period—$12 million more than what the WEDC would pay. The gap could be even more. WEDC credits were contingent on job creation and other metrics, while the workers' concessions were locked in.

When news broke that the plant would be spared, it sparked mixed emotions among the public and the workers. "It was bittersweet. I was glad to see the facility stay open," Breckheimer told me. "But there were folks that didn't want to see it being done on the backs of the taxpayers." According to a Kimberly-Clark spokesman, the company's worldwide restructuring plan had been made possible by the recently enacted Trump tax cuts. Now, liberal advocacy organization One Wisconsin Now disclosed that Kimberly-Clark had paid just one dollar in net state income tax between 2013 and 2017. Why should working families of the Fox Valley fork over millions in concessions to a multinational corporate behemoth that had already received massive tax breaks and given away hundreds of millions in stock buybacks?

Many paper workers at other mills, especially Midwest Paper Group, were pissed off. "I think it's horseshit," Jim Weyenberg told me. "Why would you help Kimberly-Clark out and not the rest of the paper mills? For that matter, why would you help Foxconn out when you watch all these paper mills fold, one after the other?"

Still, the survival of Kimberly-Clark was something to celebrate. As with Appleton Coated, labor played a crucial role in saving the plant. Labor's contributions are not limited to receivership objections. Workers made enormous sacrifices, giving up $8 million a year in wages and benefits, using these concessions as the tool and the collective bargaining process as the strategy. With the latter, they outwitted the company and the state Republicans, calling their bluff by agreeing to a contract that Walker, the GOP legislators, and Kimberly-Clark itself never thought they would ratify. This move forced the opposition's hands, saving jobs and creating the potential for the mill to add more jobs down the road.

LOST IN THE ELECTION-YEAR MELEE was Appvion. When the company came out of bankruptcy in the spring of 2018, workers were shocked to learn that their company stock was wiped out. Employees and retirees lost a combined $40 million in life savings. Those who'd plowed all their savings into company stock lost everything.

Retirements would be delayed; some would take up second jobs; lifestyles would change.

The golden years would have to wait—though not for the company's top executives.

Former CEOs Doug Buth and Mark Richards filed a combined $2.8 million in "unpaid long-term payment" claims. Buth had led the creation of the ESOP in 2000 and peddled it like a snake oil salesman. It was the ESOP that unraveled and caused the bankruptcy in the first place. Richards had sold out the company's future by authorizing the sale of Encapsys, the company's most valuable and profitable division. Workers and retirees were beside themselves.

Making matters worse, eliminating employee stock was punitive and unnecessary. In the grand scheme of things, the $40 million in writedowns barely made a dent on the company books. To put that number in perspective, it represented just eleven percent of the purchase price ($365 million) and roughly five percent of all company liabilities.

At the same time, according to *Appleton Post Crescent* reporter Maureen Wallenfang, the company was cutting jobs and moving most of their operations to Appvion's Roaring Springs, Pennsylvania, facility. Workers at Appvion couldn't catch a break. It was mind-boggling how such a tragedy could go practically unnoticed.

The USW leaders cried foul. They hired a forensic accountant, who uncovered damning evidence of executives and other top officials cashing out when the company stock peaked, apparently by taking advantage of insider information. The union promptly filed a claim to recover lost money for both USW members and salaried workers. A nationally recognized plaintiff's law firm took the case on contingency. As of this writing (fall 2020), union officials close to the case anticipate a victory and awards "in the multiples."

A FAILURE LIKE APPVION IS AN ORPHAN, but success has many parents. The comeback of Appleton Coated birthed thousands of fair-weather fans, including one governor, a congressman, a U.S. senator, a dozen legislators, and a throng of local officials.

On July 31, 2018, in the midst of the struggle to save Kimberly-Clark, Walker's hubris peaked. Flanked by GOP legislators who'd ignored Appleton Coated's pleas for help and avoided calls from the workers for weeks, Walker delivered a check for $1.8 million—0.05 percent of the Foxconn outlay—to Appleton Coated, an inconsequential sum given the substantial investments Mattes and the company were already making. Workers like Jim Weyenberg, Tony Swanningson, and Chris Bogan were disgusted: "Where were they when we needed them?!"

It goes without saying that neither I nor representatives of the USW were invited to the event. One official even asked, "Shouldn't Nelson be here?" I took it in stride. In an interview with WLUK, the local Fox affiliate, I said, "I think it's all well and good and I think it's understandable, why in an election year, a room full of politicians are trying to take credit for this, but I think it's important to take stock. We are here today because of the workers, because the entire community came together, labor and management, fought back against impossible odds and were able to . . . bring it back to life."

Appleton Coated retiree Jack DeKoch, who worked at the mill from 1945 to 1986, had a well-honed BS detector. DeKoch said, "If the politicians would have come on board sooner, they could have kept the mill running without having somebody put it on the auction block." Some of the mill's current workers were not so measured in their comments. Jim Weyenberg called out Walker for his Johnny-come-lately act: "All of a sudden the mill is up and running, and all of a sudden Walker is here putting a feather in his hat like he saved the mill."

There can be no doubt that it was the USW that saved Appleton Coated from certain death. Left to its own devices, IAC would have sold the mill's parts as scrap, and Appleton Coated would have been another casualty in the deindustrialization of American manufacturing. As newly minted Midwest Paper Group CEO Kyle Putzstuck told the *New York Times*, "No one is shocked when a paper mill closes anymore."

The USW's efforts matter all the more because the Appleton Coated case is not unique. According to USW international vice president for pulp and paper Leeann Foster, there are a host of paper mills such as Glatfelter, Flambeau River Paper, and others, that can apply the Appleton Coated model. "Receivership as a tool had not been used before," Foster told me. "And in general, it took fifteen years to figure out how to turn a negative like this into a positive. There are a lot of things to be learned out of the Appleton Coated case that we can bring forward."

Appleton Coated/Midwest Paper Group is a model of how labor can partner with management to revitalize American manufacturing, renewing its promise as a source of good-paying, family-supporting jobs. Jobs that build communities by creating the tax base to pay for good schools and vital services. Jobs that give our kids a shot at the American Dream and a chance to live up to their God-given potential.

This is the road map that built the American middle class. We did it before, we can do it again, but not without labor. As John Schmitt, president and business manager of the Wisconsin Laborers District Council, an affiliation representing roughly 9,000 Wisconsin construction workers, told me, "The unions created the middle class so the average guy can have a good job and a good wage. And that is why we need to restore the middle class and why we need strong unions. A whole community thrives because of unions."

Although Combined Locks was the first place the USW used receivership law to save a mill, it will not be the last. In the fall of 2019, the USW objected in another case, this time at Flambeau River Paper (FRP) in Park Falls, Wisconsin, on the other side of the state. I made a point of being there, attending court hearings, working closely with the USW, and facilitating meetings with aides to Governor Tony Evers and Senator Tammy Baldwin and with local and state officials—not unlike my work in Outagamie County. It was exciting for me to be on the front lines of an emerging worker-based strategy to revitalize industry that not only can help paper-centric communities like Combined Locks and Park Falls, but that can also be extended to other industries.

Some symptoms and causes of FRP's receivership would be familiar to those involved in the Appleton Coated case. Others, however, would not. The owner ignored clear signs of pending danger: the economy was taking a turn for the worse, pulp prices were due for a market correction, and the mill's chief customer was consolidating market share, putting FRP in a position of negotiating weakness. FRP had also failed to make critical investments in capital and equipment. While Appleton Coated was on the cusp of breaking through with a new product line, FRP made zero effort to diversify and had all their eggs in one basket for one customer. Worker morale was low, respect from customers and competitors alike was falling, and the mill itself looked as if it were pulled from the pages of a history book. It was not a pretty picture.

Workers paid the price for the company's negligence. "Over the years, we have given up double time," union local president John Tapplin told me. "They cut on-call pay in half to try and help the company. It's like they are jumping over a five-dollar-bill to save a nickel." "We have been told we were investing in that company, but saw zero profit, job loss, and loss of benefits," local vice president Tony Kundinger added. Worst of all, workers felt unsafe just coming to work. "The equipment was so run-down, it felt like an accident just waiting to happen," one worker told me.

These management missteps put the mill on a death watch. Only time would tell if the workers could help save their mill, as their union brethren had saved Appleton Coated.

Smart, innovative thinking can be found in union halls across the country, where labor leaders have been devising innovative strategies to reclaim a measure of economic power. In 1998, UAW workers at General Motors gave the company a dose of its own medicine, taking advantage of the company's lean supply chain network by striking at key plants and paralyzing operations across North America. At the height of the strike, twenty-seven plants had closed and 117 component suppliers around the country had suspended operations because of strikes at two facilities.

In 1991, following the deaths of five workers at the Ravenswood Aluminum Corporation (RAC) in West Virginia, USW Local 5668 demanded basic workplace safety improvements. When contract negotiations stalled, the company locked out union workers and brought in replacements. It was a vicious, ugly dispute which led to what labor historian Andrew Herod calls one of the "most imaginative campaigns implemented" by a union against its employer. The USW launched an eighteen-month, five-part plan including boycotts, legal challenges to the NLRB, "morale boosting solidarity activities" and, perhaps most innovative, "an international campaign designed to harass" RAC owner Marc Rich. This campaign took the USW and key allies to twenty-eight countries over a twenty-month period. Skillfully identifying and squeezing pressure points, USW made life miserable for Rich. It helped that Rich was a fugitive from the law, tracked by U.S. authorities for income tax evasion and violating terms of the U.S.-Iranian embargo. Any notoriety could hurt business and complicate Rich's hope of a deal with the U.S. Department of Justice.

Joining forces with unions in key locales like Switzerland and the Czech Republic, the USW boxed in Rich. Ultimately, he relented when an ally took control of RAC, fired the replacement workers, rehired the union workers, and negotiated a new contract covering union demands. Rich would be pardoned by Bill Clinton in the waning days of his presidency, thanks to his former wife Denise's stature as a major Democratic donor.

UNFORTUNATELY, SUCH STORIES OF UNION SUCCESS based on creative strategizing are more the exception than the rule.

Labor is trapped in the past, struggling to return to a time when thoughtful, progressive policymakers understood the power of unions as a force for constructive economic and social change and followed through on that belief by passing fair prolabor laws. As the New Deal advocates of the National Industrial Recovery Act and the Wagner Act recognized, according to the late distinguished labor historian Irving Bernstein, only unions could "foster economic recovery and stability" and "redress the balance of bargaining power between employees and employers arising from economic concentration."

The two New Deal labor laws deserve their place in the pantheon of labor achievement. However, the legacy of the Wagner Act is not all it is cracked up to be. For one thing, the Wagner Act is, in some respects, "profoundly racist," according to Christine Blumauer, former Executive Director of Harvard's Clean Slate Project. Industries and job categories for which immigrants and people of color make up a majority of the workforce were deliberately excluded from the legislation.

In addition, the Wagner Act and other New Deal laws helped take the steam out of the budding movement for full-scale economic reform. Social historian Frances Fox Piven and union leaders like Geenen believe that the 1930s could have been the time to revolutionize the socioeconomic structure of the United States by using the union movement to exert powerful political pressure on the country. The potential was there. It was the reason why the Congress of Industrial Organizations was established; it had previously been the mission of the Industrial Workers of the World (aka the "Wobblies"). But, instead, the mainstream labor movement shifted from the streets and picket lines into the boardrooms and courtrooms. The New Deal laws "gave workers a voice in industrial relations" and "regularize[d] management-worker relations," but they did so at the expense of "labor power," a shift which did not become obvious for some time. "Industrial peace" was the objective that corporate America sought, and the Wagner Act was the answer. As labor professor Charles Heckscher notes, the basic strategy of the Wagner Act "was to confer enough power on unions to balance and stabilize relations with corporate organizations."

Union membership and influence peaked during World War II; union density topped out at thirty-three percent in 1945. It would be downhill from there on. By 1970, just one in four workers were organized; ten years later, one in five; and at the turn of the millennium, one in ten. Labor was a hollowed-out shell of its former shell. Why?

In their article "Union Membership in the United States: The Decline Continues," authors Henry S. Farber and Alan B. Krueger summarize various theories as to explain this phenomenon. From their research, I organize the theories into three groups.

The first theory asserts that union decline stems mainly from the steady erosion of the country's manufacturing base. Even in cases where manufacturing has rebounded, many of those new jobs are at smaller firms that are mainly nonunion.

A second theory sees management hostility to unions as a driving cause. In *Failure by Design*, Josh Bivens, director of research for the Economic Policy Institute, argues that the difference in union density rates between the private sector (declining) and public sector (stable, at least before 2010) suggests that management intimidation caused decline in the private sector, since "Public employers are generally barred from fighting unionization drives as aggressively as private sector employers."

A third theory holds that private sector union growth declined because the demand for union representation fell. Based on research covering a fourteen-year period from 1977 to 1991, Farber and Kreuger themselves attribute "virtually all" union density decline to lower demand. They suggest that nonunion workers are happy with their jobs and that those new to the market are unconvinced that unions would make a difference. Other progressive economists vociferously disagree with Krueger and Farber, arguing that support for unionization has never been higher. Several studies show demand as high as fifty-five percent.

I think all three theories contain elements of truth. Practically, I think the second theory is most important. Personal experience tells me that unfair labor practices are a big problem in American industry.

Here's an anecdote that illustrates the problem. In January 2020, I went with a delegation of local leaders to meet with the management team of a company seeking to expand in our county. The meeting went well until I asked the president whether his workforce was organized. His face turned beet red. "That facility will not be union," he thundered. "I will fight it, and should it unionize, I may even close and leave. You heard it from me first." His comments were discouraging and shortsighted, to say nothing of being possibly illegal under National Labor Relations Board regulations.

To discourage such attitudes and prevent them from being acted upon by unscrupulous business leaders, the National Labor Relations Act needs to be updated and it needs extra teeth. Unfortunately, since the Reagan era, national labor policies have been steadily trending in exactly the wrong direction.

The effects of the country's right-wing, anti-union policies have been devastating and lasting. Today, most states have implemented so-called right-to-work laws whose real aim is to sabotage unions and deny workers effective representation. Some states have gone much farther. In Wisconsin, collective bargaining in the public sector was effectively banned. Scott Walker rolled back prevailing wage protection and eliminated fair share and automatic dues collections; the latter policy decimated union treasuries and memberships. Walker and the GOP legislature implemented punitive campaign laws that severely restricted union electoral activity while enabling corporations to spend unlimited amounts to advance their political ends, thanks to the U.S. Supreme Court's *Citizens United* decision (2010). As a result, labor-backed Democratic legislative candidates were starved of essential campaign resources, from dollars to door knockers, and suffered even more setbacks.

The trend continued under Donald Trump. He has appointed NLRB members who share his regressive outlook and hostility toward unions and have voted accordingly. The board has ruled against labor so many times that many unions have simply stopped bringing cases before it. Trump has also nominated Supreme Court and federal judges, rubber-stamped by the GOP majority in the U.S. Senate, who have issued rulings making it more difficult for workers to organize and collectively bargain. A disproportionate number of right-wing judges are throwing *stare decisis* out the window, chipping away at legal precedent established over the course of decades, the effects of which will be felt for generations.

The rushed confirmation of Amy Coney Barrett as an associate justice of the U.S. Supreme Court—she was sworn in on Tuesday, October 27, 2020, just one week before the presidential election—made for six conservative justices on the nine-member court. That imbalance immediately put *Roe v. Wade* and the Affordable Care Act at risk and promised a new series of deregulatory and *Citizens United*-like decisions to serve big business interests.

The decline of unions has been egged on by professors, researchers, opinion leaders, and other elites. A wide and deep body of scholarship encouraged doubts about the true value and purpose of organized labor. Despite the clear success of organized labor in building the foundation for a sustainable middle class, mainstream economic theorists decried unions as monopolies. The theorists claimed that unions had a single purpose: to extract as much money and resources from companies as possible with zero regard for the health of the business.

Economists did not consider how noneconomic matters such as quality of life, job security, improved work conditions, and community benefits might bear on worker decisions, a blindness that the economics profession has only belatedly acknowledged and begun to rectify. They also failed to consider plainly relevant economic factors such as productivity. Their one-sided, simple, and elegant theory held that unions hurt business, workers, and the economy, that they pushed out good people because of seniority rules and related subjects of bargaining, and that they unfairly dominated the labor market at the expense of nonunion workers competing for the same jobs.

Moreover, in their estimation, workers didn't really need a union. Thanks to a free market, workers could always vote with their feet and find a boss they liked, just as you would seek out the convenience store with the cheapest gas. While that may conform to the assumptions of microeconomic theory, it's not what happens in the real world. Of course, when businesses behaved like monopolies, many economists took a "boys will be boys" attitude. Firms were just trying to maximize profits, microeconomists argued. In the long run, markets would flow to perfect competition, and profits would zero out. In an age of unchecked monopolies, oligarchs, and unprecedented wealth accumulation, such a conclusion is laughable.

Compounding the woes of workers have been inventive financial instruments from Wall Street, designed to extract as much value and cash out of corporations as possible at the expense of investment—into bricks-and-mortar facilities, research and development, and the workers themselves. One of the more notorious tools today is stock buybacks. In 1982, Reagan's Securities and Exchange Commission adopted a rule that allowed company senior executives to repurchase the company's own stock up to twenty-five percent of its trading volume. The effect of the rule was to goose stock value by removing equity from the market. Supply goes down, demand rises, and prices follow. As long as the buyback program is publicly disclosed and follows a number of rules regarding price and other specification, it is perfectly legal and exposes the company to minimal legal liability, creating a so-called safe harbor.

Unfortunately, like most financial engineering inventions, the practice of stock buybacks would be abused. In 2018, corporations bought back $900 billion of their stock. To put that amount into perspective, it's the equivalent of one-third of national spending on health care. Between 2013 and 2019, Boeing spent $43.1 billion in stock buybacks, a period when they could easily have afforded to spend the $7 billion needed to fix the problems of the 737 MAX airliner and likely have avoided two crashes and a total loss of life of 346 passengers and crew members. Ten years after its taxpayer bailout, General Motors spent $10.6 billion on buybacks while closing plants and laying off workers. This amount is just under what the GM bailout cost U.S. taxpayers—$11.2 billion. And in the paper industry, Kimberly-Clark spent at least $500 million in stock buybacks—largely financed by the most recent round of corporate tax cuts—immediately before the announced closures of ten facilities, including two in the Fox Valley.

Had money not been spent on stock buybacks like these, many companies could have raised wages to "lift low-income workers out of poverty," according to Lenore Palladino of the Roosevelt Institute. For example, McDonald's could have paid each of its franchisees' 1.9 million workers $4,000 more a year, and remained profitable, had it not spent earnings on stock buybacks. Big-box retailers like Lowes and Home Depot could have given raises of "at least" $18,000 each year. Palladino found that, while payments to stockholders doubled over the last forty-five years, wages dropped twenty-one percent relative to total corporate assets.

All of this in the name of maximizing short-term profits—the sole necessary purpose of corporations, according to then-University of Rochester economist Michael Jensen in 1984. Before that year, few if any subscribed to such a theory. Many still believed that earnings should primarily be reinvested to strengthen a company. But within years, Jensen's management-friendly theory—any good executive will acknowledge that it's a whole lot easier to goose short-term profit than to build long-term value—became accepted dogma. Companies began shifting strategies from "retain-and-reinvest" to "downsize-and-distribute," as economist William Lazonick put it. With outsized executive compensation primarily coming in the form of stock options, it was no surprise that corporations became more concerned with short-term gain—hitting quarterly earnings projections—than with longer-term investment, research and development, innovation and other key capital commitments. In Lazonick's words, "value creation" lost out to "value extraction."

The theory that profit maximization for shareholders is the most important, or even the only, consideration that corporate managers should focus on was grounded in the belief that those who put down the cash to start a company in the first place and continue to invest in it are its sole risk-takers. But employees take risks, too. In her testimony before the U.S. House Committee on Financial Services in October, 2019, Lenore Palladino pointed out:

> Employees risk the loss of their sole source of income, and the entire society risks suffering negative externalities created by the production process. Stock buybacks are justified under this theory of shareholder primacy on the grounds that shareholders should be "returned" available cash when it has not found another productive use. This flawed theory not only fails to recognize that productive uses properly include other types of

corporate expenditures, including increased wages, and demands a long-term time horizon, it also gives rise to expectations by shareholders and executives that unused, and frequently borrowed, resources are "owed" to them as sole and exclusive risk-takers within a firm. Finally, it confuses shareholder purchases of new equity from a company with trading transactions that take place on the secondary market.

Stock buybacks, along with other financial practices like the trading of credit default swaps and other derivatives, have wreaked widespread havoc in the domestic economy, accelerating wealth accumulation, lowering crucial business investment, and hurting workers. This is to say nothing of precipitating worldwide financial meltdowns, including both the Asian financial crisis of 1997-1999 and the Great Recession. When the tail of financial services wags the dog of the overall economy, most people suffer, especially workers.

THE STRUGGLES OF TODAY'S WORKING FAMILIES are not solely a result of union-busting policies on the part of business leaders and politicians. They also reflect an array of right-wing shifts that date back to the era of Ronald Reagan. It was Reagan who began cutting up the social safety net, slowly chipping away at a social contract that had worked for almost seventy years. He moved the country's tax policy rightward, slashing marginal tax rates for the very rich and busting open corporate loopholes.

President George W. Bush continued where Reagan left off, passing more tax cuts that led to budget deficits and trade deficits. Starved of revenue, the federal government again took an axe to social programs. Combined with two major wars without a dedicated source of funding, the picture for the average American worsened. Already in tough shape, the gap between rich and poor grew until it seemed unbridgeable. Job insecurity plus frayed safety nets made strikes more costly and workers less likely to push back against bosses.

Our broken immigration system was deliberately neglected to serve right-wing interests by producing an abundance of workers to make it easy for businesses to lower wages and flout basic workplace safety rules. From 1994 to 1996, Barbara Jordan, the late liberal icon and the first Black congresswoman from the South, chaired the U.S. Commission on Immigration Reform. Jordan abhorred how cheap-labor immigration policies depressed wages and hurt workers. She sounded a call to action: "It is both a right and a responsibility of a democratic society to manage immigration so that it serves the national interest." Her words have gone unheeded.

Record cheap-labor immigration has long been a Republican goal. For all the Tea Party's sometimes ill-informed and mistargeted campaign rhetoric and bluster on immigration, GOP leadership has never scheduled a vote on a bill that might actually moderate immigration to a point where it no longer created an oversupply of working-age people. This is for one simple reason: it would kill their patrons' business models, exemplified by Donald Trump, whose lavish hotels and apartments were largely built by and run by immigrant labor.

Business interests hold a tight leash around their sycophants in government. Should any wayward GOP official cross them, the consequences would be swift and severe. After endorsing Scott Walker for president, Charles Koch and his brother, the now-deceased David Koch, yanked their support when he flipped on immigration and called for new restrictions. "Any call, by anyone, to further restrict legal immigration is not a viable, nor an acceptable policy remedy," said Daniel Garza, spokesman for the Koch-funded Libre Initiative. Walker's campaign never recovered. Ironically, as Walker's star fell, Trump's campaign caught fire, not because he acquiesced to the Kochs' demands but because he threw them in their face, calling for every form of immigration restriction imaginable, employing xenophobic demagoguery to boot.

As Jordan argued, a good immigration policy would be keyed to supply and demand in the labor market, calling for neither wide-open borders nor zero immigration. It would also provide a well-defined path to citizenship for undocumented workers and encourage them to organize. "Green cards and union cards" would then be the right approach.

Immigration reform should be part of a package of progressive reforms designed to help American workers. Let's adopt key planks of the AFL-CIO agenda to force upward pressure on wages. Let's raise and expand the minimum wage and reverse the race to the bottom. Let's adopt stronger workplace safety policies, repeal corporate trade pacts, and forcefully enforce and prosecute those who conduct unfair trade practices. We also need to open wide the umbrella of labor protections by expanding the Wagner Act to cover domestic work, agriculture, and other immigrant-heavy industries.

This can all be accomplished while honoring our heritage and our rich traditions of immigration. Waves of immigrants and refugees, like the Hmong refugees in my home county, have enriched our communities socially, culturally, and economically. Their forefathers fought along the U.S. in the Vietnam War and received no credit. Opening our country to them and their families after the war while other countries turned them away represented the American spirit at its best. In March 2020, the Outagamie County Board unanimously adopted, and I signed, a resolution affirming our county's support of refugee settlement. At the time, we were one of just over a hundred local units of government to open their communities to refugee settlement.

IT WASN'T UNTIL THE EARLY 1980S that Richard Freeman, James Medoff, and other labor economists began rethinking the mainstream economic paradigm of unions. They asked, aren't there some good things about unions? Isn't it a good thing in general for people to come together and build organizations to make their lives and others better? It happens all over the country with people in all walks of life: Kiwanis and Rotary clubs, parent-teacher associations, churches, credit unions, county boards, and city councils. All of these are groups of people working together for the common good, just as industrial and business interests deploy chambers of commerce, industry and trade associations, and political action committees to further their collective aims.

Freeman and Medoff went off in search of answers to those questions, and ended up writing a treatise on the value of labor unions aptly titled *What Do Unions Do?* Their answers confirmed what many of us knew all along.

Unions raise wages and benefits—for their members and often for their nonunion counterparts. They also reduce wage inequality. (Freeman and Medoff estimate that "trade unionism lowers wage disparity by 3 percent.") Unions serve as social-political vehicles to effect change in the workplace and community, for their members and all working families. They reduce profiteering by monopolies, returning hard-earned money to workers in the form of higher wages, bonuses or profit-sharing, dollars that would otherwise enrich CEOs and Wall Street. And organized labor improves productivity in the form of lower turnover, more engaged managers who include employees in crucial business planning and strategy, and overall better labor-management relations.

What Do Unions Do? made a clear and convincing argument that organized labor is a good thing. What turned heads wasn't the results or the use of sophisticated econometric analysis of new, empirical data sets, but the approach they took and the questions they asked. Instead of looking at unions as monopolies hell-bent on getting their pound of flesh, Freeman and Medoff embraced what is known as *voice theory*. In his seminal *Exit, Voice and Loyalty*, Albert Hirschman developed a conceptual framework with the proposition that one could exit a problem (for example, by emigrating, quitting a job, or choosing a different consumer brand) or try to advocate change (by protesting, filing a grievance, or running for office). That is, people can use their voice to improve their lot. Hirschman focused on the issue of emigration primarily, but the concept can be applied in many different scenarios: seeking political asylum versus fighting a corrupt regime; quitting a civic group versus running for president; relocating a business in a tax-free state versus lobbying for tax cuts.

Organizing in the workplace and immigration can be understood through the same lens. Through unions, people stay and fight back. They organize and bargain for better wages and work rules. Through immigration, people leave behind problems in search of answers elsewhere. There can be an upside to this, of course, for the lucky few that can afford to migrate to the U.S., Canada, Western Europe, and other prosperous and free regions. However, losing a nation's best and brightest provides a safety valve for corrupt, repressive regimes, which subsequently face less organized pressure to reform government.

Take, for example, a common workplace scenario: your job is decent but not great. It's close to home with some benefits, but the pay is low, the safety record is mixed, and the boss is less than endearing. Milton Friedman and his compatriots of the Chicago School, a cluster of conservative and libertarian economists, would say you should simply quit. If others share your concerns, they will follow. Eventually the company will wise up, fire the crummy boss, and spring for a raise. In turn, workers will come flocking back. Problem solved.

Hirschman, Freeman, and Medoff would say the opposite: don't leave—stay and start a union. Bargain for raises, better benefits, a grievance process, and a seat at the table in making important business decisions. Take care of the problems, prevent others before they happen (like receiverships affecting Wisconsin paper mills), and, most significantly, lock into place a governance structure to deal with future challenges. It's an approach that serves workers and helps ensure good long-term management.

More work has been done that builds on voice theory. In their book *What Workers Want*, Freeman and MacArthur fellow Joel Rogers conducted one of the more robust inquiries into the attitudes and opinions of the American worker. (The surveys are now somewhat dated, originally conducted in 1994 and last updated in 1999.) In the book, they summarize the essence of voice theory:

> Exit is an incomplete solution to workplace problems, and it's one that most workers and management reject in favor of some form of dialogue. Exit creates search costs, as workers look for a new job and management looks for new workers; it obviates the firm-specific skills that workers acquire through experience; and it is a poor way to communicate the precise nature of problems, and thus to learn how to correct them ... While voice has its own costs, in many circumstances its benefits outweigh its costs.

Other scholars followed. In a twenty-year retrospective on the publication of *What Do Unions Do?*, labor economist Barry Hirsch concluded that both "the approach adopted, and empirical regularities found by Freeman and Medoff hold up reasonably well," adding, "The empirical regularities that they identify as union effects have been sustained in subsequent research."

Around the time of Freeman and Medoff's formative work, classical economics began losing favor. In the words of respected Greek economists Stavros Drakopoulos and Ioannis Katselidis:

The orthodox "microeconomic" approach to union behavior which prevailed in the post-war decades has started to be seriously questioned. Important reasons for this were its theoretical fragility, poor predictive results and its weakness in explaining many aspects of unionism. . . . The more recent developments in the literature seem to confirm this conceptual turn in the study of unionism.

Exactly as Freeman and Medoff predicted, the power and efficacy of organized labor manifest themselves in many ways, from the conventional (raising wages, improving benefits, and making workplaces safe) to the creative and sometimes unorthodox (making common cause with management to save a business). The latter is what happened at Appleton Coated and Flambeau River Paper.

SARA NELSON (NO RELATION) has been called one of today's most important young labor leaders, turning up on many short lists for the next AFL-CIO president. International president of the Association of Flight Attendants (AFA) union since 2014, she exploded onto the national scene when she called for a general strike at the January 2019 AFL-CIO convention, right in the middle of the Trump government shutdown. Nelson's speech brought the assemblage to its feet and earned applause from coast to coast on social media. Soon after the speech, she made an appearance at the Screen Actor Guilds awards, collected speaking invitations like business cards, and was Senator Bernie Sanders's guest at the 2019 State of the Union address.

Nelson offers an interesting counterpart to the work that the USW has done at Appleton Coated and is beginning to do elsewhere. While the tool the USW used is new and innovative, Nelson has resurrected an old weapon in the union arsenal. Strikes and other kinds of job actions are a big part of AFA history. In 1986, when John Georges and International Paper were ransacking small towns and busting unions, notorious corporate raider Carl Icahn, then CEO of TWA, fired striking attendants. That experience forged a militant culture at AFA and fueled the creation of the strike tactic called Create Havoc Around Our System (CHAOS). "We don't ever announce when or where," Nelson said, explaining the tactic. "We might strike Paris. We might strike Texas."

Compared to leveraging insolvency law to keep jobs, just mentioning the word "strike" seems extreme. But the strike option should not be judged in absolute terms, but in context. Different situations require different responses and the use of different strategies and tactics.

AFA's job actions have garnered great success. So effective was a work stoppage at Alaska Airlines that CHAOS threw management into a state of mental chaos. Negotiating via fax machine, management accidentally gave some flight attendants a sixty percent raise. (Two weeks later, when management recognized its mistake, the AFA graciously agreed to correct it.) And after Nelson's 2019 speech, the mere threat of a general strike helped to change the course of a nation's economy. Within days, the government shutdown was over. Kim Kelly of *The New Republic* observed, "Individuals had been [calling in sick] sporadically since as early as January 4, but once Nelson's words rang out, the trickle became a flood." Bernie Sanders credited Nelson with helping to end the shutdown.

Nelson is convinced that a "revolution" to revitalize the labor movement is just around the corner. The conditions are "ripe," Nelson notes, with problems like stagnant wages, hollowed-out benefits, and student debt. More important, the people are primed. "You're looking at your world dying. People are ready to be asked, 'What are you willing to do to fight for what's important to you?'"

At the end of the day, unions are important because they make a difference in people's lives. When they are strong, so are working families. When they are weak, Wall Street has its way, and sooner or later sends us into recessions that strip away good jobs and throw households into bankruptcy. It's time for all of us to say, "Enough."

10.

A Labor Party for America?

I T WAS OCTOBER 2017, and a hundred recently unemployed Appleton Coated union members had gathered for an emergency meeting of USW Local 2-144 at Kaukauna's Mariner supper club. Just two years earlier, they'd celebrated their union's centennial. But tonight they were not in a celebratory mood. They were pissed off, and rightfully so. I spent the evening with them, asking them about their feelings, their plans, and their hopes for the future. What I heard would be disturbing for anyone concerned about the health of our nation.

These paper makers of Wisconsin had lost more than their jobs. They'd also lost their faith in the system—or whatever faith they'd still had after years of economic struggle. As their mill had slowly spiraled downward toward what seemed like certain death, the workers had gotten few if any calls from Republicans in government, and no concrete help. The Democrats hadn't done much better— although admittedly, there was only one elected Democrat other than me within a twenty-mile radius.

"I always had disdain for the two-party system," Kimberly-Clark–Cold Spring union president Dave Breckheimer told me on another occasion. He and his fellow workers pointed to the failure of Democrats and Republicans to work together, to politicians who apparently didn't even give a damn.

The paper workers weren't wrong to question our two-party system. The United States is unusual in not having a political party explicitly dedicated to serving the interests of working people. Nearly all advanced democracies have a labor party in name, function, or both. Great Britain has the Labor Party; Germany has the Social Democrats; Australia and New Zealand each have their own Labor Party; and Canada has the New Democratic Party, founded by a consortium of labor unions and other workers groups. These parties have no direct parallel in the United States.

Historians, political scientists, and labor advocates have pointed to several factors that short-circuited attempts to establish a labor-based party in the United States.

First, there is America's struggle with racism and bigotry, a legacy that goes back to the founding of the country. The racial schism challenged solidarity and undermined class-conscious movements. For much of American history, labor unions deliberately excluded Black workers, denying them equal access to jobs. Until the Civil Rights Act of 1964, unions in the South would not integrate. Despite their strong personal support for integration, labor leaders like John Burke and Wayne Glenn had to accept this and organize separate locals for Black workers at paper mills in the South. The culture of segregation was so deeply ingrained that one local would not integrate fully until 1988.

During a conversation at his home, Glenn recalled for me how, during his stint as AFL-CIO chairman for Arkansas, he publicly condemned Governor Orval Faubus's decision to use the National Guard to keep Black children from integrating Little Rock's schools in 1957. Faubus tried to return the favor by having a segregationist candidate run against Glenn for state AFL-CIO chair. Glenn won re-election as chair, and although his pro-integration stance brought him a lot of scorn from White Arkansans, he earned a reputation as a labor leader that communities of color could trust. That proved helpful in integrating locals after 1964. Yet it also must be acknowledged that few union leaders in the 1950s and 1960s were as progressive and forward thinking on race as Burke and Glenn.

At different eras in our history, both the Democratic Party and the Republican Party have used racism to appeal to poor, working, and middle-class white Americans at the expense of Black Americans. It is not so long ago that Democratic presidential candidates blew racist dog whistles. The Democratic Party would like everyone to forget that in a May 31, 1968, debate in California against Eugene McCarthy, Robert F. Kennedy Jr. scorned calls for housing justice by stating, "You say you are going to take ten thousand black people and move them into Orange County? It is just going to be catastrophic." In 1976, Jimmy Carter said of residential segregation, "I see nothing wrong with ethnic purity being maintained." In 2020, we heard the words of Kennedy and Carter, and other Democrats of years past, echoing in Donald Trump's insistence that any effort to promote racial justice in housing would destroy "our beautiful [white] suburbs."

Richard Rothstein's 2017 book, *The Color of Law*, documents the ugly truth that the all-white suburbs were created and maintained by racist federal government policies that remained on the books until the 1970s. These laws, which made federally subsidized mortgages available only to white Americans, kept Black Americans from leaving the inner cities to follow automaking and other good, often unionized jobs as corporations moved plants and factories out of urban areas following World War II. "White flight" was not simply a matter of individual choice; it was a federally sanctioned and enforced policy that, among other pernicious consequences, maintained and even worsened a tragic split between Black and white American workers.

Second, unlike America, where two parties have always dominated and no third party has ever gained a significant number of seats in Congress, many other countries have vibrant multiparty legislatures. Third-party success stories in the United States, such as Theodore Roosevelt's Bull Moose Party and Ross Perot's Reform Party, are all short-lived exceptions. In a multiparty legislature, a labor-based party can amass seats and help to form a coalition government, bringing to bear substantial labor influence.

Third, cultural factors play a part. The American belief in so-called rugged individualism has undermined efforts to build a collaborative movement among workers based on their shared interests and mutual interdependence as an economic class. Since Nixon, the Republican Party has excelled at using the ongoing culture war to induce socially conservative working-class and middle-class white Americans to vote against their own economic interests.

In short, labor has had to cut through the deafening noise of American ethnic, social, and religious controversies in its effort to build a national workers' movement. And the rich have successfully practiced divide-and-conquer class warfare from above to frustrate that effort.

Robin Archer's book *Why Is There No Labor Party in the United States?* acknowledges these factors, but points to two other "proximate causes." First, in the United States, unlike in other western democracies, business interests met organized labor with overwhelming force—in many cases not just with laws that undermined unions but with brute physical force, especially the notorious Pinkertons and other hired guns around the country. Business interests have also been creative in frustrating workers' efforts to organize. For example, the Western Paper Makers Association flipped the union playbook on its head and organized paper companies against unions, creating what Robert Ozanne in his account of Wisconsin labor history calls the most "elaborate" and "vivid" system of management-led repression at the time.

Second, labor leaders were paralyzed by the fear that a labor-based party would divide workers along political, religious, and geographic lines: Democratic-Republican, Catholic-Protestant, and urban-rural. Believing that a nascent labor movement could ill afford to offend and lose membership for any reason, American Federation of Labor (AFL) founder Samuel Gompers and other AFL leaders declared that partisan politics would generate "tremendous disruption," "split up the labor movement," "destroy [a] great machine," introduce a "disease," and cause the movement to be "torn asunder."

The attitude taken by labor leaders was terribly unfortunate, because Gompers and the AFL held a lot of sway. Once, on the strength of a letter to members, Gompers swung an entire congressional election. Imagine what he and his union could have done if they'd embraced electoral politics rather than shunning it.

The failure to organize a labor party represented an enormous missed opportunity for American workers. A labor party could have forged a strong and durable coalition of liberals, socialists, and progressives in support of elusive social and economic goals. As Archer writes, "If a labor party had been established, it is highly likely that business interests would have had less influence over public policy, that income and wealth would have been more equally distributed, that trade unions would have been stronger, and that a more comprehensive welfare state would have developed." Like all other advanced democracies, we would have established national health insurance, a stronger social safety net, and better labor-management relations. The absence of a labor party helps to explain why these issues continue to vex us.

IT DIDN'T HAVE TO BE THIS WAY. At several points in our nation's history, we had the opportunity to form a labor-based party in the United States; on a few occasions, we came awfully close to doing so. In 1894, AFL founder Samuel Gompers expressly chose not to establish a labor party. In fact, he had to quell an insurgent grassroots campaign among the rank and file that was demanding such a party; some had already established local party organizations. But Gompers wanted the labor movement to remain completely outside the political realm. In his view, the labor movement was a big tent; workers of all political stripes were welcome. "Party politics whether democratic, republican, socialistic, prohibition, or any other, should have no place in the convention of the AFL," read the resolution that Gompers supported.

In the 1930s, socialists and progressives in Wisconsin came close to founding a labor party. In 1944, the Minnesota Democrats created a class-based party, the Democratic Farmer-Labor party, which still exists today. More recently, in the wake of the Act 10 protests in 2011 (opposing the law signed by Walker that gutted collective bargaining rights for state workers) and the Occupy Wall Street movement of 2012, organized labor with help from Wisconsin Democrats planted the seeds that could have bloomed into a labor-based party. Nearly every aspect of Wisconsin's 2011 Democratic state convention was geared to labor and its struggles in the immediate aftermath of Act 10. The party was also preparing for a series of recalls in the state senate, which they'd come achingly close to retaking. I was a guest speaker at that convention, and I had been the only Democrat outside Milwaukee and Madison who won election in the state during that year's spring elections.

That was a heady time. You couldn't turn the dial without seeing Madison native and progressive author John Nichols on the twenty-four-hour news channels and talk shows; his voice echoed in countless blogs and Facebook pages. Along with courageous legislative leaders like my old colleagues Peter Barca and Donna

Seidel, the assembly minority leader and assistant minority leader, respectively, and state senators Mark Miller and Jon Erpenbach, John Nichols was the face of the Resistance long before that term came to dominate American politics. No other commentator, activist, and organizer better represented and explained the massive outcry.

That it happened in Wisconsin should not come as a surprise. Nichols's work was a natural expression of what Nichols himself called the state's "distinct radical history."

The roots of Wisconsin's labor-political culture date back to the late 1800s, when the state's labor community organized and chartered a federation under the AFL. One of the first major goals of the Wisconsin State Federation of Labor (WSFL) was to establish "a political arm ... to achieve reforms through use of the ballot."

The state federation became a driving force in state politics. This would have been an auspicious moment for forging a labor-farmer alliance, combining the urban Milwaukee socialists, Robert LaFollette's progressives, and farm and labor organizations. But parochialism and self-interest won out. Milwaukee politicians were unwilling to give up their party affiliation, and the progressives didn't want to work with others.

Still, the left-leaning parties continued to rack up victories, helping in 1930 to elect progressive governor Phillip F. LaFollette (son of Robert) as well as Socialist Party candidates up and down the ballot in Milwaukee. And in out-state areas like Outagamie County, they built a political party from scratch—the Farmer-Labor League, which helped elect Republicans including papermaker and WSFL board member George Schneider.

In the throes of the Great Depression, the WSFL all but declared a revolution:

Unless there is an immediate and radical change for the better, revolution is imminent ... We do not mean a political revolution by ousting one political party and installing another. We mean "revolution" set in motion by hungry, dejected, and demoralized humans who seek to overthrow a government that fails to furnish them the wherewithal to live and to take them out of their misery.

But still they could not shake their habits, and the WSFL "were not ready to break from the Socialist party." Evidently, key leaders viewed the Socialists as the Labor Party in all but name. Jacob Friedrick, executive officer of the WSFL, told his labor brethren, "[I]n voting the straight Socialist ticket you will be voting for an organized political movement of the working class." Until 1934, WSFL continued to support quixotic campaigns by statewide candidates and in so doing "weaken[ed] [their] ability to exercise statewide political power."

In 1934, Robert Jr. and Philip LaFollette founded the Progressive Party. This was a natural and logical extension of the movement, but for the time it was a power play to ward off an emerging third party led by WSFL board member Henry Ohl. Ohl and the WSFL judged the time ripe to fuse labor and farm interests; this time they were right, just a bit late.

The Progressive Party immediately took flight. That year, Philip LaFollette was elected governor again, now on the Progressive slate (he'd been elected as a Republican in 1930), and Robert Jr. was returned to the U.S. Senate. Ohl and other WSFL members felt betrayed. They were the ones who'd "nursed and groomed" the movement for years, testing and trialing to find just the right time. When they finally did, the LaFollettes swooped in. The two camps learned a hard lesson in the 1935 legislative session when a conservative legislature shot down New Deal-like legislation including a "Little Wagner Act," a jobs bill, and a law to "slow down farm foreclosures."

As historian Robert Ozanne observed, "when the liberal vote was split between Socialist and Progressive candidates, candidates with a name like 'LaFollette' could win statewide races, but conservative Democrats and Republicans would win enough legislative seats to defeat legislation wanted by labor, by farmers and by the unemployed."

In time, the two camps got together, hashed out their differences, and created the Farmer-Labor Progressive Federation. Building this coalition was an especially difficult task, because it meant pulling together nine economic and political groups, many of which had been around for years and had worked hard to build their own brands; they felt they had earned the right to lead a third party. But the existential threat of a failing economy and tough legislative losses at the hands of conservative Republicans and Democrats were enough to get them together. Bringing everyone together on one ticket gave the liberal federation significant resources and focused them in one direction. Their experiment succeeded. In 1936, the Progressive Party took control of the legislature and maintained its hold on the governorship. For labor the victory meant passage of important legislation—the WSFL introduced forty bills, and almost all passed—as well as unprecedented power in state electoral politics. There was a lesson to be learned: you can't have labor power without political power.

The grand coalition and its attendant victories would prove fleeting. The merger broke apart the following year when the anti-union *Milwaukee Journal* and other state newspapers printed inflammatory stories that stoked dissension between farm and labor interests. It didn't help that the CIO raided AFL-chartered unions, taking them away from the AFL and bringing them into the CIO's fold. A conservative backlash, a new recession, a series of strikes, and La Follette's failed launch of a national Progressive Party conspired to defeat most labor-backed candidates. The Republicans swept statewide offices and, with the help of conservative Democrats, took control of the legislature. What labor had gained in the 1937 legislative session, it lost in the 1939 session.

In many respects, what happened then was "a kind of precursor to Walker's triumph generations later," wrote *Milwaukee Journal-Sentinel* capitol reporters Jason Stein and Patrick Marley in their acclaimed account of the Act 10 protests, *More Than They Bargained For*. The Little Wagner Act and other newly adopted labor laws were rolled back. In its place, the state-level precursor to Taft-Hartley, the Wisconsin Employment Peace Act, was adopted, severely restricting union activity.

The 1936 election cycled marked the last time labor would come close to forming its own political party. It would take another twenty years before it had a taste of political power and savored thrilling legislative victories. It took a little-known legislator and transplant from Northwoods' Clear Lake to revive the state's liberal traditions and resurrect the state's moribund Democratic Party.

As recounted by John Nichols in *Uprising: How Wisconsin Renewed the Politics of Protest, from Madison to Wall Street*, the 1958 election of Governor Gaylord Nelson bookended Act 10. In his first year in office, Nelson signed into law the country's first collective bargaining law for local government employees and teachers, the law that would flourish for decades until Act 10 replaced it. Nelson's election was part of "a fighting liberal movement" that touched off grassroots action and mass mobilization while also sweeping Democrats into office, including many who would serve for years, like Senator Bill Proxmire (1957-88) or the country's longest-serving state legislator, Senator Fred Risser (1957-2021). As Nichols observes, the combination of "street heat and electoral action" was the secret to winning elections, wresting power away from corporate and right-wing interests, and passing progressive laws that moved state and national politics leftward.

ROBIN ARCHER HAS POSTULATED that one of the ways labor could launch a nationwide political movement would be through "the successful establishment of a model party in one or more key states: a model that [would be] emulated and spread to others." Unfortunately, however, the success of Wisconsin's Progressive Party has had no parallel on a national level.

Nonetheless, the absence of a labor-based party in the United States doesn't mean that labor has no political voice. Labor has always been a key part of the Democratic Party and the American left, as the story of my own political career illustrates.

When I'm running for office, I always make labor my first stop for one simple reason: it's who I am, the reason I entered public life in the first place. My core inspiration has been the men and women who work in the paper mills, doing difficult jobs well. Growing up, I respected them, and later in life I came to appreciate their way of life even more. I think of Nick Weyenberg of Midwest Paper Group, grinding it out in the wood yard under a punishing midsummer sun; a single mom like Jessica Schiessl, who pulls night shifts at Procter & Gamble's Green Bay paper mill so she can provide for her son; or Ned Wittman, the Kimberly-NewPage worker who shut down the boilers and turned off the lights, who had passed on a promising military career to follow in his old man's footsteps.

My encouragement is not just the people but the communities they created. There is a reason why my dad started his mission church in Combined Locks. The people there welcomed and embraced him; they respected his ministry call, even though Lutheranism was a bit unusual for the village at the time. In that respect, he was not unlike another outsider, John W. Van Nortwick of Illinois, who a century earlier had rolled the dice in the Paper Valley and won big.

There is also the political reality that, if you want to go anywhere in Democratic politics, you need labor support, and the more the better. This remains true despite declining union membership and depleted treasuries. Labor is even more important than hot-button issues like abortion, once thought to be a dealbreaker for Democrats in a solidly blue-collar, Catholic district like mine. I was the first prochoice Democrat to represent the fifth assembly district. But I could not and would not cross labor; and that core commitment has made me a better public servant.

Unfortunately, this is not the case in other parts of the country. Across the nation, the relatively conservative New Democratic caucus in the U.S. Congress rivals the Progressive caucus in its size and power. The New Dems have their roots in the moderate Democratic Leadership Council whose philosophy drove the Clinton administration's domestic policy agenda, which embraced such Republican policies as welfare "reform," school choice, and free trade rather than a progressive, labor-based economic plan.

The South is generally hostile to labor, except for pockets like the Gulf Coast of Alabama, with its unique and rich trade union heritage. Beginning in the 1960s, scores of northern manufacturers took their businesses and jobs to the South in search of cheap labor, one strategy for dealing with heightened international competition and tight profit margins—both convenient excuses to rid themselves of union workforces.

By contrast, regions like the Northeast and Northwest carry rich and vibrant union traditions. The labor history of the Northeast includes steelworkers in western Pennsylvania, shoe factory workers in Massachusetts, longshoreman on the coast, lobstermen in Maine, Teamsters up and down I-95, and the building trades in the big cities. While union membership has shrunk in recent years, it holds its own in the Northeast. Except for Delaware and New Hampshire, every Northeast state has a union density greater than the national average (10.5 percent). Public-sector unions are vibrant and growing, especially among local and state employees and health care workers, not only in the Northeast but elsewhere. The West Virginia teachers, the second lowest-paid educators in the nation, gained nationwide attention in 2018 when they struck over wages and health insurance, inspiring teachers across the country, many of whom followed in their footsteps, including teachers' unions in Los Angeles and Chicago. One year later, grocery store clerks and stockers of the Stop & Shop chain struck against wage and benefit cuts—and won.

The West Coast, too, has an outsize union presence. Oregon boasts a 13 percent union density rate; Washington, a 19.8 percent rate; and Hawaii, 23.1 percent—twice the national average. The paper industry in the West has a dynamic union history. In the 1960s, forty-nine locals and 21,375 members of the Brotherhood of Sulfite, Pulp and Paper Workers in Oregon and Washington split from the international because of decisions made without their approval. According to Harry Graham, author of *The Paper Rebellion*, "a union schism of [that] size had never taken place before." The locals reorganized under the Association of Western Pulp and Paper Workers, which is still active.

For the most part, the Midwest remains a labor bastion, including in national politics. Senator Tammy Baldwin of Wisconsin is a stalwart advocate for labor. Senator Sherrod Brown of Ohio is a favorite of labor, especially the industrial unions like the UAW and USW. I was one of many disappointed he did not run for president in 2020. The Minnesota Democratic Party clings to its roots and its identity as the Democratic Farmer-Labor Party. This is the party that helped launched the political career of the late senator and unabashed liberal Paul Wellstone. As I tell my colleagues, "Before there was Bernie Sanders, there was Paul Wellstone." And as I've explained, Madison, Wisconsin, was the site of the great Act 10 protests of 2011, which marked a tectonic shift in American politics—labor finally fighting back against right-wing culture-war "populism" that only serves the rich, not working people and their families.

Today, with Act 10 shrinking in the rearview mirror, Nichols's central question takes on even greater importance. What potential is there to build a movement to "transform America . . . and form a grand coalition for economic and social justice"? I would add, how do we refashion a major political party in labor's image, if not in name?

Sara Nelson, the upstart president of the AFA, would assert that we are on our way. The time is ripe, and we are blessed with a deep bench of stalwart progressives in labor's ranks and in the Democratic Party. And while we live in a time when right-wing forces continue to do damage to our national fabric, we can't afford to give in to hopelessness. As historians Daniel Katz and Richard A. Greenwald observed, some of the "thrilling moments of labor's rise . . . succeeded long periods of despair." In the coming decade, labor and Democrats have a special chance to finish what was started in 2011. But first, the Democratic Party must come to terms with their history with labor, to see it through their eyes.

One reason labor leaders are rightfully frustrated with our electoral system is the nonstop fundraising it requires. I've heard countless labor leaders and activists complain about Democratic politicians, "They're only being nice to us because they want our money. They're always asking for one more check: 'I really need your help, I need to keep the ads up on TV.'" I wish I could say those complaints are wrong.

There's no doubt that labor offers important electoral resources that Democratic politicians rely upon. Labor can't compete with corporate America's bottomless reservoir of cash, but it owns the ground game, pushing its members to the polls and providing bodies for phone banks, literature drops, and door knocking. But Democratic candidates don't give grassroots campaigners the respect they deserve. I should know. When I ran for Congress, the old hands made it perfectly clear to me that, while parades, door knocking, town halls, and other forms of voter outreach were important, the focus must be fundraising.

"If people don't see the dollars, they won't take you seriously," one high-ranking party official told me when I started that congressional run. I saluted and made 60,000 fundraising calls during my seven-month campaign. I felt I had no choice. Most candidates loathe call time, and some have left office because of it. But I'll be honest, I'm a bit odd when it comes to fundraising—I like it. I'm not talking about funneling millions into an outside group or exchanging checks for votes—that's not fundraising, that's bribery. I'm talking about building a campaign one call, one knock, and one vote at a time, whether by walking in parades or glad-handing football fans outside Lambeau Field. For every Bernie Sanders or Donald Trump who catches fire, there are a thousand Tom Nelsons who must grind it out on the phones. It's common for congressional candidates to spend six or even eight hours a day in call-time; my record is nine hours and forty-five minutes, not including bathroom and lunch breaks. It's an ethic I learned working on my uncle's farm, the summer after my freshman year in college, when I "learned how to work," as my late grandfather told me. Indeed, my fundraising was on par with the number of miles I racked up running for lieutenant governor (62,000) and in the doors I knocked in my three successful races for the state assembly (70,000).

For Democratic leaders, labor is a crucial part of this retail relationship-building.

So, every election year, union leaders like the Laborers' John Schmitt, local presidents like Kimberly-Clark–Cold Spring's Dave Breckheimer and Midwest Paper Group's Mack MacDonald, and USW international representatives like Sally Feistel and Denny Lauer are pummeled with "asks." I'm no exception; I don't think there is a single union I have not asked for support.

But I try to do it the right way. For many candidates, it's trans-actional: money in, votes out. That's cynical and it's wrong. And this is where the fissures in Democratic-labor relationships appear. The candidate has a weak understanding of the labor movement and how it is inextricably part of a larger socioeconomic organism. Labor's issues get swallowed up in a kaleidoscope of bills and resolutions.

Like everyone else—save for the big corporate donors—labor must take a number and get in line.

A more enlightened view would realize that labor itself is at the heart of all those other issues. Indeed, if the U.S. had a labor-based party, this view would be widely shared—as it should be.

GOOD POLITICS LEADS TO GOOD POLICY. A strong Democratic Party means a strong labor movement. Was it a coincidence that when the Wisconsin Democratic Party was at its peak in the mid-1970s—when they controlled every statewide office, commanded super-majorities in both legislative houses and owned seven of nine congressional districts—labor was at its height, too? As Ozanne puts it, "The legislative influence of the State AFL-CIO from the mid-1960s through 1977 has been rivaled only by the legislative influence of the WSFL under [Henry] Ohl in 1932 and 1937-39"—the years when labor was on the verge of launching its own party.

The 1970s was also the time when John Schmitt's father and namesake held sway over labor and Democratic politics in Wisconsin as the state federation president (1964-84). Schmitt was a kingmaker among Democrats and a force in state politics in general, but he refused to wield his power like a cudgel. "My dad always had an open door up at the capitol for Republicans and Democrats," his son told me. "He worked well with both sides."

Recent years have brought a bit of hope for a resurgence of truly progressive policies among national Democrats. Events like the election of Elizabeth Warren to the U.S. Senate from Massachusetts in 2012, Senator Bernie Sanders's launch of his presidential campaign in 2015, and the election of "the Squad" (Alexandria Ocasio-Cortez, New York; Ilhan Omar, Minnesota; Ayanna Presley, Massachusetts; and Rashida Tlaib, Michigan) to the U.S. House of Representatives in 2018 are all positive signs.

But it remains undeniable that, in the years since the 1970s, the political power of labor has sharply declined. For decades, the Democratic Party was stuck right of center, rarely making the effort to advance a progressive economic agenda that put labor in the forefront. Labor suffered a kind of purgatory in the Clinton years with the administration's right-leaning policies on free trade, welfare "reform," and school choice. Later, labor leaders applauded several Obama achievements—the Lilly Ledbetter Act, the GM bailout, and health care reform—but were let down when he failed to get legislation passed that would preserve card check, which allows work places to become unionized when a majority of workers sign cards in favor of the union. Obama's vigorous support for the Trans-Pacific Partnership—a kind of NAFTA for Southeast Asia—soured the relationship further.

Rather than lifting voters with an inspiring vision, too many candidates dumb down their campaigns with pabulum: "I'm for Social Security." "Collective bargaining is important." "Let's raise the minimum wage."

No wonder labor leaders are disenchanted with both major parties. Dan Kaufman's The Fall of Wisconsin quotes one labor leader after another criticizing the Democratic Party. Dave Poklinkoski, president of Madison-based IBEW Local 2304, claims to have a hard time distinguishing Scott Walker from his predecessor, former Democratic Governor Jim Doyle. He calls Walker "son of Doyle," highlighting Doyle's promise to shrink the state's workforce by 10,000. Local 8 Ironworker and renowned labor activist Randy Bryce says, "Too often we hear during a campaign about what someone will do for us. I'm done hearing words. I'm done." Bryce mocks Obama's promise to put on a "comfortable pair of shoes . . . [and] walk on that picket line with you as president of the United States of America," if workers were "denied their right to organize and collectively bargain." When Obama was a no-show during the Act 10 debate,

Bryce, on a trip to Washington, tied a pair of shoes together and hung them on the White House fence.

Longtime Milwaukee Labor Council secretary-treasurer and COO Sheila Cochran shared similar frustrations with me over coffee at Rise and Grind Café, an institution on Milwaukee's near north side. "We would be the doorknockers, the leaflet droppers, and the lit droppers," she said. "We would do the legwork for whoever was the candidate. They would come in and present their own little platform or whatever it was. We'd like what they would have to say and we'd go out and work for them."

Cochran continued: "So, the candidate would be heavily reliant on us to get them into office. But what the candidate did not do was look at that workforce and say, all right, we have twenty-five people sitting in this room, twenty-five people from all different walks of life. What do these twenty-five people think I should be doing once I get into office?"

Labor has had enough. Union leaders feel like "cogs in party machines." "Workers today do not have nationally recognizable advocates," say Katz and Greenwald. "Politicians have given up on them, preferring to talk about middle-class issues, never about the working class, or at most referring sometimes to working families."

AFL-CIO president Richard Trumka has put Democrats on notice:

> We have listened hard, and what workers want is an independent labor movement that builds the power of working people—in the workplace and political life. Our role is not to build the power of a political party or a candidate. It is to improve the lives of working families and strengthen our country.... We'll be less inclined to support people in the future that aren't standing up and actually supporting job creation and the type of things that we're talking about. It doesn't matter what party they come from.

Trumka's call was not lost on his members. That same month, the International Association of Fire Fighters "indefinitely suspended all contributions to federal candidates," instead choosing to focus resources on state and local issues and races.

Labor leaders are right to insist that the Democratic Party stop treating workers as mere sources of money and unpaid labor. Labor and the Democratic Party need one another. The proven method to win elections, get into power, and make constructive social and economic change is the one John Nichols advocated: "street heat and electoral action"—a confluence of the strengths of both groups.

The career of the late Paul Wellstone, who served as Minnesota's senator for nearly two terms (1991-2002) (he died in a plane crash eleven days before the 2002 election that might have given him a third term), best exemplifies Nichols's strategy and provides a blueprint to build a labor-based party.

Jeff Blodgett, Wellstone's campaign manager and former student, both witnessed and contributed to Wellstone's transition from activism to electoral politics. "Paul had written off electoral change as a viable option for affecting change," Blodgett told me. "He was all about protest, grassroots action, and organizing. Really, it wasn't until I took his class, The Politics of Protest, that I gained an appreciation for movement politics and he, electoral politics."

Soon after Blodgett graduated from Carleton College in 1982, Wellstone launched an unsuccessful campaign for state auditor. Eight years later, he came back, ran for the U.S. Senate, and pulled off the biggest electoral upset of 1990, one that captivated the imagination of countless young progressives and spurred me into public service. I chose to attend Carleton myself largely because of my admiration for Wellstone, and when I ran for state assembly my campaign yard signs mimicked Wellstone's campaign logo, down to the exclamation mark. Wellstone became one of the country's most outspoken liberal leaders, one who made labor and farmers the centerpiece of his agenda and his own progressive coalition, the Wellstone Alliance.

Wellstone recognized that the key to gaining power and making constructive economic and social change was "street heat and electoral action." Wellstone more than any other politician identified the "burgeoning power of the class issue" and capitalized on it. As Wellstone said to a packed capitol rotunda of supporters the day after his 1990 election victory, "A day of reckoning is approaching."

A classic illustration of Paul Wellstone's fierce progressive integrity is the story of the Hormel workers strike of 1985.

It started after the United Food and Commercial Workers (UFCW) had agreed to "chain concessions" that affected all Hormel locals. Most of the workers acquiesced. But Local 9, representing workers at the Hormel Factory in Austin, Minnesota, refused to go along, because they had just forked over $15,000 apiece through paycheck deductions to help build Hormel's newest facility. They also viewed themselves as leaders and considered the industry-wide ramifications of their choices. "If the newest plant in the industry takes a cut in wages," said then-union president Jim Guyette, "then the other plants are going to say they can't compete. If concessions are going to stop, then they are going to have to stop at the most profitable company with the newest plant."

The P-9ers, as they were affectionately known, understood that if someone didn't take a stand, labor would lose a lot of what they'd fought for and earned.

While others in labor did not agree with the P-9ers, including the UFCW leaders who'd brokered the deal and the conservative-leaning state AFL-CIO and Teamsters, Paul Wellstone did. After one particularly raucous day on the picket line, Wellstone went to jail for them, an act that nearly derailed his senatorial bid. When Hormel broke the strike and union, Wellstone took the loss hard.

But the Hormel strike was just one example of Wellstone's tenacity. He helped to organize struggling single moms shut out by county and state human services agencies and unable to provide for their families. He stood alongside the farming community as they protested the construction of an interstate power line and battled the banks as farms were foreclosed. "Politics is about the improvement of people's lives," Wellstone taught his students. It was a mantra he repeated time and again in the classroom and one he took to heart.

In *Professor Wellstone Goes to Washington*, a chronicle of his 1990 campaign, *Minneapolis Star Tribune* reporters Dennis J. McGrath and Dane Smith note that Wellstone practiced "a politics of economic and social justice, first, last and foremost." Echoing John Nichols, the authors described a radical philosophy "grounded in an appreciation of history. The foundation was populism and progressivism, the insurgent movements of turn-of-the-century farmers, workers, and altruistic reformers who rose up together to challenge the accumulation of wealth and power of the robber barons of the late 1800s."

It was on this foundation of class- and labor-based politics combined with social and economic justice that Wellstone built what McGrath and Smith call "an alliance that included hard hats, gays and lesbians, inner-city poor people, middle-class suburbanites and maturing baby boomers, black and Hispanic minorities, family farmers, feminists, environmentalists, and sundry farmers." In 1992, a similar alliance was created next door in Wisconsin, when underdog Russ Feingold won a seat in the U.S. Senate along with left-leaning Democrats Ben Nighthorse Campbell (Colorado), Carol Mosely-Braun (Illinois), and Barbara Boxer (California). In Washington, Feingold joined Midwest populist senators Tom Harkin (Iowa), Byron Dorgan (North Dakota), and Tom Daschle (South Dakota). Bernie Sanders entered the national stage in 1990 as a congressman-elect from Vermont.

These and other left-leaning candidates hit bumps along the way—especially in the elections of 1994, 2010, and 2016—but the long arc of history is bending toward a class or labor-based politics. In 2020, seventeen years after Wellstone's untimely death, his U.S. Senate seat remains in Democratic hands, and his Democratic Farmer-Labor Party is still intact and solid. Minnesota Democrats have a monopoly on all statewide offices and control a majority in the state house of representatives. They hold four of eight seats in the U.S. house of representatives, and they hold both U.S. senate seats, including that of one of 2020's top-tier presidential candidates, Senator Amy Klobuchar. Not a bad legacy.

IN THE CONCLUDING CHAPTER of *Uprising*, John Nichols writes, "Real movements must be built in the states and hold officials to account and keep low-income and working-class Americans engaged as they push ideas up from the local and state levels to the federal level." I can't think of a better contemporary example of local people holding officials accountable and pushing new ideas than Appleton Coated. In that way, not only is Appleton Coated a model for productive labor-management-government relations, it is a model for building a grassroots and political movement that can help change our country. Now, if only our state and federal officials will take notice and listen to us.

11.

In the Vanguard

THE OLD SAYING HAS IT that "to the victor go the spoils." Sometimes, it's true. In pro sports, players that win Super Bowls and World Series trophies usually earn bonuses and lucrative contracts. But the same doesn't hold true for labor. When a company succeeds, workers too often receive a pittance compared to the windfall that owners, shareholders, and investors enjoy—to say nothing of the tax breaks they get. Workers are supposed to feel fortunate if they get to stay a step or two ahead of inflation and their quality of life ticks up. They may get a little more time off, a shortened work week, and a modest profit-sharing plan. Nothing to write home about.

In late December 2019, owner Steve Mattes flipped Midwest Paper Group, formerly known as Appleton Coated, for at least $70 million in profit, according to one source close to the sale. Mattes's company had owned the business for just over two years. When Appvion came out of bankruptcy, the company wiped out $40 million in employee retirement funds, while most executives had cashed out long before, allegedly taking advantage of insider information. (The matter is subject to a pending lawsuit.) When Kimberly-Clark accepted a proposed state aid package to keep its Cold Springs facility open, it did so only after the workers agreed to substantial concessions. When the legislature failed to pass generous tax breaks and credits, the state aid package was renegotiated between Governor Scott Walker and Kimberly-Clark—but the union concessions were not renegotiated. In the end, as I've noted, the union contributed some $12 million more than the state.

Cases like these illuminate how corporate America really works. When companies succeed, workers do not reap the benefits. But when companies go under, workers lose their jobs and usually have to settle for new ones that pay less and offer fewer benefits or none at all—while CEOs take million-dollar payouts, and speculators sell stock short or write off the losses.

In the case of Appleton Coated, only pressure from the union, the village, and a handful of determined leaders prevented a new owner from shuttering the mill and selling its parts as scrap.

But these cases can also be considered green shoots poking out through the infertile soil of corporate greed and showing what can be done to change the destructive dynamic that currently dominates the American economy.

The subtitle of this book points the way: *How one union local saved a mill and changed an industry.* It's not about one leader, one manager, or even one group of workers, but rather a union local, the formal, legally recognized association of employees. Only through that vehicle could the resources, network, institutional knowledge, and collective will be mobilized to undertake the monumental task of re-opening the all-but-abandoned Appleton Coated mill.

Conceptually, the same holds true with the Kimberly-Clark workers. Their creativity, initiative, and strategic prowess won the day. They gave up more than their fair share of wage and vacation concessions; they took control when the state senate left them hanging; they applied pressure to get a contract signed; and they ground away on company papers like a corporate litigator doing discovery, changing the course of negotiations. Without the union representing workers and focusing their energies, none of this could have happened.

Even the Appvion case reinforces the same lesson. The current union lawsuit against top-level company executives is aimed at righting a wrong that has cost union and non-union workers some $40 million. That lawsuit has not yet succeeded—but if and when it does, it will be another victory for union solidarity over the forces of legalized greed.

The good news is that an infrastructure exists by which the rights of working people can be vindicated.

Unions have stood the test of time. They've been a concept since the trade guilds of fourteenth-century Europe and legally protected entities in the United States since the National Labor Relations Act of 1935. Paper unions have proven especially resilient. In Wisconsin, they've persevered through seemingly insurmountable obstacles, including what economist Robert W. Ozanne called "an epic 40-year labor-management struggle" against the early twentieth-century corporate cartel the Western Paper Makers Association. Today, paper is the only major U.S. industry except the auto business that is solidly unionized.

If any industry is tailor-made to show America how to chart a new and better economic direction, it is paper.

Unions themselves are not the only piece of existing socioeconomic infrastructure we can use as tools of reform. Another is the collective bargaining law created during the Great Depression to balance private sector power. Although Franklin D. Roosevelt was never an avid union supporter, he still endorsed and signed the National Industrial Recovery Act and the Wagner Act to ensure that labor would have a voice in the workplace and enjoy equitable gains as businesses and their owners thrived. Neither bill benefited workers at the expense of owners; both were designed to make possible productive relationships that would help both sides. That's exactly what the heady challenges of today's economy call for. Neither labor nor management can go it alone—the problems we face are too big and too complex. Organized labor is the model, and collective bargaining is the vehicle.

When businesses are in trouble because of strategic missteps, market shifts, or technological changes, labor and management must work together to find solutions. This doesn't require any major changes to existing law. We just need to allow, and incentivize, unions to challenge plant closures, as the USW did in the Appleton Coated case, and then to help identify new ownership and new business models that will allow companies to remain in business. Labor leaders already want to participate in these positive steps— during the Appleton Coated receivership, union leader Jon Geenen and I spent an entire day fielding calls from prospective buyers. Why not let unions and the workers they represent participate more fully in the economic benefits these efforts make possible?

Similarly, concessions agreed to by workers when companies are in distress should be tied into pricing and value added. Every dollar sacrificed by the employees should be used to make the company more competitive, and when the company achieves an agreed-upon level of profitability, workers should recover lost pay and benefits. In this way, concessions will be treated properly as a form of investment.

Furthermore, in special cases like Kimberly-Clark, when government aid packages are renegotiated, union concessions should be reopened and renegotiated to reflect the same change. When the state development corporation's contribution to Kimberly-Clark decreased by seventy percent, the union concessions stayed the same. That is patently unfair.

Adjustments like these will not give unions an unfair advantage over management, nor will they create incentives for labor leaders to raise frivolous objections to corporate plans. The Appleton Coated saga amply illustrates the fact that challenging a receivership sale and trying to force a company to reconsider its plans is far from riskless.

First, there are no guarantees of success. Delaying the sale prolongs an otherwise painful ordeal for employees. Workers are caught in a kind of purgatory. They hope their workplace will be spared, but at the same time, they need to get on with their lives and seek out a new job or go back to school. Remaining betwixt and between, hoping for a positive outcome, is incredibly painful for them. A union must balance the pros and cons of objecting to a sale just as they would with any other risk they take—for example, when considering bringing an unfair trade practice claim before the International Trade Commission, a process that can take years and millions of dollars. And if objecting to a sale ends in failure, this outcome would be viewed as a loss for the individual union and for labor as a whole, a painful blow to a movement already reeling from decades of orchestrated decline.

There's a socially accepted paradigm of risk: "Big risk, big reward." But in receivership cases, the paradigm is turned upside down: Unions are forced to take a big risk in hopes of little reward. On the other side of the table, the big banks that are usually involved enjoy the most perverse version of all—no risk, all reward. These unfair realities need to change.

The innovative use of the receivership objection strategy in the Appleton Coated case can serve as a prototype for other unions and communities where plant shutdowns threaten to wreak economic havoc. Others are already beginning to learn from it. Across the state, Flambeau River Paper (FRP)—another century-old mill—fell into receivership in late spring 2019. Despite warnings from the USW, owner Butch Johnson voluntarily chose receivership, even though he had enough capital to go through a bankruptcy. (He has a poor reputation in the community, and it was not surprising for him to blow off advice.) He soon regretted his decision and ultimately was out of the picture when a new group of investors, Faith Asset Management, took control in November 2019.

Unlike in the Appleton Coated case, the receivership process at FRP dragged on for well over a year. In fall 2020, FRP reopened. (It's now called Park Falls Pulp and Paper.) Faith Asset Management, led by New Jersey businessman Yong Liu, imple-mented a business plan authored by former Appleton Coated CEO and *Post Crescent* "Man of the Year" Doug Osterberg. But Osterberg's clients only succeeded in gaining control of the mill because the receiver was sympathetic to the workers and community. The stalking horse bid for FRP was a scant $1 million. However, the receiver allowed the receivership process to continue until a job-saving solution emerged. That was thanks mostly to the USW's adroit use of the community-impact provision in Wisconsin's receivership law and the workers themselves. The workers never lost faith in the viability of their mill and they kept it on a hot idle, so a new owner could step in and run it immediately, rather than give up and look for other, lesser jobs. Just like the Appleton Coated workers, the FRP workers were unsung heroes. They had no part in the ribbon-cutting ceremony when their mill reopened.

The Appleton Coated and FRP stories show how, once union objections are taken seriously, labor and management can begin to work together to create win-win solutions that save businesses, jobs, and communities. And if a positive labor-management model can be forged in the crucible of a mill closure, certainly it can work with the comparatively mundane, day-to-day issues that unions typically face—worker grievances, work rule changes, and the like. Just knowing the union can save a mill from shutdown changes the labor-management dynamic for the better. Workers can focus on their jobs without wondering whether they will be out on the street in a month. Managers can sleep better at night knowing they have a built-in consultancy that will work with them to help make them successful.

In addition, the symbolic value for the labor movement of victories like Appleton Coated can't be overstated. With all the setbacks labor has suffered in recent years—Act 10, right to work, prevailing wage rollbacks—even a small change in momentum has the potential to breathe new life into the movement. This is especially urgent in a time when labor is struggling to win victories through the electoral and democratic process. In Wisconsin, for example, it will take years—perhaps a generation—to reverse the damage done by Republican dominance of state government. For the time being, gerrymandering has put the state assembly out of reach; the Republicans are within striking distance of an unstoppable super-majority, and they have a budget to raise $13 million in dark money to get there. Much the same goes for the state senate.

The solution is for labor to get creative. Sale objections, entrepreneurship, legal action, shrewd negotiation tactics, and other approaches must all be on the table, along with traditional tools like the strike. Most union officials, especially those in the paper industry, have shied away from the strike, and for good reason—it hasn't worked well. Historically, strikes by paper workers have led to big defeats. The five-year strike against International Paper in the 1920s almost broke the union; it would take seven years to recover. Another big strike in the mid-1980s cost about $1 billion, according to former United Paperworkers International Union president Wayne Glenn, and poisoned labor-management relations for years.

But times are changing. We've seen how leaders of the West Virginia and Los Angeles teachers used strikes effectively, and how Sara Nelson's call for a general strike at the 2019 annual winter AFL-CIO meeting helped to end the Trump government shutdown. In the right time and place, a strike can be a powerfully effective union weapon.

As we consider the path forward toward a more just and equitable economic model, it's important to remember that labor and management are just two legs of a stool. The third leg is government—and in too many cases, local governments have failed to take action when businesses, jobs, and economic growth are at stake.

To some extent, this is an understandable byproduct of a legal system that disadvantages workers and communities in favor of management, investors, and creditors. When companies are in distress, workers are last in line to get paid, and community impacts are generally ignored. According to attorney Tim Nixon, in insolvency cases in the United States, labor unions only get to weigh in on the fate of pension funds, which have little bearing on the insolvency process because they are protected by the federal Pension and Benefit Guaranty Corporation (PBGC). Otherwise, Nixon explains, "Labor, in the United States, does not play a legal role in insolvency proceedings. You as a community don't have any standing in the United States to raise the social fabric community issues—unlike in Europe, where they would recognize these stakes." It would be a great step forward for the United States to modify its laws to mandate, or at least encourage, corporations to give labor representatives seats on corporate boards, so the interests and ideas of workers can be considered routinely rather than ignored in all but the most dire circumstances.

In any case, local government agencies and community leaders must play a more active role in addressing corporate actions that threaten worker livelihoods. The Appleton Coated and FRP cases illuminate this problem. In both instances, local governments and chambers of commerce showed little interest, considering a possible plant shutdown a *fait accompli* or focusing excessively on poor city-company relations rather than seeking to alter the overall dynamic. (However, once the problematical longtime owner of FRP was out of the picture, local officials, especially Mayor Michael Bablick of Park Falls, worked day and night to help the new ownership group and the USW resuscitate the mill as a going concern.) Again, the Appleton Coated story shows the way. It illustrates what can be done when labor and government leaders join forces to press businesses to take community interests seriously.

ANOTHER IMPORTANT ELEMENT IN CRAFTING a better economic future for our country is a more robust program of private and public research and development. Forging strong relationships among managers, owners, and labor is important, but unless there are products in the pipeline that consumers want to buy, it is all for naught.

Fortunately, the paper industry—like most American industries—has its share of visionary thinkers. I'm thinking of people like Paul Fowler of the Wisconsin Institute for Sustainable Technology (WIST) at the University of Wisconsin–Stevens Point. He's a creative, forward-thinking expert who is trying to get leaders from industry and government to pay attention to his urgent message.

In his Cold War–era office at UW–Stevens Point, whose forestry and paper science department was once the country's best, Fowler is making the most of a decade-old congressional earmark, living and working grant to grant. In 2017, Scott Walker line-item-vetoed and zeroed out a full year's appropriation for WIST, forcing Fowler to lay off staff and become an institute of one. State representative Katrina Shankland (D-Stevens Point), who had carved out a niche as an authority on papermaking issues, fought hard against Walker's cut, but the governor was so punitive he added insult to injury by leaving a gratuitous "0" in the budget line for WIST.

Few public-private partnerships beyond WIST exist in the state. Fowler is trying to fill the void left when the storied Institute of Paper Chemistry fled south to Georgia Tech in the early 1990s.

For decades, the Institute of Paper Chemistry sat atop the banks of the Fox River with a vista of a half dozen mills. At its peak, the institute boasted 86 member-companies making regular financial contributions. That provided a baseline of research and development support in addition to training the next generation of paper scientists, engineers, and leaders. The institute attracted the likes of Harry Spiegelberg, who previously had had no real interest in the business. He enrolled because he wanted to work for Kimberly-Clark, and he wanted to make a difference. He went on to oversee the invention and development of breakthrough products. He spent a career in research and development, leading a team of brilliant researchers who invented super-absorbent technology, creating billion-dollar product lines. This is the kind of innovation paper needs today.

Paul Fowler has been urging the creation of a "new center of excellence" for the paper business. Let's stock it with some the world's best and brightest—paper chemists, scientists, researchers, and policy directors. Get Uncle Sam to pitch in, or kill the Foxconn deal, and allocate a modest ten percent of the $3.5 billion outlay to a new paper research facility. For $350 million, Wisconsin could again become the undisputed king of the industry.

The paper industry also needs to start making big capital investments—new plants, new machines, and new equipment. According to the Center for Paper Business and Industry Studies, paper is the most capital-intensive industry in the manufacturing sector; machines, equipment, and related infrastructure represent about eighty-five percent of the industry's cost structure. Paper companies live or die by the quality of their machines and equipment.

And it's not as though the industry leaders cannot afford to invest. Wisconsin offers paper companies generous tax breaks, most notably the personal property exemption that has taken millions of dollars of machines and equipment off the tax rolls. More recently, the legislature adopted a law that eliminated all tax liability for mills and other manufacturers. The money saved should be invested in infrastructure upgrades—new plants and machinery that will be more efficient, more productive, safer, and more environmentally friendly.

In addition, the paper companies themselves need to pour resources into product innovation and development. According to Fowler, a lot of it is happening "on the fly," with paper makers responding to customer needs on an ad hoc basis. "It's a customer saying to them, 'How can you help us with this problem?' or 'This is the sort of material, the sort of product we like.' So it's entirely responsive." This was Doug Osterberg's experience at Appleton Coated: prospective customers sought out original cardboard products and coated paper sheets for one-of-a-kind printing machines. Those hints from customer requests pointed the way toward new lines of business that mapped a profitable future for the company.

Asked about potentially disruptive products that the paper industry could be investing in, Fowler points to a nanocellulose crash program at the University of Maine. Taking cellulose down to its smallest component, just above the molecular level, researchers have identified film-like properties that could help the paper industry go into the space of flexible packaging, a market estimated to yield double-digit growth for the next decade or more. Nanocellulose technology can also be applied to improve products like tires, latex gloves, paint, and cement. Each of these products would normally depend on fossil fuel or plastic-based materials. By contrast, paper is environmentally sound; it displaces harmful chemicals. Nanocellulose is a nascent technology that may take years to perfect, but now is the time to invest in it.

Another promising material is lignin, left over when fiber is extracted from wood. For years, it was used as fuel or simply discarded. Now scientists are figuring out better ways to use it. Lignin can be used as a resin, adhesive, or surfactant; it can serve as a substitute to make fertilizer or help bind cement. This product will only grow in importance, provided businesses invest in perfecting and developing it. Indeed, it is the centerpiece of Flambeau River Paper's new business model.

Developing the technology for tomorrow's paper industry doesn't end with upgraded machinery and new product ideas. It also includes deeper changes that will bring paper into what many experts are calling Industry 4.0.

Along with other advanced nations, the United States has already passed through a series of industrial revolutions. They involved the development and widespread adoption of technologies like the steam engine, mass production, electricity, and the assembly line. More recently, our economy and our way of life have been transformed by the rise of computing, the digitization of manufacturing, and the Internet.

The emerging revolution called Industry 4.0 builds on these previous revolutions to bring a new degree of automation, speed, and efficiency to industrial production. It uses the emerging Internet of Things, which connects far-flung machines, processes, and people in a seamless web. What happens in the physical space happens in the virtual space, and vice-versa. The resulting Cyber Physical Systems turn the traditional factory into a kind of living, breathing organism. In the case of a paper mill, the pulper, disc refiner, fourdrinier machine (which creates the continuous paper web), calendar, convertor, and wood yard are integrated into other systems charged with receiving, distributing, and converting products into a single complex system. All these pieces of equipment are wired together, working in harmony, and talking to each other. The smart factory system is designed to identify patterns and to act on acquired data to improve operational efficiencies, to weed out deficient products, to anticipate mechanical breakdowns, and to reduce or eliminate unplanned work stoppages.

Smart factories along these lines are already in operation around the world. But American industry as a whole, and the paper industry in particular, has not yet caught up.

Today, Germany devotes $1 billion annually toward Industry 4.0 alone. By contrast, the U.S. government's principal manufacturing research and development program, Manufacturing USA, spends about $121 million each year, not including cost shares with the private sector. Thus, Germany's investment is about eight times larger than ours, despite the fact that the German economy is one-fifth the size of ours.

What's more, our foreign rivals are already applying Industry 4.0 insights to the same challenges U.S. paper makers face. The German company Voith has designed a program called Papermaking 4.0 that connects sub-processes, making more efficient use of inputs like energy, chemicals, and fibers. With continued investment, Voith predicts a ten percent increase in productivity and a ten percent decrease in overall costs. A case study conducted by the Finnish company Stora Enso focused on energy monitoring systems at a papermaking plant built in 1917 that makes and exports one of the same paper grades Midwest Paper Group produces—carton board. According to the study's author, Industry 4.0 systems for data collection and automation will enable the plant to increase its efficiency significantly.

These findings are consistent with the observations of Gerry Ring, a professor of paper science at the University of Wisconsin-Stevens Point. Ring notes that the paper industry's success over time has been due to innovation, especially in material and energy efficiencies. Similarly, industry analyst Dan Miklovic notes that the industry is "perennially plagued by extremely tight margins, a variable material supply chain, the need to run many operations 24 × 7, and highly capital intensive." Because energy and environmental compliance are significant cost drivers in the paper industry, he concludes that "asset performance management enabled by [the Internet of Things] promises to deliver lower costs with higher yields."

The global consulting firm of McKinsey and Company makes the same points in its analysis of the paper industry:

> The paper and forest-products industry is often labeled a "traditional" industry. Yet given the confluence of technological changes, demographic changes, and resource concerns that we anticipate over the next decade, we believe the industry will have to embrace change that is, in character, as well as pace, vastly different from what we have seen before—and anything but traditional. . . . By radically rethinking the operating model, companies can significantly shift their fixed-cost structure.

The report concludes that, by leveraging what McKinsey terms "digital manufacturing," paper companies can save as much as fifteen percent.

The evidence, then, is clear. If American manufacturing, and the paper industry in particular, want to remain competitive in an increasingly global economy, nothing short of a full-scale industry-wide revolution must happen soon. Of course, this is easier said than done; implementing Industry 4.0 is incredibly expensive. Most paper industry leaders would begin conversion immediately if they could. When I asked John Corrigall, human resources director for Midwest Paper Group, about Industry 4.0, he replied, "Could Midwest Paper Group do that? Sure. How big of a check book do you have?"

Given the recent history of papermaking in the Fox Valley, with multiple companies battered by receivership, bankruptcy, closures, and close calls, it is unlikely that many operations will be investing heavily in Industry 4.0. Most are living hand to mouth and simply cannot afford it. This is why government needs to step up.

Finally, the innovation needed to prepare the pulp and paper industry for the future also includes environmental safeguards. Like many other industries, the pulp and paper industry has left behind a residue of environmental problems—negative externalities, as economists call them—that future generations must rectify. The twenty-year PCB cleanup project in the Fox Valley dealt only with the most visible and significant environmental problem that the paper industry has created. The cleanup effort began in 1998 with pilot projects and continued with early phase cleanups in 2004; the final phase began in 2009 in DePere and Green Bay, where most PCBs had accumulated and settled. By late 2020, the dredging process was finally nearing its end.

Equally important, thanks to the 2019 settlement of a nine-year-old lawsuit by the U.S. and Wisconsin departments of justice, it is now clear that the last phase of the cleanup will be funded exclusively by the defendants—the polluting companies. Attorney General Josh Kaul was understandably proud of this accomplishment as he closed the book on the twenty-four-year-long journey, including the intensive dredging phase that began during the attorney general tenure of his mother, the late Peg Lautenschlager.

The Fox River cleanup project is a model that can and should be replicated elsewhere. While it took time, eventually all stakeholders came to the table and hashed out a solution. Of course, it required political and public pressure on the companies that created the problem in the first place. Dave Ullrich of the EPA got it half right: "Hats off to the companies that paid the money. They should have [paid for the cleanup], and they should have done it sooner, but they did it."

The core lesson of the Fox River cleanup is that strong public-private partnerships are possible and can be highly effective. In the words of Charlie Frisk, a member of the Clean Water Action Council, "Good things happen when there's the political will and people work together."

I CAN'T LEAVE THIS DISCUSSION about the future of the paper industry without a word about the kind of people needed to make that future a reality.

Years ago, Cornell professor Lee Adler taught paper workers at the university's Industrial and Labor Relations School. At a recent industry conference, he ran into some former students. This time Adler was the student; paper workers, the teachers. He quickly realized they were a completely different kind of paper worker. They had an incredible command of the technology, chemistry, and operations of their plant, virtually on a par with their professional counterparts—chemists, engineers, and technicians. Their technological prowess reflected changes in the industry. Paper plants are becoming more capital intensive and dependent on new technology. Paper workers now control complex, half-billion-dollar machines whose operation demands significant skill and knowledge.

It all means that tomorrow's paper industry needs to invest not just in machinery, technology, and innovative ideas, but also in its people—in the workers whose dedication, skill, and hard work drive productivity to new heights. There's a fantastic future ahead for the paper business in Wisconsin and the world, as long as we begin preparing for it now.

If we combine the innovative technological thinking we can produce through expanded investments in education, scientific research, and product development with today's deeper understanding of and commitment to environmental sustainability, there is no reason the Fox Valley cannot be in the vanguard of the Green New Deal revolution. We can overhaul our country's energy and economic policies, control carbon emissions, slow climate change, and reduce income inequality, all while building the industries of tomorrow, expanding employment, and giving working men and women a say in the futures of their communities.

It all starts in the Paper Valley. We led our nation's economic and social progress before. We can do it again.

Acknowledgments

THE APPLETON COATED FIGHT is the highlight of my public service to date, and the lack of support for its workers from so many quarters inspired me to get involved. You get into politics to right wrongs, to stand up for those who cannot stand up for themselves, and to fight for the little guy. Those are also the reasons why I wrote this book.

It was essential to get the Appleton Coated story right along with the broader story of the labor movement in the paper industry and the Fox Valley and how our little corner of the world can help renew the promise of American manufacturing—including the good jobs that built my hometown of Little Chute. To that end, I interviewed sixty-eight paper workers, executives, historians, scholars, labor leaders, and elected officials, in the process logging over one hundred and thirty hours of interviews and countless texts, emails and follow-up calls. I am eternally grateful to all those who made themselves available to me.

I want to mention a few in particular, beginning with longtime friend and mentor Jon Geenen and new friend Doug Osterberg, one of Appleton Coated's former owner-managers. Jon has been by my side for all my campaigns, a source of encouragement and an invaluable liaison with the labor community. Doug responded to *every* email, call, and text—and kept everything on the record. He shared intimate details few were privy to.

The United Steelworkers (USW) fought valiantly to save Appleton Coated, and both local members and senior officials shared their experiences and insights with me. Michael Bolton, director of USW District 2 (Wisconsin and Michigan), has built an amazing organization. In the wake of Act 10, it was Bolton and USW District 2 that came in and filled the void when the public-sector unions in Wisconsin were decimated. Today, the USW is the state's largest and most influential union.

Mike's staff and members were generous with their time: Sally Feistel, Denny Lauer, Dan VandenBush (retired), and Ross Winklbauer. So was USW international vice-president for pulp and paper Leeann Foster, who offered important national and international perspectives that made clear what innovative work Mike and others have been doing in Wisconsin.

Several Local 2-144 (Appleton Coated) members deserve special mention: Jim Weyenberg, Nick Weyenberg, Tony Swanningson, Mike "Mack" MacDonald, Jack DeKoch, and Chris Bogan.

Other USW members at other locals were helpful, too, including Jessica Schiessl and Dave Breckheimer of Kimberly-Clark–Cold Spring Local 2-482; Andy Nirschl, Mark VanStappen, and Ned Wittman of Kimberly NewPage Local 2-9, RIP; and John Tapplin and Tony Kundinger of Flambeau River Paper Local 2-445.

Former UPIU president Wayne Glenn—a pioneering labor leader who should be known and honored as a national treasure—graciously welcomed me into his home in suburban Nashville and delivered a riveting six-hour rendition of his life and the history of paper and its labor movement. I was saddened by his passing in January, 2021, as this book was being completed.

Sara Geenen, the USW's able co-counsel for the receivership case, gave me valuable insight into the legal strategies that enabled Appleton Coated's workers to save their mill.

Acknowledgments

In addition to Doug Osterberg, other former Appleton Coated owner-managers provided crucial insights into the inner workings of the company, particularly in the period just before and after the start of its receivership: Ed Bush, John Corrigal, Mike Rask, Marianne Sterr, and Ann Whalen. Like the workers of Appleton Coated, they showed commitment and faith in the mill that were second to none.

Fox Valley paper industry leaders Bob DeKoch, Kathi Seifert, Harry Spiegelberger, Charles Klass, and Pat Maley gave me the benefit of their expertise and historical perspective.

Jay Grosskopf of Bold Construction and Patrick Pelky of the Oneida Nation helped me understand the PCB cleanup history.

Several labor leaders of note shed revealing light on the history and current situation of labor in Wisconsin and the nation: Kilah Engelke (OPCMIA), John Schmitt (Laborers), Sheila Cochran (former Milwaukee Labor Council and UAW), Sara Nelson (AFA-CWA), Dennis Delie (USW, AFL-CIO), John Zapfel (IBEW Local 484) and Terry Hayden (United Association).

State representatives Katrina Shankland and Greta Neubauer offered their insights on the paper industry and Foxconn, respectively.

Chuck Rundquist graciously sat for an extended interview. He was a pillar of the community in Kimberly and a founding member of my dad's church. His effervescent smile saw our church through dark days and brightened all our lives. He passed away a few months after our meeting. We will miss him.

Paul Fowler of the Wisconsin Institute for Sustainable Technology at the University of Wisconsin–Stevens Point shared his well-supported vision of how the paper industry can evolve to keep pace with, and help lead, important trends in manufacturing.

Combined Locks president John Neumeier and administrator Racquel Shampo-Giese shared their feelings about and insights into the receivership that threatened the economic heart of their community.

Paper and labor experts including Andrew Herod, University of Georgia; Mike Kocurek, North Carolina State University; Gerry Ring, UW–Stevens Point; Lee Adler, Cornell University; Katie Weichelt, UW–Eau Claire; Irving Brotslaw (retired), UW-Extension and UW-Parkside; Michael Hillard, University of Southern Maine; and Christine Blumauer, Harvard University, all provided important background and perspective.

Longtime friend and collaborator Jeff Gillis provided invaluable advice during both the Kimberly NewPage and Appleton Coated fights. He would make "*the* Mayor," Henry Maier, proud.

David Halbrooks handled all the legal issues connected with the book. He is a talented attorney and, above all, a loyal friend.

David Strange, scion of the Van Nortwick family that founded the Combined Locks mill, shared priceless family heirlooms and old mill records. He and his wife, Shirley, generously responded to all of my inquiries and offered candid insights. Hearthstone Historic House Museum executive director George Schroeder went over the history chapter with a fine-toothed comb. Ann Kloehn, local historian and Appleton Coated expert, shared clippings from the time of the mill's founding to the present day.

As chapter 1 recounts, brilliant attorney and friend Tim Nixon first gave me the idea of objecting to the sale of Appleton Coated to a scrap dealer. Had it not been for our September 2017 lunch meeting—one that had been rescheduled a few times—the story told here might never have happened. Things happen for a reason, and that includes Taco Thursdays.

Over the years, I have been blessed with great teachers who have been tremendous sources of inspiration. While it is an incomplete list, some special ones deserve mention: Jo Gehl, Margaret McMahon, Jane and Bob Klozotsky, Margaret Callies, Mr. Poupore, Bob Frankenberg, Steve Timm, and Richard Bender. Thanks are owed to Carleton College professor Richard Keiser who nurtured my interest in labor policy.

Also in the mix are teachers and mentors from my latter years: Ann Corwin, Dean Cecilia Rouse and Professors Anne Case and Daniel Kahneman of the Princeton School of Public and International Affairs.

Not a day goes by that I do not think of my late Grandma and Grandpa Nelson. I hope I've made them proud.

The book would not have been possible without a great editor, Hilary Hinzmann. Hilary took my cold call when the project was on ice in May of 2019. He saw an important story that had to be told and helped me tell it in a way that I could not have done on my own. More, he renewed my love of writing and storytelling and helped me make an important life decision: when I grow up, I'm going to be a writer.

Gratitude is also owed to Karl Weber, editor-publisher of Rivertowns Books, who helped structure and streamline the narrative and produced the beautifully printed and bound book you hold in your hands.

I must also mention another literary figure, Larry Tye. He took me under his wing and guided me through the initial stages of the project, and he was always there to answer questions and get me out of slumps along the way.

Endless thanks to my wife, Maria, for lending her support and for understanding that I needed to do this project. And last but not least, my bestest buddies in the whole wide world, Mare-Mare and Georgie—they are my sunrise and sunset. (Lucy isn't too far behind.)

Thomas M. Nelson
Outagamie County, Wisconsin
January 2021

Source Notes and Bibliography

I HAVE WRITTEN THIS BOOK as a participant-observer in the events connected with Appleton Coated's receivership and the mill's rebirth as Midwest Paper Group. In addition to my own notes and recollections, I have drawn on interviews and correspondence with mill workers and managers, local and national labor leaders, paper industry executives, elected officials, and relevant subject matter experts and on a wide range of published and archived sources. I identify these people and documentary sources where I quote or mention them in the main text.

The list of personal communications below gives dates of interviews in parentheses. Where no dates are indicated, emails exchanged over a period of time are involved.

The bibliography gives full citations for published and archived sources, including URL links where available.

What follows is a selected list of the most important sources for each chapter. Dates of interviews are given in parentheses.

1. On the Brink

The chapter draws on interviews and correspondence with Ed Bush (March 10 and December 7, 2019), Jon Geenen (May 21, 2019), Tim Nixon (June 28, 2019), and Doug Osterberg (July 15, 2019). For Foxconn's record as a corporate citizen, see Todd Frankel, "How Foxconn's Broken Pledges in Pennsylvania Cast Doubt on Trump's Jobs Plan," *Washington Post*, March 3, 2017, and Brian Merchant, "Life and Death in Apple's Forbidden City," *Guardian* (US edition), June 18, 2017.

2. Like Day into Night

The chapter draws on interviews and correspondence with Ed Bush (March 10 and December 7, 2019), Doug Osterberg (July 15, 2019), Marianne Sterr (May 29, 2019), Tony Swanningson (June 26, 2019), Nick Weyenberg (August 22, 2019), and Ann Whalen (June 12, 2019).

3. Auctioning Off a Legacy

The chapter draws on interviews and correspondence with Todd DiBenedetto (June 2, 2020), Jon Geenen (May 21, 2019), Michael "Mack" MacDonald (July 12, 2019), Mike Rask (June 15, 2020), Marianne Sterr (May 29, 2019), Jim Weyenberg (July 18, 2019), and Ann Whalen (June 12, 2019). For information on John Cuneo's ownership of Appleton Coated, see the bibliography entry for Cuneo Studio Materials.

4. Profits, People, and Planet

The chapter draws on interviews and correspondence with Ed Bush (March 10 and December 7, 2019), Wayne Glenn (May 15, 2019),

George Schroeder (August 23, 2019), and David Strange (August 7, 2019). Studies by Dorothy Heesakker and Ellen Kort were helpful for the history of the Fox River Valley. Gregory Summers' *Consuming Nature* cast light on the history of Wisconsin's environmental movement, and Robert W. Ozanne's *The Labor Movement in Wisconsin* provided important background on the history of the state's paper workers unions. Works by Roy Beck, Jerry Kammer, and Larry Tye offered different useful perspectives on immigration and labor market issues. Reports to Congress and other materials related to the 1994 U.S. Commission on Immigration Reform (the "Jordan Commission") are available online at the University of Texas Libraries. For more information, see the bibliography.

5. The Ghosts of Kimberly-NewPage

The chapter draws on interviews and correspondence with Sally Feistel (June 13, 2019), Michael Hillard (June 7, 2019), Pat Maley (July 27, 2019), Andy Nirschl (June 12 and 20, 2019), Mark Van Stappen (July 23, 2019), and Ned Wittman (August 6, 2019).

6. The Voice of God

The chapter draws on interviews and correspondence with Ed Bush (March 10 and December 7, 2019), Todd DiBenedetto (June 2, 2020), Jon Geenen (May 21, 2019), Sara Geenen, Mack MacDonald (July 12, 2019), Tim Nixon (June 28, 2019), Doug Osterberg (July 15, 2019), Marianne Sterr (May 29, 2019), Tony Swanningson (June 26, 2019), and Ann Whalen (June 12, 209). All quotations from the September 2017 hearings in Outagamie Circuit Court come from the court transcript (see bibliography).

7. On Our Own

The chapter draws on interviews and correspondence with Chris Bogan (August 16, 2019), Doug Osterberg (July 15, 2019), and Racquel Shampo-Giese (August 28, 2019) and on reporting by Wisconsin news outlets (see bibliography).

8. Foxconn for Kimberly-Clark

The chapter draws on interviews and correspondence with Chris Bogan, Bob DeKoch (September 3, 2019), Jack DeKoch (September 9, 2019), Jessica Schiessl (August 26, 2019), Racquel Shampo-Giese (August 28, 2019), and Jim Weyenberg (July 18, 2019) and on reporting by Wisconsin news outlets (see bibliography). The information on immigration-related wage depression comes from data assembled for the National Academies of Sciences, Engineering, and Medicine report *The Economic and Fiscal Consequences of Immigration*, Francine D. Blau and Christopher Mackie, editors (see bibliography).

9. State of the Unions

The chapter draws on interviews and correspondence with Christine Blumauer, Chris Bogan (August 16, 2019), Dave Breckheimer (August 5, 2019), Jack DeKoch (September 9, 2019), Leeann Foster (August 30, 2019), Andrew Herod (May 7, 2019), Tony Kundinger (October 3, 2019), John Tapplin (October 3, 2019), Jessica Schiessl (August 26, 2019), Racquel Shampo-Giese (August 28, 2019), and Jim Weyenberg (July 18, 2019) and on reporting by Wisconsin and national news outlets (see bibliography).

Studies and commentary by a diverse group of historians and economists—Irving Bernstein, Josh Bivens, Henry Farber (alone and with Alan Krueger), Richard Freeman (alone and with James Medoff or Joel Rogers), Charles Heckscher, Andrew Herod, Barry Hirsch, Albert O. Hirschman, and Frances Fox Piven, among others—provided valuable insight and information into organized labor's achievements and challenges (see bibliography).

10. A Labor Party in America?

The chapter draws on interviews and correspondence with Dave Breckheimer (August 5, 2019), Sheila Cochran (October 11, 2019), and Wayne Glenn (May 15, 2019). Studies by Robin Archer, Harry Graham, Richard Greenwald and Daniel Katz, Dan Kaufman, John Nichols, Robert Ozanne, and Jason Stein and Patrick Marley provided especially useful information and perspective (see bibliography).

11. In the Vanguard

The chapter draws on interviews and correspondence with Lee Adler (April 10, 2019), John Corrigall (April 19, 2019), Paul Fowler (April 15, 2019), Gerry Ring (March 29, 2019), and Harry Spiegelberg (May 2, 2019).

Personal Communications

Lee Adler (April 10, 2019)
Chris Bogan (August 16, 2019)
Jeff Blodgett
Christine Blumauer
Dave Breckheimer (August 5, 2019)
Ed Bush (March 10 and December 7, 2019)
Sheila Cochran (October 11, 2019)
John Corrigall (April 19, 2019)
Bob DeKoch (September 3, 2019)
Jack DeKoch (September 9, 2019)
Todd DiBenedetto (June 2, 2020)

Sally Feistel (June 13, 2019)

Leeann Foster (August 30, 2019)

Paul Fowler (April 15, 2019)

Jon Geenen (May 21, 2019)

Sara Geenen

Wayne Glenn (May 15, 2019)

Mike Grones (October 7, 2019)

Jay Grosskopf (December 13, 2019)

Andrew Herod (May 7, 2019)

Michael Hillard (June 7, 2019)

Gordon Hintz (January 21, 2020)

Charles Klass (February 24, 2019)

Tony Kundinger (October 3, 2019)

Michael "Mack" MacDonald (July 12, 2019)

Pat Maley (July 27, 2019)

Craig Moser

Ben Nerad

John Neumeier (August 28, 2019)

Andy Nirschl (June 12 & 20, 2019)

Tim Nixon (June 28, 2019)

Doug Osterberg (July 15, 2019)

Patrick Pelky (January 14, 2020)

Mike Rask (June 15, 2020)

Gerry Ring (March 29, 2019)

Dan Sawall

Jessica Schiessl (August 26, 2019)

George Schroeder (August 23, 2019)

John Schmitt (October 2, 2019)

Racquel Shampo-Giese (August 28, 2019)

Harry Spiegelberg (May 2, 2019)

Marianne Sterr (May 29, 2019)

David Strange (August 7, 2019)

Tony Swanningson (June 26, 2019)

John Tapplin (October 3, 2019)
Mark Van Stappen (July 23, 2019)
Jim Weyenberg (July 18, 2019)
Nick Weyenberg (August 22, 2019)
Ann Whalen (June 12, 2019)
Ned Wittman (August 6, 2019)

Bibliography

Alanen, Arnold R., and Joseph A. Eden. *Main Street Ready-Made: The New Deal Community of Greendale, Wisconsin.* Madison: State Historical Society of Wisconsin, 1987.

American RadioWorks. "Bridge to Somewhere: Public Works Administration." *Blueprint America: PBS Reports on Infrastructure.* PBS, June 5, 2009. https://www.pbs.org/wnet/blueprintamerica/reports/by-topic/growth-development/profiles-from-the-recession-report-bridge-to-somewhere-public-works-administration/693/.

Andrews, Valeri, and Karen Bartosh, Nicole Gunderson, Katelin Holm, Katie Larson, Tina Spielmann, and Elizabeth Wiedell. "Contamination of Polychlorinated Biphenyls in the Fox River, Northeastern Wisconsin." Fox River PCB timeline prepared for Introduction to Environmental and Public Health course, University of Wisconsin-Eau Claire, fall 2003. https://people.uwec.edu/piercech/PCBs/.

Appleton Post Crescent. "16-foot-thick wall split open." September 26, 1989.

Appleton Post Crescent. "Appleton Coated Comes Back to Life with Worker Recalls, Machine Re-starts." March 27, 2018. https://www.postcrescent.com/story/news/2018/03/27/appleton-coated-comes-back-life-worker-recalls-machine-re-starts/442190002/.

Appleton Papers. "100 Years of Progress: Locks Mill Centennial Anniversary: 1889-1989." Combined Locks: Appleton Papers, 1989.

Appleton Public Library. "Joint Local Government Resolution Supporting Fox River PCB Cleanup Settlement." Appleton Common Council, July 1, 1998. https://apl.org/pcb-resolution.

Appvion. "Appvion Receives Court Approval of First Day Motions to Support Ongoing Operations." October 3, 2017. http://www.appvion.com/en-us/Documents/Historical%20News/Appvion_Receives_Court_Approval_First_Day_Motions_Support_Ongoing_Operations.pdf.

Appvion. "Appvion to Consolidate Carbonless Paper Manufacturing Operations." November 9, 2017. http://www.appvion.com/en-us/Documents/Historical%20News/News_Release_Appvion_Consolidate_Carbonless_Paper_Manufacturing_Operations.pdf.

Archer, Robin. *Why Is There No Labor Party in the United States?* Princeton, NJ: Princeton University Press, 2007.

Ashby, Steven, and C.J. Hawking. *Staley: The Fight for a New American Labor Movement*. Champaign: University of Illinois Press, 2009.

Associated Press. "Record High Gas Prices in Wisconsin." WKBT (News8000.com), May 4, 2011. https://www.news8000.com/record-high-gas-prices-in-wisconsin/.

Bach, Pete. "Union Leaders Push Legislative Action to Bring NewPage Mill in Kimberly Back under New Owner." *Appleton Post Crescent*, August 14, 2008.

Baldwin, Tammy (Senator). "With Over 600 Wisconsin Workers Facing Lay-offs in Fox Valley, Senator Tammy Baldwin Questions the Use of Corporate Tax Cuts for Stock Buybacks." Press release, February 8, 2018. https://www.baldwin.senate.gov/press-releases/baldwin-questions-kimberly-clark-use-of-corporate-tax-cuts-for-stock-buybacks.

Banham, Russ. *Appleton: Applying Technology for Performance.* Nashville, TN: Greenwich Publishing, 2007.

Barrett, Rick. "Kimberly-Clark Closing 2 Wisconsin Plants, Cutting 600 Jobs." *Milwaukee Journal Sentinel*, January 31, 2018. https://www.jsonline.com/story/money/business/2018/01/31/k imberly-clark-closing-two-plants-neenah/1082701001/.

Batavia Historical Society. "Famous Batavians: The Van Nortwick Industrial Empire." http://www.bataviahistoricalsociety.org/exhibits-collections/batavians-overview/the-vannortwick-family/.

Bauer, Scott. "Political analysis: Foxconn hands Scott Walker a 'grand slam home run.'" *Wisconsin State Journal* (Associated Press), July 27, 2017. https://madison.com/wsj/news/local/govt-and-politics/political-analysis-foxconn-hands-scott-walker-a-grand-slam-home/article_724e22df-fd51-55f8-b912-9846cd5db454.html.

Beck, Molly. "Foxconn Legal Appeals Go Straight to Supreme Court under GOP Proposal." *Wisconsin State Journal*, September 6, 2017. https://madison.com/wsj/news/local/govt-and-politics/foxconn-legal-appeals-go-straight-to-supreme-court-under-gop/article_b342dd57-a5b3-568c-b56a-4d10077cbd23.html.

Beck, Molly, and Patrick Marley. "Kimberly-Clark to Receive $28 Million in Taxpayer Funds under New Deal from Scott Walker." *Milwaukee Journal Sentinel*, December 13, 2018. https://www.jsonline.com/story/news/politics/2018/12/13/scot t-walker-give-kimberly-clark-25-million-taxpayer-funds/2292678002/.

Beck, Roy. *The Case Against Immigration: The Moral, Economic, Social, and Environmental Reasons for Reducing U.S. Immigration Back to Traditional Levels.* New York: W. W. Norton, 1996.

Beckett, Andrew. "Assembly Approves Tax Incentives for Kimberly-Clark." Wisconsin Radio Network, February 23, 2018. https://www.wrn.com/2018/02/assembly-approves-tax-incentives-for-kimberly-clark/.

Beech, Eric. "US Government Says It Lost $11.2 Billion on GM Bailout." *Reuters*, April 30, 2014. https://www.reuters.com/article/us-autos-gm-treasury/u-s-government-says-it-lost-11-2-billion-on-gm-bailout-idUSBREA3T0MR20140430.

Behr, Madeleine. "Appleton Coated Workers Hopeful, But Uncertain, about Future." *Appleton Post Crescent*, September 22, 2017. https://www.postcrescent.com/story/news/2017/09/22/appleton-coated-workers-hopeful-but-uncertain-future/693097001/.

Behr, Madeleine. "Despite Appvion and Appleton Coated Troubles, Paper Industry Thriving Overall, Leaders Say." *Appleton Post Crescent*, October 6, 2017. https://www.postcrescent.com/story/news/2017/10/06/despite-appvion-and-appleton-coated-troubles-paper-industry-thriving-overall-leaders-say/727512001/.

Behr, Madeleine. "Walker, Nelson Letters Discuss Paper Industry Woes." *Appleton Post Crescent*, November 22, 2017. https://www.postcrescent.com/story/news/2017/11/22/gov-walker-tom-nelson-exchange-letters-appleton-coated-economic-issues/890129001/.

Behr, Madeleine. "Walker: 'Hard to Tell' If K-C Takes Tax Deal." *Appleton Post Crescent*, February 15, 2018. https://www.postcrescent.com/story/news/2018/02/15/walker-hard-tell-whether-kimberly-clark-take-tax-deal-keep-plants-open/338959002/.

Berg, Peter, and Oskar Linqvist. "Pulp, Paper, and Packaging in the Next Decade: Transformational Change." McKinsey & Company, August 7, 2019.

https://www.mckinsey.com/industries/paper-forest-products-and-packaging/our-insights/pulp-paper-and-packaging-in-the-next-decade-transformational-change#.

Bergquist, Lee. "Wisconsin Still at Center of Water Battles 10 Years After Passage of Great Lakes Compact." *Mikwaukee Journal Sentinel*, October 2, 2018. https://www.jsonline.com/story/news/2018/10/02/wisconsin-center-water-battles-decade-after-great-lakes-compact/1492177002/.

Bergquist, Lee. "Final Settlement Reached over Costs in Massive Cleanup of the Fox River in Green Bay." *Milwaukee Journal Sentinel*, March 15, 2019. https://www.jsonline.com/story/news/local/wisconsin/2019/03/15/final-settlement-reached-cleanup-fox-river-green-bay/3179716002/,

Bernstein, Irving. *The Turbulent Years: A History of the American Worker, 1933-1940*. Chicago: Haymarket Books, 2010 (Reissue).

Bernstein, Mark, and William Hoest. *Paper with Presence: A Gilbert Century*. Menasha: Gilbert Paper, 1987.

Bivens, Josh. *Failure by Design: The Story Behind America's Broken Economy*. Ithaca, NY: ILR Press/Cornell University Press, 2011.

Blau, Francine D., and Christopher Mackie, eds. *The Economic and Fiscal Consequences of Immigration*. Washington DC: National Academies Press, 2016.

Borjas, George J. "Labor Market Impact of Immigration: A Summary of the Evidence." Presentation to the Congressional Budget Office's Macroeconomics Advisory Panel, June 14, 2013.

Borjas, George J. *We Wanted Workers: Unraveling the Immigration Narrative*. New York: W. W. Norton, 2016.

Bremer, William W., and Holly J. Lyon. *A Little Ways Ahead: The Centennial History of Thilmany Pulp & Paper Company*. Kaukauna: Thilmany Pulp & Paper, 1983.

Brown, Courtenay. "U.S. Manufacturing Activity Hits Worst Level Since 2009." Axios, January 3, 2020. https://www.axios.com/us-manufacturing-index-ism-lowest-great-recession-af6fb388-9cee-4944-8955-6aec166671ea.html.

Burke, Michael. "Foxconn Chooses Mount Pleasant." *Journal Times* (Racine, WI), October 5, 2017. https://journaltimes.com/news/local/foxconn-chooses-mount-pleasant/article_8c4af8b4-bbc4-5b64-b343-f23a70879374.html.

Burnley, Alexandra. "620 employees temporarily laid off at Appleton Coated." WFRV (wearegreenbay.com), September 22, 2017. https://www.wearegreenbay.com/news/local-news/620-employees-temporarily-laid-off-at-appleton-coated/.

Burnley, Alexandra. "Appleton Coated Will Temporarily Re-Hire 50 Employees for Three Months." WFRV (wearegreenbay.com), December 6, 2017. https://www.wearegreenbay.com/news/local-news/appleton-coated-will-temporarily-re-hire-50-employees-for-three-months/.

Card, Andrew, and Alan B. Krueger. "Minimum Wages and Employment: A Case Study of the Fast-Food Industry in New Jersey and Pennsylvania." National Bureau of Economic Research Working Paper, October 1993. https://www.nber.org/papers/w4509.

Case, Anne, and Angus Deaton. "Rising Morbidity and Mortality in Midlife among White Non-Hispanic Americans in the 21st Century." *PNAS*, 112 no. 49: 15078-15083. https://doi.org/10.1073/pnas.1518393112.

Case, Anne, and Angus Deaton. *Deaths of Despair and the Future of Capitalism*. Princeton, NJ: Princeton University Press, 2020.

Combined Locks. "Golden Jubilee: Combined Locks, Wisconsin." Combined Locks, 1970. [This is the Village of Combined Locks as author/publisher.]

Combined Locks Mill. Minutes of Board Meetings: 1916-1935. Personal collection of David Strange.

Corkery, Michael. "The Great American Cardboard Comeback." *New York Times*, March 22, 2019. https://www.nytimes.com/2019/03/22/business/cardboard.html.

Cotton, Brad. "Ohio, Rutherford B. Hayes and the Great Railroad Strike of 1877." *Circleville (OH) Herald*, September 2, 2015. https://www.circlevilleherald.com/comment/editorials/ohio-rutherford-b-hayes-and-the-great-railroad-strike-of/article_a22d4aa6-f78f-5bdb-9935-775e00be9715.html

Cowie, Jefferson. "'A One-Sided Class War': Rethinking Doug Fraser's 1978 Resignation from the Labor-Management Group." *Journal of Labor History*, 44 no. 3 (2003): 307-314. https://www.tandfonline.com/doi/abs/10.1080/002365603200012928.

Cowie, Jefferson. *Stayin' Alive: The 1970s and the Last Days of the Working Class*. New York: New Press, 2010.

Cuneo Studio Materials. Charles Deering McCormick Library of Special Collections, Northwestern University. https://findingaids.library.northwestern.edu/agents/corporate_entities/1528.

DeFour, Matthew. "Workers Wanted: Wisconsin Businesses Grapple with a Growing Worker Shortage." *Wisconsin State Journal*, September 11, 2017. https://madison.com/wsj/business/wisconsin-businesses-grapple-with-a-growing-worker-shortage/article_3ef1000e-c18b-5f72-bbcd-720ee2456111.html.

DeFour, Matthew. "WEDC Delays Vote on Foxconn Contract After Discovering Problem." *Wisconsin State Journal*, October 18, 2017. https://madison.com/wsj/news/local/govt-and-politics/wedc-delays-vote-on-foxconn-contract-after-discovering-problem/article_4f15f3d6-3121-5d6f-80fd-cf8f56b9d743.html.

DeFour, Matthew. "Foxconn Contract Contained 'Nuclear Bomb' That Left Taxpayers Exposed, WEDC Board Member Says." *Wisconsin State Journal*, October 25, 2017. https://madison.com/wsj/news/local/govt-and-politics/foxconn-contract-contained-nuclear-bomb-that-left-taxpayers-exposed-wedc/article_be03bc7a-3ee1-5d92-8bb9-ff740e8718c6.html.

DeFour, Matthew. "WEDC Board Approves Foxconn Contract, Which Includes CEO's Personal Guarantee." *Wisconsin State Journal*, November 9, 2017. https://madison.com/wsj/news/local/govt-and-politics/wedc-board-approves-foxconn-contract-which-includes-ceo-s-personal/article_0f45ad70-6e3b-5fc8-b65f-1fa9adcab11b.html.

DeFour, Matthew. "Fiscal Bureau: Foxconn Roads Could Draw $134 Million from Other State Highway Projects." *Wisconsin State Journal*, December 16, 2017. https://madison.com/wsj/news/local/govt-and-politics/fiscal-bureau-foxconn-roads-could-draw-million-from-other-state/article_f7a8a608-c245-5dce-acf3-7f83a19e615e.html.

DeSilver, Drew. "Most Americans View Unions Favorably, Though Few Workers Belong to One." Pew Research Center, August 30, 2018. https://www.pewresearch.org/fact-tank/2018/08/30/union-membership-2/.

Dickens, William T., and Jonathan S. Leonard. "Accounting for the Decline in Union Membership, 1950-1980." *Industrial and Labor Relations Review* 38 (April 1985): 323-334.

Drakopoulos, Stavros, and Ioannis Katselidis. "The Development of Trade Union Theory and Mainstream Economic Methodology." *Journal of Economic Issues* 48 no. 4 (2014): 1133-1149. https://doi.org/10.2753/JEI0021-3624480413.

Epstein, Reid J. "Scott Walker's Immigration Shift at Odds with Koch Group." Washington Wire *Wall Street Journal*, April 21,

2015. https://blogs.wsj.com/washwire/2015/04/21/scott-walkers-immigration-shift-at-odds-with-koch-group/.

Farber, Henry S. "The Recent Decline of Unionization in the United States." *Science* 13 (November 1987): 915-920.

Farber, Henry S. "Trends in Worker Demand for Union Representation." *American Economic Review* 79 (May 1989): 166-171.

Farber, Henry S. "The Decline in Unionization in the United States: What Can Be Learned from Recent Experience?" *Journal of Labor Economics* 8 (January 1990): S75-S105.

Farber, Henry S., and Alan B. Krueger. "Union Membership in the United States: The Decline Continues." National Bureau of Economic Research Working Paper, November 1992. https://www.nber.org/papers/w4216.

Featherstone, Liza. "How Flight Attendants Grounded Trump's Shutdown." *Jacobin*, February 8, 2019. https://jacobinmag.com/2019/02/flight-attendants-union-sara-nelson-shutdown.

Federal Reserve Bank of St. Louis. "Producer Price Index by Commodity: Pulp, Paper, and Allied Products: Wood Pulp." https://fred.stlouisfed.org/series/WPU0911.

Ford, Brittany. "Gov. Walker Makes Campaign Stop in Fox Valley." WLUK, November 7, 2017. https://fox11online.com/news/election/governor-walker-makes-campaign-stop-in-fox-valley.

Frankel, Todd C. "How Foxconn's Broken Pledges in Pennsylvania Cast Doubt on Trump's Jobs Plan." *Washington Post*, March 3, 2017. https://www.washingtonpost.com/business/economy/how-foxconns-broken-pledges-in-pennsylvania-cast-doubt-on-trumps-jobs-plan/2017/03/03/0189f3de-ee3a-11e6-9973-c5efb7ccfb0d_story.html.

Freeman, Richard B., "Contraction and Expansion: The Divergence of Private Sector and Public Sector Unionism in the United States." *Journal of Economic Perspectives* 2 (Spring 1988): 63-88.

Freeman, Richard B., and James L. Medoff. *What Do Unions Do?* New York: Basic Books, 1985.

Freeman, Richard B., and Joel Rogers. *What Workers Want.* Ithaca, NY: ILR Press/Cornell University Press, 1999.

Freifeld, Karen. "Deutsche Bank Signs $7.2 Billion Deal with U.S. over Risky Mortgages." *Reuters*, January 17, 2017. https://www.reuters.com/article/us-deutsche-bank-mortgage-settlement-idUSKBN1512UC.

Furay, Catherine. "Chapter 128: A change would do us good." *Wisconsin Lawyer*, June 12, 2019. https://www.wisbar.org/NewsPublications/WisconsinLawyer/Pages/Article.aspx?Volume=92&Issue=6&ArticleID=27061.

Geoghegan, Thomas. *Only One Thing Can Save Us: Why America Needs a New Kind of Labor Movement.* New York: New Press, 2014.

Getman, Julius. *The Betrayal of Local 14: Paperworkers, Politics, and Permanent Replacements.* Ithaca, NY: Cornell University Press, 1998.

Gnau, Thomas. "Appvion Cuts 200 Jobs But Spares West Carrollton Plant." WHIO, November 9, 2017.

Goldstein, Amy. *Janesville: An American Story.* New York: Simon & Schuster, 2017.

Graham, Harry E. *The Paper Rebellion: Development and Upheaval in Pulp and Paper Unionism.* Iowa City: University of Iowa Press, 1970.

Greenwald, Richard, and Daniel Katz, eds. *Labor Rising: The Past and Future of Working People in America.* New York: New Press, 2012.

Gross, James A. "The Making and Shaping of Unionism in the Pulp and Paper Industry." *Labor History* 5 no. 2 (April 1964): 183-208.

Harrington, Moira. "Largest PCB Cleanup in the World Winding Down." Sea Grant, University of Wisconsin-Madison,

November 6, 2019.
https://www.seagrant.wisc.edu/news/largest-pcb-cleanup-in-the-world-winding-down/.

Hearthstone Historic House and Museum. "Illuminating Our Heritage: Electricity and Our Place in History." Hearthstone Historic House and Museum. https://www.hearthstonemuseum.org/house-and-grounds.

Heckscher, Charles. *The New Unionism: Employee Involvement in the Changing Corporation.* Ithaca, NY: ILR Press/Cornell University Press, 1996 (Reissue).

Heesakker, Dorothy, "The Paper Mill Industry in the Lower Fox River Valley, Wisconsin, 1872-1890." Master's thesis, Loyola University Chicago, 1926. http://ecommons.luc.edu/luc_theses/1926.

Herod, Andrew. "Local Political Practice in Response to a Manufacturing Plant Closure: How Geography Complicates Class Analysis." *Antipode* 23 no. 4 (October 1991): 385-402. https://onlinelibrary.wiley.com/doi/abs/10.1111/j.1467-8330.1991.tb00420.x.

Herod, Andrew. "Further Reflections on Organized Labor and Deindustrialization in the United States." *Antipode* 26 no. 1 (January 1994): 77-95. https://www.researchgate.net/publication/227981914_Further_reflections_on_organized_labor_and_deindustrialization_in_t he_United_States.

Herod, Andrew. "Labor's Spatial Praxis and the Geography of Contract Bargaining in the US East Coast Longshore Industry, 1953-89." *Political Geography* 16 no. 2 (February 1997): 145-169. https://www.researchgate.net/publication/248441787_Labor's_spatial_praxis_and_the_geography_of_contract_bargaining_in _the_US_east_coast_longshore_industry_1953-89.

Herod, Andrew. "Labor Internationalism and the Contradictions of Globalization: Or, Why the Local Is Sometimes Still Important in a Global Economy." *Antipode* 33 no. 3 (July 2001): 407-426. https://www.researchgate.net/publication/227521498_Labor_I nternationalism_and_the_Contradictions_of_Globalization_O r_Why_the_Local_Is_Sometimes_Still_Important_in_a_Global _Economy.

Hirsch, Barry T. "What Do Unions Do for Economic Performance?" *Journal of Labor Research* 25 no. 3 (Summer 2004): 415-455.

Hirsch, Barry T., David Macpherson, and Wayne G. Vroman. "Estimates of Union Density by State." *Monthly Labor Review*, July 2001. Annually updated Excel spreadsheet, "Union Density Estimates by State." http://www.unionstats.com/MonthlyLaborReviewArticle.htm; MLR_7-01_StateUnionDensity.pdf.

Hirschman, Albert O. *Exit, Voice, and Loyalty: Responses to Decline in Firms, Organizations, and States.* Cambridge, MA: Harvard University Press, 1970.

Holter, Darryl. *Workers and Unions in Wisconsin: A Labor History Anthology.* Madison: Wisconsin Historical Society, 1999.

Hornacek, Robert. "Fox 11 Investigates: Clean-up of PCBs in Fox River." WLUK, May 16, 2019. https://fox11online.com/news/fox-11-investigates/fox-11-investigates-clean-up-of-pcbs-in-fox-river.

Howard, Vicki. "The Rise and Fall of Sears." *Smithsonian*, July 25, 2017. https://www.smithsonianmag.com/history/rise-and-fall-sears-180964181/.

IndustriALL. "IndustriALL Global Union and UNI Global Union Condemn Kimberly-Clark's Lack of Respect for Workers." September 6, 2018. http://www.industriall-union.org/industriall-global-union-and-uni-global-union-condemn-kimberly-clarks-lack-of-respect-for-workers.

International Brotherhood of Paper Makers. Local 1 (Eagle Lodge: Holyoke, Mass.) Records. Special Collections and University

Archives, University Libraries, University of Massachusetts-Amherst. http://findingaids.library.umass.edu/ead/mums081.

Jagoda, Naomi. "Kimberly-Clark to Use Savings from Tax Cuts to Pay for Layoffs." *Hill* (Washington, DC), January 24, 2018. https://thehill.com/policy/finance/370498-kimberly-clark-to-use-savings-from-tax-cuts-to-pay-for-layoffs.

Jordan, Barbara. Testimony before U.S. Senate Committee on the Judiciary, Subcommittee on Immigration and Refugee Affairs, August 3, 1994. *See* U.S. Commission on Immigration Reform (the "Jordan Commission").

Kaeding, Danielle. "Demand for Paper Mills Decline [sic] While Market for Tissue, Sanitary Paper Is Expected to Rise." Wisconsin Public Radio, October 25, 2017. https://www.wpr.org/demand-paper-mills-decline-while-market-tissue-sanitary-paper-expected-rise.

Kagermann, Henning, Wolfgang Wahlster, and Johannes Helbig. "Securing the Future of [the] German Manufacturing Industry: Recommendations for Implementing the Strategic Initiative Industrie [sic] 4.0; Final Report of the Industrie 4.0 Working Group." Forschungsunion and National Academy of Science and Engineering (Germany), April 2003. https://www.din.de/blob/76902/e8cac883f42bf28536e7e8165993f1fd/recommendations-for-implementing-industry-4-0-data.pdf

Kammer, Jerry. "The Hart-Celler Immigration Act of 1965." Center for Immigration Studies, October 2015. https://cis.org/sites/cis.org/files/kammer-hart-celler.pdf.

Katada, Saori N. *Banking on Stability: Japan and the Cross-Pacific Dynamics of International Financial Crisis Management.* Ann Arbor: University of Michigan Press, 2001.

Kaufman, Dan. *The Fall of Wisconsin: The Conservative Conquest of a Progressive Bastion and the Future of American Politics.* New York: W. W. Norton, 2018.

Kelly, Heather. "Amazon wants you to start a business to deliver its packages." CNN Business, June 28, 2018. https://money.cnn.com/2018/06/28/technology/amazon-delivery-partners/index.html.

Kelly, Kim. "Sara Nelson's Art of War." *The New Republic*, May 13, 2019. https://newrepublic.com/tags/sara-nelson.

Kitroeff, Natalie. "The Shutdown Made Sara Nelson into America's Most Powerful Flight Attendant." *New York Times*, February 22, 2019. https://www.nytimes.com/2019/02/22/business/sara-nelson-flight-attendant-union.html.

Klingenberg, Cristina. "Industry 4.0: What Makes It a Revolution." EurOMA conference presentation, July 2017. https://www.researchgate.net/publication/319127784_Industry_40_what_makes_it_a_revolution.

Kloehn, Ann. Personal collection of newspaper clippings.

Kort, Ellen. *The Fox Heritage: A History of Wisconsin's Fox Cities.* Woodland Hills, CA: Windsor Publications, 1984.

Lazonick, William. "Stock Buybacks: From Retain-and-Reinvest to Downsize-and-Distribute." Brookings Institution, Center for Effective Public Management, April 2015. https://www.brookings.edu/research/stock-buybacks-from-retain-and-reinvest-to-downsize-and-distribute/.

Lind, Michael. "How Reaganism Actually Started with Carter." Salon.com, February 8, 2011. https://www.salon.com/2011/02/08/lind_reaganism_carter/.

Lofy, Bill. *Paul Wellstone: The Life of a Passionate Progressive.* Ann Arbor: University of Michigan Press, 2005.

MacIver Institute. "Union Membership Rises as Wisconsin Economy Creates Thousands of Blue Collar Jobs." January 19, 2018. https://www.maciverinstitute.com/2018/01/union-membership-rises-as-wisconsin-economy-creates-thousands-of-blue-collar-jobs/.

McGrath, Dennis J., and Dane Smith. *Professor Wellstone Goes to Washington: The Inside Story of a Grassroots U.S. Senate Campaign.* Minneapolis: University of Minnesota Press, 1995.

Matesic, Emily, Brittany Schmidt, and Jason Zimmerman. "Judge Approves Sale of Appleton Coated." WBAY, October 5, 2017. https://www.wbay.com/content/news/Judge-approves-sale-of-Appleton-Coated-449623153.html.

Matesic, Emily, and Jason Zimmerman. "Kimberly-Clark Plant Closures to Impact 600 Local Workers." WBAY (Green Bay), January 31, 2018. https://www.wbay.com/content/news/Kimberly-Clark-to-close-two-Fox-Cities-facilities-471966083.html.

Mays, Gabrielle. "Temporary layoffs confirmed at Appleton Coated, unclear how many." WLUK (Green Bay), September 21, 2017. https://fox11online.com/news/local/temporary-layoffs-confirmed-at-appleton-coated-unclear-how-many.

Mays, Gabrielle. "Walker Says There's a Future for the Papermaking Industry in Fox Valley." WLUK, February 2, 2018. https://fox11online.com/news/local/walker-says-theres-a-future-for-papermaking-industry-in-fox-valley.

Merchant, Brian. "Life and Death in Apple's Forbidden City." *Guardian* (US edition), June 18, 2017. https://www.theguardian.com/technology/2017/jun/18/foxconn-life-death-forbidden-city-longhua-suicide-apple-iphone-brian-merchant-one-device-extract.

Miklovic, Dan. "IIoT, Smart Connected Assets, and the Pulp & Paper Industry." LNS Research Industrial Transformation Blog, August 11, 2015. https://blog.lnsresearch.com/iiot-smart-connected-assets-and-the-pulp-paper-industry.

Mizan, Nusaiba. "Kimberly-Clark made big promises in exchange for state incentives. At Its Cold Spring Facility, It's Following Through." *Appleton Post Crescent*, November 4, 2019. https://www.postcrescent.com/story/money/2019/11/04/kimbe

rly-clark-cold-spring-facility-add-four-production-line-warehouse-to-fulfill-its-115-million-in/4084248002/.

Morales, Aisha. "Green Bay Packaging to Build New $500 Million Facility." WBAY (Green Bay), June 12, 2018. https://www.wbay.com/content/news/Green-Bay-Packaging-to-build-new-500-million-facility--485249631.html.

Murphy, Bruce. "Wisconsin's $4.1 billion boondoggle." *Verge*, October 29, 2018. https://www.theverge.com/2018/10/29/18027032/foxconn-wisconsin-plant-jobs-deal-subsidy-governor-scott-walker.

National Research Council. *Funding a Revolution: Government Support for Computing Research.* Washington, DC: National Academy Press, 1999. https://doi.org/10.17226/6323.

NBC26 (WGBA). "U.S. Paper Converters Inc. Joins Other Fox Valley Paper Companies in Layoffs." October 24, 2017. https://www.nbc26.com/news/us-paper-converters-inc-joins-other-fox-valley-paper-companies-in-layoffs.

Nelson Institute for Environmental Studies. "Gaylord Nelson and Earth Day." Nelson Institute for Environmental Studies, University of Wisconsin-Madison. http://www.nelsonearthday.net/nelson/

Nichols, John. *Uprising: How Wisconsin Renewed the Politics of Protest, from Madison to Wall Street.* New York: Bold Type Books, 2012.

One Wisconsin Now. "GOP Pushes Tax Giveaway Plan That Pays More for Fewer Jobs." November 14, 2018. https://onewisconsinnow.org/press/gop-pushes-tax-giveaway-plan-that-pays-more-for-fewer-jobs/.

Orendorff, Aaron. "Global Ecommerce Statistics and Trends to Launch Your Business Beyond Borders." Shopify.com, February 14, 2019. https://www.shopify.com/enterprise/global-ecommerce-statistics.

Outagamie County (WI) Circuit Court Branch 4. In re: Appleton
   Coated LLC, Case Number 17CV760, September 12, 20, 22, and
   25, 2017.

Ozanne, Robert W. *The Labor Movement in Wisconsin: A History.*
   Madison: State Historical Society of Wisconsin, 1984.

Palladino, Lenore. Testimony before the House Financial Services
   Committee Subcommittee on Investor Protection,
   Entrepreneurship, and Capital Markets, 116th Congress,
   October 17, 2019. https://financialservices.house.gov; hhrg-116-
   ba16-wstate-palladinol-20191017.pdf.

Piven, Frances Fox. Introduction to *The Turbulent Years: A History of
   the American Worker, 1933-1940*, by Irving Bernstein. Chicago:
   Haymarket Books, 2010 (Reissue).

PRNewswire. "Final Determination by U.S. International Trade
   Commission Confirm [sic] Coated Free Sheet Paper Imports
   from China & Indonesia Cause Injury to U.S. Workers; Duties
   to Be Applied." NewPage Corporation, October 22, 2010.
   https://www.prnewswire.com/news-releases/final-
   determination-by-us-international-trade-commission-
   confirm-coated-free-sheet-paper-imports-from-china--
   indonesia-cause-injury-to-us-producers-workers-duties-to-be-
   applied-105552498.html.

PRNewswire. "Appvion Enters into Sale Agreement to Position
   Business for Long-Term Success: Group of Lenders to Provide
   Stalking Horse Bid in Court-Supervised Sale Process." Appvion,
   February 8, 2018. https://www.prnewswire.com/news-
   releases/appvion-enters-into-sale-agreement-to-position-
   business-for-long-term-success-300596315.html.

PRNewswire. "USW Calls on Wisconsin Senate to Vote on
   Kimberly-Clark Plan." United Steelworkers, April 16, 2018.
   https://www.prnewswire.com/news-releases/usw-calls-on-
   wisconsin-senate-to-vote-on-kimberly-clark-plan-
   300630577.html.

ProPublica. Bailout Tracker.
https://projects.propublica.org/bailout/list.

Richmond, Todd. "Judge OKs Deal for PCB Polluters to Cover Fox
River Clean-Up." *U.S. News & World Report* (Associated Press),
March 15, 2019. https://www.usnews.com/news/best-
states/wisconsin/articles/2019-03-15/judge-oks-deal-for-pcb-
polluters-to-cover-fox-river-clean-up.

Rogoway, Mike. "West Linn Paper will shut mill after 128 years."
Oregonian (Portland, OR), October 17, 2017.
https://www.oregonlive.com/business/2017/10/west_linn_pap
er_will_shut_down.html.

Romell, Rick. "Foxconn Would Get $140 Million Electricity Project."
Milwaukee Journal Sentinel, December 12, 2017.
https://www.jsonline.com/story/money/business/2017/12/12/f
oxconn-would-get-140-million-electricity-project-use-more-
power-than-any-plant-state/944403001/.

Ronallo, Alex. "Hearing Ends, Now a Different Path for Appleton
Coated's Future." WLUK, September 25, 2017.
https://fox11online.com/news/local/appleton-coated-hearing-
underway.

Rosswurm, Steve. "Congress of Industrial Organizations." In
Encyclopedia of Chicago, edited by Janice L. Reigg, Ann Durkin
Keating, and James R. Grossman. Chicago Historical Society,
2005.

Roth, Roger (@SenatorRoth). Twitter post, February 5, 2018.
https://twitter.com/SenatorRoth.

Rothstein, Richard. *The Color of Law: A Forgotten History of How Our
Government Segregated America*. New York: Liveright, 2017.

Rushe, Dominic. "'It's a Huge Subsidy': The $4.8 Bn Gamble to Lure
Foxconn to America." *Guardian* (US edition), July 2, 2018.
https://www.theguardian.com/cities/2018/jul/02/its-a-huge-
subsidy-the-48bn-gamble-to-lure-foxconn-to-america.

Ryan, Courtney. "Uncertainty remains for 600 employees pending sale of Appleton Coated." WLUK, September 20, 2017. https://fox11online.com/news/local/uncertainty-remains-for-600-employees-amid-pending-sale-of-appleton-coated.

Scheiber, Noam. "Candidates Grow Bolder on Labor, and Not Just Bernie Sanders." *New York Times*, October 11, 2019. https://www.nytimes.com/2019/10/11/business/economy/democratic-candidates-labor-unions.html.

Schroeder, George. "Nomination of William M. Van Nortwick, John S. Van Nortwick, and Henry J. Rogers to the Paper Industry International Hall of Fame." Unpublished essay, 2019.

Somerhauser, Mark. "Memo: Foxconn Cost to Public Nearing $4.5 Billion." *Journal Times* (Racine, WI), January 17, 2018. https://journaltimes.com/business/local/memo-foxconn-cost-to-public-nearing-billion/article_26ee82a2-f12b-5c3e-a600-036ee900d01a.html.

Spears, Ellen Griffith. *Baptized in PCBs: Race, Pollution, and Justice in an All-American Town*. New Directions in Southern Studies. Chapel Hill: University of North Carolina Press, 2014.

Stein, Jason. "GOP: Dems Could Upset $3 Billion Deal with Foxconn." *Milwaukee Journal Sentinel*, November 21, 2017. https://www.jsonline.com/story/news/politics/2017/11/21/gop-democrats-could-bring-3-billion-jobs-deal-foxconn-halt/884628001/.

Stein, Jason, and Patrick Marley. *More Than They Bargained For: Scott Walker, Unions, and the Fight for Wisconsin*. Madison: University of Wisconsin Press, 2013.

Stein, Judith. *Pivotal Decade: How the United States Traded Factories for Finance in the Seventies*. New Haven, CT: Yale University Press, 2010.

Stevens Point News. "Legislators Announce Bipartisan Wisconsin Paper Caucus." March 12, 2019.

https://stevenspoint.news/2019/03/12/legislators-announce-bipartisan-wisconsin-paper-caucus/.

Stiglitz, Joseph. "Interview: Joseph Stiglitz." "The Warning," *Frontline*, PBS, October 20, 2009. https://www.pbs.org/wgbh/pages/frontline/warning/interviews/stiglitz.html.

Strange, Mary. "Background of the Van Nortwick Family and the Combined Locks Paper Company." Unpublished essay, personal collection of David Strange.

Strouse, Jean. *Morgan: American Financier*. New York: Random House, 1999.

Summers, Gregory. *Consuming Nature: Environmentalism in the Fox River Valley, 1850-1950*. Lawrence: University Press of Kansas, 2006.

Taylor, Erinn. "Officials Reflect on the Future of the Fox Valley's Paper Industry." WFRV (wearegreenbay.com), February 3, 2018. https://www.wearegreenbay.com/news/local-news/officials-reflect-on-the-future-of-the-fox-valleys-paper-industry/.

Thompson, Maury. "An Unknown Celebrity." *Post-Star* (Glen Falls, NY), September 3, 2007. https://poststar.com/news/local/an-unknown-celebrity/article_b582a3dc-5859-57d3-b545-06b236c55730.html.

Torres, Ricardo. "Family Spent Years Building Custom Home They Will Lose to Foxconn." *Journal Times* (Racine, WI), January 2, 2018. https://madison.com/business/family-spent-years-building-custom-home-they-will-lose-to/article_6325ffad-709a-562f-93b7-4fcbbe14c28a.html?mode=comments.

Tye, Larry. *Rising from the Rails: Pullman Porters and the Making of the Black Middle Class*. New York: Henry Holt, 2004.

U.S. Bureau of Labor Statistics. https://www.bls.gov/bls/proghome.htm.

U.S. Commission on Immigration Reform (the "Jordan Commission"). Repository for the commission's reports to

Congress and related documents, University of Texas Libraries, University of Texas-Austin. https://repositories.lib.utexas.edu/handle/2152/64167.

United Steelworkers Local 2-0009. "Kimberly Mill." New member orientation, 2005-2008.

United Steelworkers. "Wisconsin Paper Mill Workers Rallying at State Capitol to Save Kimberly Mill Jobs." United Steelworkers News, October 2008. https://m.usw.org/news/media-center/releases/2008/wisconsin-paper-mill-workers-rallying-at-state-capitol-to-save-kimberly-mill-jobs.

United Steelworkers. "USW Locals 1421, 1575, 10-448, 2-86, & 2-482—Kimberley-Clark—Mobile, Ala., ... & Neenah/Menasha, Wis.—USW, IndustriALL Global Union and UNI Global Union Condemn Kimberly-Clark's Walmart-Style Treatment of Workers." Monday Morning Minute: September 10, 2018. https://www.usw.org/news/publications/monday-morning-minute/monday-morning-minute-sept-10-2018.

Urdaneta, Mario. "Funding for Federal Manufacturing Technology R&D." Blogpost, July 10, 2019. https://medium.com/@MForesight/funding-for-federal-manufacturing-technology-r-d-58bfccaf3d1c.

Verburg, Steven. "First Environmental Exemption Clears Foxconn to Fill 26 Acres of Wetlands." *Wisconsin State Journal*, January 4, 2018. https://madison.com/wsj/news/local/govt-and-politics/first-environmental-exemption-clears-foxconn-to-fill-acres-of-wetlands/article_c5b0dd02-dd4b-5f38-8686-00c58d7354f8.html.

Walker, Scott (@ScottWalker). Twitter posts, January 16 and September 13, 2018. https://twitter.com/ScottWalker.

Wall Street Journal. "Scott Walker's Subsidy Blowback." Editorial, February 8, 2018. https://www.wsj.com/articles/scott-walkers-subsidy-blowback-1518135455.

Wallenfang, Maureen. "Appleton Coated seeks buyer, files for receivership." *Appleton Post Crescent*, August 18, 2017.

Wallenfang, Maureen. "Appleton Mill Gets 45-Day Extension." *Appleton Post Crescent*, September 26, 2017. https://www.postcrescent.com/story/news/2017/09/26/relief-hope-and-anger-follow-news-appleton-coated-mill-45-day-extension/705359001/.

Wallenfang, Maureen. "Appvion Files for Bankruptcy Protection." *Appleton Post Crescent*, October 2, 2017. https://www.postcrescent.com/story/news/2017/10/02/appvion-files-bankruptcy-protection-looks-reorganize/722487001/.

Wallenfang, Maureen. "Appleton Coated Sale 'Like a Death in the Family,' Worker Says After Thursday Ruling." *Appleton Post Crescent*, October 5, 2017. https://www.postcrescent.com/story/news/2017/10/05/appleton-coated-sale-like-death-family-worker-says-after-thursday-ruling/735928001/.

Wallenfang, Maureen. "Encapsys Moves into New $17.5 Million Headquarters." *Appleton Post Crescent*, December 5, 2017. https://www.postcrescent.com/story/news/2017/12/05/encapsys-moves-into-new-17-5-m-headquarters-appleton/924182001/.

Wallenfang, Maureen. "Appleton Coated Employees Get More Benefits." *Appleton Post Crescent*, February 7, 2018. https://www.postcrescent.com/story/news/2018/02/07/appleton-coated-employees-eligible-additional-benefits/316303002/.

Wallenfang, Maureen. "Appvion Workers Learn Stock Is Likely Worthless." *Appleton Post Crescent*, February 14, 2018. https://www.postcrescent.com/story/money/2018/02/14/appvion-workers-employee-stock-ownership-plan-likely-worthless/334960002/.

Wallenfang, Maureen. "Angry K-C Workers Vent about Planned Closures." *Appleton Post Crescent*, February 16, 2018. https://www.postcrescent.com/story/news/2018/02/16/angry-kimberly-clark-workers-vent-planned-mill-closures-fox-cities/344705002/.

Wallenfang, Maureen. "Assembly Passes Plan to Aid Kimberly-Clark." *Appleton Post Crescent*, February 22, 2018. https://www.postcrescent.com/story/news/2018/02/22/wiscon sin-assembly-takes-up-efforts-aid-kimberly-clark/364575002/.

Wallenfang, Maureen. "Senate Skips Vote on Kimberly-Clark Bailout." *Appleton Post Crescent*, March 20, 2018. https://www.postcrescent.com/story/news/2018/03/20/state-senate-skips-vote-kimberly-clark-bailout-fox-valley/443312002/.

WBAY (Green Bay). "Kimberly-Clark Posts First Quarter Sales Increase." April 25, 2018. https://www.wbay.com/content/news/Kimberly-Clark-posts-First-Quarter-sales-increase-480821431.html.

Weiler, Paul C. *Governing the Workplace: The Future of Labor and Employment Law*. Cambridge, MA: Harvard University Press, 1990.

WHBY (Green Bay). "Walker Reacts to K-C Cuts." January 31, 2018.

WisPolitics.com. "Dems Today Used a May Audit to Cast Doubt on Whether the State's Job Agency Is Up to Overseeing the $3 Billion Foxconn Incentive Package in the Coming Years." Email newsletter, October 24, 2017.

WisPolitics.com. "The State Jobs Agency Pointed to the State's Break-Even Point under the Foxconn Deal As One of the Agreement's 'Weaknesses,' According to the Staff Review Board Members Approved Last Week." Email newsletter, November 13, 2017.

WisPolitics.com. "Gov. Scott Walker Today Announced He'll Ask the Legislature to Approve $6.8 Million in Taxpayer Money for an Advertising Campaign Aimed at Attracting Workers to Wisconsin." Email newsletter, November 29, 2017.

WisPolitics.com. "Sen. Fitzgerald: Statement on Kimberly-Clark Discussions." August 1, 2018. https://www.wispolitics.com/2018/sen-fitzgerald-statement-on-kimberly-clark-discussions/.

WisPolitics.com. "Sen. Roth: Releases Statement after Kimberly-Clark Discussions." August 1, 2018. https://www.wispolitics.com/2018/sen-roth-releases-statement-after-kimberly-clark-discussions/.

WLUK. "Midwest Paper Group to Add 321 Jobs at Former Appleton Coated." July 30, 2018. https://fox11online.com/news/local/future-plans-for-combined-locks-paper-mill-to-be-announced.

Woodward, Bob. *The Agenda: Inside the Clinton White House.* New York: Simon & Schuster, 1994.

Zieger, Robert H. *Rebuilding the Pulp and Paper Workers' Union, 1933-1941.* Knoxville: University of Tennessee Press, 1984.

Zimmerman, Jason. "Appleton Coated Paper Mill to Stay Open As Potential Buyer Is Sought." WBAY, September 25, 2017. https://www.wbay.com/content/news/Hearing-on-Appleton-Coated-paper-mill--447797063.html.

Zimmerman, Jason. "Union Wants Vote on Kimberly-Clark Bill: Senate Says Not Yet." WBAY, April 18, 2018. https://www.wbay.com/content/news/Union-wants-vote-on-Kimberly-Clark-bill-Senate-says-not-yet--480190673.html.

Index

Index

Index

About the Author

THOMAS M. NELSON HAS BEEN County Executive of Outagamie County, Wisconsin since 2011. He served three terms in the state assembly, including one as majority leader, one of the youngest in state history. He developed his passion for public service from his parents, who founded a Lutheran mission church in Combined Locks, in the shadow of Appleton Coated. Nelson holds degrees from Carleton College (BA) and the Princeton School of Public and International Affairs (MPA). He lives in Appleton, Wisconsin, with his wife, Maria, and their two children, Mary and George, and Lucy, a Yorkshire Terrier.

A Note on the Design of this Book

TWO TYPEFACES HAVE BEEN USED in the design of this book: Faustina for the main body text, and Avenir Next for the chapter titles, running heads, and other display purposes.

Faustina is a strong, elegant square-serif typeface designed by Alfonso Garcia for the Omnibus-Type Press Series. It was originally used mainly in newspaper printing, but it has now been widely adopted for use in magazines and books. Omnibus-Type is a collective type foundry organization based in Buenos Aires, Argentina.

Avenir is a geometric sans-serif typeface designed by the influential Swiss designer Adrian Frutiger (1928–2015). He is said to have regarded Avenir as his single greatest achievement. Between 2004 and 2007, Frutiger worked with Linotype's in-house designer Akira Kobayashi to expand Avenir to include a broader range of weights and features. The result is Avenir Next, which is used in this book.

CPSIA information can be obtained
at www.ICGtesting.com
Printed in the USA
LVHW031653190421
684910LV00002B/269